Writing against the Curriculum

Cultural Studies/Pedagogy/Activism

Series Editors
Rachel Riedner, The George Washington University
Randi Gray Kristensen, The George Washington University
Kevin Mahoney, Kutztown University

Advisory Board
Paul Apostolidis, Whitman College; Byron Hawk, George Mason University; Susan Jarratt, University of California, Irvine; Robert McRuer, The George Washington University; Dan Moshenberg, The George Washington University; Pegeen Reichert Powell, Columbia College; Dan Smith, University of South Carolina; Susan Wells, Temple University

The Lexington Press book series Cultural Studies/Pedagogy/Activism offers books that engage questions in contemporary cultural studies, critical pedagogy, and activism. Books in the series will be of interest to interdisciplinary audiences in cultural studies, feminism, political theory, political economy, rhetoric and composition, postcolonial theory, transnational studies, literature, philosophy, sociology, Latino Studies, and many more.

Titles in Series:

Cultural Studies and the Corporate University, by Rachel Riedner and Kevin Mahoney

Democracies to Come: Rhetorical Action, Neoliberalism, and Communities of Resistance, by Rachel Riedner and Kevin Mahoney

Writing against the Curriculum: Anti-Disciplinarity in the Writing and Cultural Studies Classroom, edited by Randi Gray Kristensen and Ryan M. Claycomb

Writing against the Curriculum

Anti-Disciplinarity in the Writing and Cultural Studies Classroom

Edited by
Randi Gray Kristensen
and
Ryan M. Claycomb

LEXINGTON BOOKS
A division of
ROWMAN & LITTLEFIELD PUBLISHERS, INC.
Lanham • Boulder • New York • Toronto • Plymouth, UK

Published by Lexington Books
A division of Rowman & Littlefield Publishers, Inc.
A wholly owned subsidiary of The Rowman & Littlefield Publishing Group, Inc.
4501 Forbes Boulevard, Suite 200, Lanham, Maryland 20706
http://www.lexingtonbooks.com

Estover Road, Plymouth PL6 7PY, United Kingdom

Copyright © 2010 by Lexington Books

British Library Cataloguing in Publication Information Available

Library of Congress Cataloging-in-Publication Data

Writing against the curriculum : anti-disciplinarity in the writing and cultural studies classroom / edited by Randi Gray Kristensen and Ryan M. Claycomb.
  p. cm. — (Cultural studies/pedagogy/activism)
 Includes bibliographical references and index.
 ISBN 978-0-7391-2800-8 (cloth : alk. paper)
 ISBN 978-0-7391-4279-0 (electronic)
 1. English language—Rhetoric—Study and teaching (Higher) 2. English language—Composition and exercise—Study and teaching (Higher) 3. Interdisciplinary approach in education. I. Kristensen, Randi Gray, 1960– II. Claycomb, Ryan M., 1974–
 PE1404.W6932 2009
 808'.0420711—dc22   2009029655

The paper used in this publication meets the minimum requirements of American National Standard for Information Sciences—Permanence of Paper for Printed Library Materials, ANSI/NISO Z39.48-1992.

Printed in the United States of America

Contents

Acknowledgments

This project began as collaboration, and has remained collaboration in various ways from start to finish. We would therefore like to acknowledge those whose collaboration, input, and assistance have been invaluable. First, as editors, we would like to thank each contributor whose work has made this collection possible. We would also like to extend particular thanks to series editors Rachel Riedner and Kevin Mahoney, whose guidance, encouragement, and support on the project has brought it to this point, as well as our colleagues in the University Writing Program at The George Washington University and the English Department at West Virginia University for their committed and inspiring teaching. Other important support came from participants in the Cultural Studies and Critical Pedagogies Symposium at the George Washington University in 2006 and 2007, the Faculty Research Group in the Department of English at West Virginia University, Donald E. Hall at West Virginia University, and Joseph Parry and the staff at Lexington Books. Ryan would also like to extend personal gratitude to Ann who has been an intellectual and editorial sounding board throughout this process.

We would also like to thank the Columbian College at the George Washington University for sabbatical support for Randi, and for subvention support for the production of this volume.

Finally, three pieces in this volume appeared in earlier form in the journal *Enculturation*. Chapter 2, Ryan Claycomb and Rachel Riedner's "Toward an Anti-Disciplinary Nexus: Cultural Studies, Rhetoric Studies, and Composition" appeared in issue 5.2 (2004), while both chapter 10, Randi Gray Kristensen's "From *Things Fall Apart* to *Freedom Dreams*: Black Studies and Cultural Studies in the Composition Classroom," and chapter 11, Ryan Claycomb's "Performing/Teaching/Writing: Performance Studies in the Critical Composition Classroom," appeared in issue 6.1 (2008). Special thanks to Byron Hawk for both editorial guidance and for permission from *Enculturation* to present this work in its expanded form.

Chapter One
Introduction:
Writing against the Curriculum

Randi Gray Kristensen and Ryan Claycomb

In his 2006 essay, "Composing Bodies; or, De-Composition," Robert McRuer describes the recent institutional history of the writing program at The George Washington University (GWU), where he teaches. He describes the process as one where a vibrant program that fostered critical awareness for its student writers was "dismantled" in favor of "a less unruly alternative."[1] That less unruly alternative is the University Writing Program (UWP) that both of us were hired into, Randi coming over from the previous incarnation of the writing requirement at GWU, and Ryan fresh from PhD work in English. McRuer lists several of the ways in which the constitution of the new program sought to more rigorously police writing, but he also notes that "specters of disability and queerness have appeared at the margins of the new program, and how those specters will impact its current corpo-reality remains to be seen," and that the questions raised by these specters represent "de-composing processes" with which he hopes to "affirm, in the face of dangerous transitions, what Paolo Freire called a 'pedagogy of hope.'"[2]

At the same moment when McRuer was laying out his manifesto for de-composition, Ryan was working with Rachel Riedner on "Cultural Studies, Rhetoric Studies, and Composition: Towards an Anti-Disciplinary Nexus," a short response essay for the online journal *Enculturation*, expanded for this collection. That essay seeks to position Cultural Studies alongside rhetoric and composition in order to open up the disciplinarity of those converging fields, even as such a nexus might be used to challenge disciplinary boundaries across the academy through critical writing, teaching, and thinking. While that essay engaged directly with an essay by Sharon Crowley in the same volume of *Enculturation*, it also reflected the kind of attitude we were working toward locally at GWU. Many of us present in the first semesters of the University Writing Program experienced—despite the dystopian surveillance of the program's constitution—something of a utopian moment, asked to re-imagine writing pedagogy from within. We wanted, among other things, to re-imagine the instrumentalist, pre-disciplinary first-year writing course as a resistant, anti-disciplinary space.

We found ourselves teaching UW20, the initiatory element of a university-wide revision of the literacy curriculum requirement. All incoming freshmen and nearly all transfer students are required to take the course and pass it with a C- or better before taking one "Writing in the Disciplines" (WID) course in the sophomore and junior years. The expectation is that majors will have some sort of discipline-specific writing-intensive project in the senior year. Thus, writing becomes a privileged site of learning throughout students' university careers, but also a privileged mechanism for disciplinary and, we would assert, socially disciplined knowledge production.

As instructors in the first-year writing course, we were uncertain how to characterize our course. Given the obvious hierarchical implications of the WID classes—advanced, higher-level, and *in* the disciplines—what were we doing? Was our course, like our faculty, multi-disciplinary? Given the range of writing genres offered not only between, but within, each of our classes, was our course pre-, inter-, trans-, multi-, or even post-disciplinary? On the one hand, early language of the program asserted that we worked in a "pre-disciplinary" classroom, which at once suggested a disciplinary vacuum and, at the same time, an inexorable and seemingly unproblematized movement toward writing within disciplinary academic frameworks. Meanwhile, since a number of faculty came from a Cultural Studies background, the preparation that students found in recognizing rhetorical genres and conventions fit into the Cultural Studies project of disciplinary critique—an anti-disciplinary stance—ironic for students being directed into WID classes.

This collection is the outgrowth of the conversations that began in the hallways of the UWP, and extended outward to faculty who had worked in similar programs (Pegeen Reichert Powell and David Kellogg both taught in the University Writing Program at Duke University, one of the models for GWU's reconstituted program), to colleagues at the new institutional homes of these faculty, eventually including other teacher-scholars using writing in anti-disciplinary contexts. Collectively, we take a wide range of approaches to disciplinarity—multi-, inter-, pre-, post-, trans-, and anti-disciplinarity—as grounds to think through writing and the writing-intensive classroom as spaces in which to challenge the conventional organization and ghettoization of knowledges and epistemologies into discrete and highly regulated disciplines.

Building on the work of critical educators, Cultural Studies scholars, and composition theorists, this collection imagines "disciplinary" writing as "disciplined" writing,[3] in both of the senses that Michel Foucault uses the term in *The Archaeology of Knowledge* and *Discipline and Punish*; that is, writing produced under the auspices of highly controlled and tightly guarded disciplines is subject to surveillance and restriction that governs what knowledge can be made, under what conditions it can be made, and how it is authorized. These processes are enacted by the bodies in the classroom—faculty and student—that are subtly and not-so-subtly trained to conform to the instrumental requirements of capital that drive contemporary higher education. Both faculty and students are rewarded for performance to institutional expectations of cooperation with, and limited challenge to, the production of classed, raced, and gendered subjects prepared to support the status quo. Therefore, we see writing courses (now more and more considered to be pre-disciplinary, and therefore outside the disciplines), and writing-intensive courses that use Cultural Studies and other discipline-challenging methodologies, as rich spaces to enact a resistant pedagogy that asks faculty and students to think beyond and against the disciplinary conventions which govern the vast majority of higher education pedagogies.

Writing against the Curriculum has also been assembled in response to the growing popularity of Writing Across the Curriculum (WAC) and Writing in the Disciplines (WID) programs in universities and colleges across the United States. Many of these programs employ both a pre-disciplinary "Introduction to Writing" course, followed by a sequence or selection of writing-intensive courses housed within academic departments. Thus, they simultaneously offer opportunities to subvert disciplinary knowledge production in the earlier course, even as they reaffirm those divisions in their later requirements. We argue that these introductory composition classrooms make excellent spaces to question disciplinarity through the study of rhetoric, the attention to invention and intervention, the emphasis on critical thinking, and a curricular flexibility that enables a pedagogy that can be applied to a wide variety of topics, before students experience disciplinary enforcement most intensely in the advanced classes.

This volume, then, proposes to intervene in the current discourses of theory and practice in the related fields of composition and Cultural Studies. Each of these discourses weighs the relationship of theory and practice differently: where composition emphasizes practice, Cultural Studies has relied more heavily on its theoretical challenges to epistemological and political thought. Simultaneous attention to both fields offers important possibilities for the activist enactment of Cultural Studies' theoretical ambitions, and for more completely interrogating the theoretical, and particularly the political, implications of composition practices, while leveraging composition's emphasis on pedagogical praxis, and its applicability to activities across the disciplines and beyond the academy.

In their 1986 *Dalhousie Review* essay, "The Need for Cultural Studies," Henry Giroux, David Shumway, Paul Smith, and James Sosnoski lay out some of the possibilities and likely obstacles to be faced by Cultural Studies in its attempt to find an institutional location in the US academy. Along the way, they make the important distinction between Cultural Studies as "project" vs. "program," and the ways that various "projects" have become "programs," i.e. Black Studies, Women's Studies, and so forth, and how inter- and multi-disciplinary efforts have had multiple effects. Giroux et al. begin with the critique of the

fragmented nature of cultural critique because of the segmentation of the study
of culture among numerous disciplines. They argue that:

> The historical development of insulated disciplines housed in segregated de-
> partments has produced a legitimating ideology that in effect suppresses critical
> thought. Rationalized as the protection of the integrity of specific disciplines,
> the departmentalization of inquiry has contributed to the reproduction of the
> dominant culture by isolating its critics from each other.[4]

This isolation enables the silencing of critique, as each division of study ignores
the other's assertions in the name of a "live and let live" approach to academic
freedom, and each winds up engaged in the description of culture on its own
disciplinary terms, rather than a potentially transformative critique. While each
approach participates in the "production of culture," the authors argue that description enables reproduction, while critique enables transformation. Finally,
they call for a "counter-disciplinary praxis" that enables "collective inquiry into
social ills."[5]

Clearly, "The Need for Cultural Studies" does call for a transformative vision of the university. It calls for a revised understanding of our work as "producers of culture," and assigns a particular aim to that production, that of "collective inquiry into social ills."[6] It expects intellectuals to become "resisting
intellectuals" participating in the public sphere, and it expects such work to occur across, and to challenge, disciplinary borders.[7] To accomplish these goals,
the authors concentrate on pedagogical praxis. Rather than participating in the
reproduction of the status quo by reinforcing hierarchy through teaching a static
idea of culture, Cultural Studies practitioners can maintain their role in resistance "by investigating and teaching the claim that culture is in a real sense *unfinished*."[8] They make the strong pedagogical claim that "in order to retain its
theoretical and political integrity, Cultural Studies must develop forms of critical
knowledge as well as a critique of knowledge itself," while simultaneously practicing its own "oppositional discourse and a counter-disciplinary praxis."[9] In
other words, while the danger always remains for Cultural Studies to ossify into
disciplinarity, its pedagogical practices must resist this process from within the
space of the classroom: the only inoculation against disciplinarity is anti-
disciplinarity. These aims sound very much like the aims of many of our contributors: to engage students as producers, not just reproducers, of knowledge;
and to draw their attention to the ways that knowledge is legitimated in the academic context.

Taking up similar questions, Louis Menand suggests that the traditional disciplines have become a fragile fiction. He notes that in the postwar period, cultural differences that were supposed to be effaced by exposure to the "Great
Books" tradition of core competencies in Western culture were not so easily
displaced. Instead, theoretical and practical attention turned to anti-disciplinary
skepticism: "Antidisciplinarity arose from the marriage of the theoretical posi-

tion that the disciplines are arbitrary (or at least limiting and artificial) ways to organize knowledge, with the institutional failure to integrate new areas of inquiry adequately into the traditional disciplines."[10] In today's academic climate, we can at least observe some of the effects of this double valence, wherein critical practices have become infused in the *modi operandi* of academic practices, i.e. various forms of service-learning, attention to the values of multiculturalism and other forms of diversity, lip-service support to interdisciplinary initiatives, and so forth. Yet such an infusion of Cultural Studies practices hides the underlying political project even as those practices become more institutionalized, usually at the cost of overt political critique.

Menand argues for the emergence of yet another dispensation: the post-disciplinary. On the one hand, this may mean doing work outside of the discipline of one's training; more often, though, "it simply means a determined eclecticism about methods and subject matter."[11] He asserts, correctly, that the disciplines are a recent bureaucratic invention; that referring to the current organization of knowledge as interdisciplinary is incorrect, as "the very term implies respect for the discrete perspectives of different disciplines. You can't have interdisciplinarity, or multidisciplinarity, without disciplines";[12] and that postdisciplinarity is the practice of the second book, as graduate education has not caught up to the shifts in the profession. That is, graduate students and, as we shall discuss, undergraduates, are still trained "in the disciplines," although the content of that disciplinary instruction can vary substantially among comparable universities.

Here we should pause to clarify some of the distinctions between the anti-disciplinary and the post-disciplinary as articulated by Menand. While the anti-disciplinary actively challenges the taxonomic effort to organize, categorize, and delimit knowledge into discrete, sanctioned modes of inquiry, the post-disciplinary (or its rough cognate, the trans-disciplinary) functions as if those discrete modes no longer matter. To construct a perhaps simplistic narrative of such a progression, we might suggest that disciplinarity has come under critique from an anti-disciplinary stance, which initially gave rise to the current rhetoric in favor of multi- and inter-disciplinary approaches, approaches that respectively combine and cross methodologies, but that still adhere to the significance of disciplines in the first place, including their importance to the material structures that govern the hiring and tenuring of individuals within disciplinarily defined departments and programs. The post-disciplinary, then, is the perhaps utopian goal of the anti-disciplinary critique, a state of knowledge production that draws on the potential of multi- and inter-disciplinary inquiry without the professional surveillance and institutional policing that remains implicit in most forms of those modes.

Meanwhile, as each of these notions suggests a stance in relationship to disciplinarity, we might locate within the discourse of anti-disciplinarity the idea of actual anti-disciplines. On the one hand, to call a methodology an anti-discipline seems to set it already at the brink of disciplinary ossification, precisely where we can currently locate Cultural Studies and any number of its cousins—Black Studies, Post-Colonial Studies, Women's Studies, Queer Studies, Disability Studies, and so forth. Yet, given the admittedly tenuous position of many of these discourses, it would then be useful to offer a prescriptive definition of the anti-discipline as a mode of inquiry that combines the intellectual resources of many disciplines (the multi-disciplinary), can be applied to other work that is being generated within existing disciplines (the interdisciplinary), provides the grounds for a critique of the limits on knowledge production in other disciplines (the anti-disciplinary) and, finally, resists being co-opted into the dominant framework of disciplinary organization itself, striving to achieve and maintain the radical intellectual freedom promised by the post-disciplinary.

In *Writing/Disciplinarity,* Paul Prior asserts that writing is the primary locus for academic enculturation into disciplinary practices. By analyzing several case studies of graduate students in multiple disciplines, he traces how acts of writing, the contextual activities (research, workshopping, and so forth) surrounding and impacting those acts of writing, and the agency exercised in those acts of writing, all participate in discipline formation and disciplinary enculturation. The primary processes of disciplinary activity are, to Prior, "Appropriation, externalization and alignment in and through which persons, artifacts, practices, institutions, and communities are being produced, reproduced, and transformed in complexly laminated social and material worlds."[13] Within this observation one can find any number of operations of social control, and yet his analysis views disciplines optimistically, as "open and relational," and as dialogic, heterogeneous, and pluralistic.[14]

While his sociohistoric account analyzes the microstructures of the scene of writing, he spends less time evaluating the larger institutional investments in disciplinarity, and the degree to which institutional enforcement of those boundaries—some of which are explored compellingly by Joe Parker below—guide the seemingly benign activities of the writing seminar. What Prior describes as an openness of disciplinarity to the shifting activities of individual scholars might be more skeptically read as the capacity for dominant discourse to co-opt resistant modes of thinking; what he describes as the shared culture generated by the "co-genesis" of mediated literate activity might similarly be interpreted as structures in place to apply discipline to disciplinary transgression, rather than those which can accept such transgression openly. That is, while Prior finds in the permeability of disciplinary writing activity cause for celebration, we might simultaneously locate the traces of hegemonic control over knowledge production in that activity.

If writing remains a crucial locus for enforcing disciplinarity, it must also be a potential site for resisting those processes. Giroux describes precisely this process for his graduate Cultural Studies classes. In "Disturbing the Peace: Writing in the Cultural Studies Classroom," Giroux renews his call to re-center pedagogy within Cultural Studies contexts, noting that Cultural Studies still typically "fails to [. . .] critically address a major prop of disciplinarity, which is the notion of pedagogy as an unproblematic vehicle for transmitting knowledge."[15] This he attributes to the denigrated status of pedagogy studies, below that even of popular Cultural Studies. Indeed, composition studies (similarly disparaged, to Giroux) is the only humanities site that Giroux says takes pedagogy seriously. With that confluence in mind, he describes what he calls border writing, "a form of cultural production forged among the shifting borderlands of a politics of representation, identity, and struggle."[16] Such a border writing practice is embodied in:

> an ongoing attempt to get the students to learn from each other, to decenter the power in the classroom, to challenge disciplinary borders, to create a borderland where new hybridized identities might emerge, to take up in a problematic way the relationship between language and experience, and to appropriate knowledge as part of a broader effort at self-definition and ethical responsibility. Border writing in this case became a type of hybridized, border literacy, a form of cultural production and pedagogical practice where otherness becomes comprehensible, collective memory rewrites the narratives of insurgent social movements, and students travel between diverse theoretical and cultural zones of difference and, in doing so, generate a space where new intersections between identity and culture emerge.[17]

While Giroux is eager to locate in writing the possibility for rupture of the disciplinary tendencies of writing, his own pedagogy described here is at the graduate level, at once freer from certain kinds of institutional surveillance and from imperatives to develop assignments "as technical exercises in skill development."[18]

What we hope to foster here, then, is to expand Giroux's conversation, imagining writing pedagogy as a critical practice against discipline, and towards postdisciplinarity. Given the tensions of the political, the professional, and the financial, and the uneven distribution of disciplinary positions towards postdisciplinarity, what work should an undergraduate writing intensive classroom do? And who should do it? And how? This volume takes up these very questions, and seeks to locate that activity in multiple classroom locations—in the predisciplinary, first-year composition classroom; in other writing intensive classrooms in and across the disciplines; and in classrooms in the anti-disciplines, where literate activity and cultural productions of many sorts may occur as political interventions—and into the culture beyond those classroom walls.

Throughout this volume, one of the most common sets of writing pathways to achieve such goals are described alternately as reflective or self-reflexive writing strategies. While these terms fluctuate slightly in their usages, we tend to follow David Kellogg, who, in chapter 6, uses Donna Qualley's definitions to tease out these terms. He writes:

This distinction also implicitly offers four ways reflection and reflexivity might be observed in composition courses.

Non-reflexive reflection. This is common in writing classes that include reflection papers, especially those sponsoring end-of-term reflective papers that collapse inevitably into simple narratives of progress or conversion. Examples are many and familiar. . . .

Reflexive reflection. This is the kind of reflection teachers covet but rarely receive. Unlike non-reflexive reflection, reflexive reflection gives an impression of a student having changed in the process rather than going through the motions or engaging in tacit negotiation for a higher grade.

Reflexive non-reflection. Reflexivity without reflection can be hard to recognize because unlike reflection, reflexivity is not identified with a particular genre. But we should learn to recognize such moments because they point toward an encounter with an other that is not necessarily expected or sought—the encounter that may be more "authentic" or destabilizing (in a positive sense). We can see such moments in some student texts that struggle and break down in ways suggestive of a difficult encounter with an Other. Such "failures" in student writing can be evaluated positively as we see how new meanings generated by this encounter seem to escape the student's ability to capture them. Indeed, reflexive non-reflection may name the very kind of openness that a writing class focusing on discovery and invention hopes to foster.

Non-reflexive non-reflection. This is the default position of student writing: the unchallenged, unchallenging paper. This is the student argument that rehearses known positions, that may succeed on superficial grounds such as correctness and length, and that showcases held knowledge rather than creates new knowledge.[19]

Kellogg here begins to describe the ways that such writing *in writing classrooms* might be used to disrupt the interpellation of students into a disciplined culture.

And yet, in the perceptions and practices of first-year writing in particular, disciplinarity is already problematically deployed on a number of intersecting, contentious levels that impact programs, faculty, students and curricula. All are affected by the ongoing significance of disciplinarity for institutional identity, and the flows of power and resources that disciplinarity determines. The question of power and resources are particularly germane to first-year writing classes because they have been the frontline for the reconfiguration of higher education towards a market model that privileges managerial (administrative) control of flexible resources (faculty) for customer (student) service. David B. Downing ties disciplinarity to Fordist notions of management science, which has disadvantaged humanistic inquiry as a basis for disciplinary knowledge production in favor of labor efficiency in higher education, and the production of efficient labor for the market place. Since mid-century, this has solidified in English through a process in which "tenured senior professors replicate themselves through apprenticeship programs whereby graduate students teach the composition courses while professors develop literary research. . . . [setting] the criteria by which the 'less-disciplined' could be exploited."[20] As this model has flourished, it has expanded to exploit "less-disciplined" labor in the form of adjuncts, and non-tenurable contract faculty. Marc Bousquet describes the historical process for writing programs:

> While the [first year] writing course was commonly staffed by full-time lecturers and tenure-stream faculty until the 1940s, the expansion of higher education under the G.I. Bill initiated the practice of adjunct hiring and reliance on graduate employees to teach the course. By the mid 1960s, the casualization of writing instruction was institutionalized and massively expanded. . . . During this expansion, a significant fraction of the collective labor of rhetoric and composition specialists was devoted to supervising and training the casualized first-year writing staff.
>
> As a result, the disciplinary identity of tenurable faculty in rhetoric and composition has emerged in close relation to the permatemping of the labor force for first-year writing.[21]

The assertion of disciplinary identity for composition/rhetoric is an important strategic value in an institutional setting that relies on disciplinary configurations. But it poses problems for writing faculty who may perceive of their work as including the project of introducing student scholars to the fictions of disciplinarity and the ways that knowledge creation exceeds, changes, and challenges disciplinary boundaries.

The tension of discipline vs. field/project/program is exacerbated by the material conditions under which most writing faculty labor. Bousquet notes:

> According to the Coalition on the Academic Workforce survey of 2000, for instance, fewer than one-third of the responding programs paid first-year writing instructors more than $2,500 a class; nearly half (47.6 percent) paid these instructors less than $2,000 per class (American Historical Association). At that rate, teaching a full-time load of eight classes nets less that $16,000 annually and includes no benefits.[22]

Downing argues, therefore, for the "task of altering the strictly hierarchical role of disciplinarity itself in determining the range of institutionally authorized labor practices," hoping then to work toward an ideal "spectrum of practices that take place along a horizontal continuum from disciplinary to postdisciplinary, or even antidisciplinary modes."[23] However, faculty in the tenuous conditions Bousquet describes, often hired into positions that privilege teaching and offer little administrative input through service roles, are unlikely to be able to play a shaping role in program development, let alone tenure-and-promotion granting. This vacuum in faculty self-governance becomes occupied by university administrators who may know little about composition as a field or practice, and writing program administrators who must cultivate a disciplinary identity to be, as Bousquet puts it, "one of the gang."[24] This in turn impacts questions of curriculum and student learning in first-year writing classes.

One of the challenges, of course, is that, like any other discipline, composition and rhetoric are evolving fields. As O'Neill and Crow point out:

> As a field, we even debate issues such as the relationship between rhetoric and composition, between literary theory and composition, between "applied" specialties (such as technical and professional writing) and more "theoretical" work (for example, cultural studies). We even disagree on what to call our discipline: composition studies, composition and rhetoric, or rhetoric and composition. . . . While differences and debates are not new or necessarily bad, they are complicated by the changing nature of the university and higher education, changes that are most noticeably manifest through funding and decision-making.[25]

Thus, curricula face monolithic disciplinary or service expectations for the first-year writing classroom in a context of material and political pressures. Aronson and Hansen note the pressures in an independent writing program where they assert they "have identified a disciplinary core . . . driven by questions that are familiar to most writing professionals."[26] However, they add:

> We do acknowledge real tensions between what we consider our disciplinary efforts in the department and our service function. We see Crowley's point of view when she says that "the imagined construction of composition as 'low' work exerts so much ideological force within the academy that even if composition were to achieve a disciplinary status that is recognized beyond its own borders, its image might not alter appreciably within the academy."[27]

Under these circumstances, writing faculty and/or administrators design curricula that struggle to negotiate the ongoing tension between multiple meanings of disciplinarity and service expectations. In an increasingly assessment-driven environment, program and faculty evaluation also struggle to measure often complex aims, particularly for first-year courses: critical thinking or comma placement? Correct citation or questioning assumptions? These questions hint at the underlying, usually unanswered question, for first-year writing instruction: What are we introducing students to? Even if the goal is proper grammatical usage, to what end?

Which brings us to the third party in the faculty-curricula-student triangle of the first year writing classroom: the students. Student input into first-year writing seems to be relegated to evaluating what administrators and faculty have set out to achieve, rather than student ambitions for their introductory writing class. Do they want to be junior scholars, informed citizens, employable, a passing grade, all or none of the above? As the essays in this volume demonstrate, the infusion of Cultural Studies in the writing classroom opens up these questions against the constraints of disciplinarity, and offers at least the possibility of inquiry into student agency in their educations.

Recently, much of the consideration of disciplinarity in writing has come through considerations of the related and overlapping WAC and WID movements. The WAC movement, in particular, has offered openings for critical pedagogy across disciplines. In his history of writing in the disciplines, for example, David R. Russell identifies 60s radicalism in the 70s rebirth of the WAC movement through "its focus on the classroom as community; its student-centered pedagogy, often with a subversive tinge; and its neo-romantic, expressivist assumptions."[28] Similarly, critical educator Ira Shor notes that WAC "challenges the standard curriculum, which separates academic courses from language study" and asserts that, through WAC pedagogies, "every content area . . . can pose its subject matter as critical problems related to social conditions and to student experience."[29] Essentially, WAC initiatives that broadly integrate an attention to language, pedagogy, and reflection, and movement away from instrumentalist writing toward the idea of "writing to think"—all components of Toby Fulwiler's touchstone conception of WAC pedagogy[30]—can be leveraged in service of resistant pedagogies and politics that both call attention to the disciplining of knowledge along sociopolitical lines and, in the case of academic disciplinarity, along epistemological lines.

But the potential for such resistance in WAC scenarios is by no means a necessary or even common feature of writing in various disciplinary scenes. Indeed, this very fact becomes a basis upon which some compositionists draw lines between WAC, which might be said to imagine writing as a transdisciplinary activity, and WID, which tends to place writing instruction firmly within disciplinary contexts, as a component of induction into the discipline. Russell is dismissive of this salient distinction, characteristic of his approach to resistant pedagogies generally. Yet he notes:

> Expressivists, such as Kurt Spellmeyer, argue that students should be encouraged to do personal writing (the personal essay of the belletristic tradition, mainly) *instead of* learning to write in the public genres of the disciplines, a practice that in his view "encourages both conformity and submission" through a naïve and formulaic "cookie cutter" approach to composition.[31]

Russell does point out that some critiques that insist on the "WAC/WID distinction," which distinguish general education from professional education, are short on "ideological edge and 'institutional critique.'"[32]

The lack of an institutional critique, then, forms the very basis for this project's concern about the proliferation of WID initiatives. One need look no further than William Keep's description of WID in a business school to see WID's potential complicity with the corporatization of the university and its use of writing as an instrumentalist component of the production of labor capital for the workforce: "Both the variety of writing situations and the discipline-specific context within which business students write are critical. . . . We need to talk specifically about writing for students in finance, accounting, management, marketing, international business, and computer information systems."[33] Here the process of disciplinary compartmentalization is linked directly to transactional writing designed specifically for use in the marketplace. Russell here defends such an approach to WID, noting that without it:

> Students rarely have a chance to develop in a systematic way over their undergraduate years the kinds of writing they will need when they leave higher education, where they will have to write to audiences other than the instructor or students. Nor do they see the textual ways a discipline carries on its work and (re)produces its ideology.[34]

Russell's invocation of what students "will need when they leave higher education" is a frequently-deployed defense of instrumentalist writing pedagogy, quite the opposite of the border writing that Giroux deploys in his classroom. Moreover, while students may see how a discipline works in such classrooms, the odds that the reproduction of ideology will be made visible often seems unlikely in classrooms like those described by Keep. Indeed, here the ongoing processes by which the mechanisms of capitalism are obfuscated seem to be upheld, rather than exposed.

Under such initiatives, then, Spellmeyer's critique (quoted above in Russell) seems on the mark: that instrumentalist approaches to WID do encourage student docility, for as Keep describes his program "about to move deeper into the respective disciplines,"[35] Russell acknowledges that

> the instructor's role has been traditionally (and logically) defined in terms of 'discipline': showing students the 'right' way within the constraints of that discipline. Thus he [sic] may find his identity as a teacher of a discipline challenged by student responses that propose answers or use evidence or methods of inquiry not accepted by the discipline.[36]

Russell's concern here seems evident: challenges to disciplinarity are often concomitant with challenges to the power structures of traditional schooling, including the intellectual authority of the instructor as representative of disciplinary knowledge.

Yet, while WID can hardly be conceived as a necessary challenge to disciplinary authority, neither is it *ipso facto* complicit with a rigid disciplinarity. For example, Chris Thaiss and Terry Myers Zawacki note, in *Engaged Writers and Dynamic Disciplines*, that while many WID faculty "may themselves write within the conventions of their disciplines, [they] do not necessarily want undergraduates to write within these conventions,"[37] and that the kinds of choices that such faculty themselves face, "choosing to write for different audiences meant that they might have had to break disciplinary conventions in many ways," including "allowing themselves to write with greater emotional intensity and with a clearer political bias."[38] While Thaiss and Zawacki themselves hardly advocate for breaking such boundaries, they implicitly acknowledge certain political implications to writing and teaching beyond the disciplines.

Similarly, WID programs can be imagined as ways of destabilizing the disciplines, or at least highlighting the arbitrariness and instability of disciplinary thinking. Jonathan Monroe, director of the John S. Knight Institute for Writing in the Disciplines at Cornell University (like Duke's University Writing Program, a model for GWU's program), notes this in his introduction to *Writing and Revising the Disciplines*, drawn from a series of talks given by faculty working in Cornell's WID program. He writes:

> Given the current pace of change in the academy, even the broad traditional terms designating the tripartite organization of the present volume—the "physical sciences," the "social sciences," and the "humanities"—cannot help but register . . . as at once picture and frame of scholarly activities and forms of writing that have emerged from, exemplify, and exceed individual disciplines, cross-, and even anti-disciplinary formations.[39]

His statement here acknowledges the degree to which such writing both exists within and pushes against disciplinarity, where either individual disciplines or anti-disciplines might be exemplified or exceeded in such a configuration. Furthermore, he notes that "as Cultural Studies and other disciplinary and interdisciplinary approaches have helped us to understand, the production of knowledge and the production of culture, the writing and revising of knowledges and cultures, go hand in hand."[40]

Drawing on this push and pull of knowledges and cultures, of disciplinarity and writing, this volume draws on writing from a variety of locations to continue to destabilize efforts to "move deeper into the . . . disciplines" as a component of an instrumentalist pedagogy for the corporate marketplace. As such, these essays privilege writing that examines and contests the production of knowledge as a function of the production of docile bodies in the service of a totalizing market economy. The student writing described here is politically engaged, self-reflexive, excessive, and public in its scope, and throughout inflected by an emphasis on pedagogy as a crucial element of a liberatory education.

The first section of the collection, "What is this Writing for?" focuses on a variety of pedagogical practices that can be drawn on in imagining and practicing anti-disciplinarity in composition and other classes where writing takes place. Each essay in this section struggles with the usually unspoken question of "what is this writing for?" by drawing attention to who is writing, in what context, and to what end. Their answers vary in attention to material conditions, theoretical positions, and writing practices, foreclosing any single response by juxtaposing multiple possibilities that are intended to be suggestive and provocative, not prescriptive.

In chapter 2, Ryan Claycomb and Rachel Riedner's "Cultural Studies, Rhetorical Studies, and Composition: Towards an Anti-Disciplinary Nexus" elevates

Cultural Studies scholarship from the shadows of the rhet/comp dyad to imagine the ways that, as a triad of modes of inquiry (not discrete disciplines), rhetoric, composition, and Cultural Studies might invigorate one another in service of an anti-disciplinary politics in the classroom and in our scholarship, and extend the scope of the composition classroom across the borders of the classroom, the academic institution, and even the local public.

In chapter 3, "Subjugated Knowledges and Dedisciplinarity in a Cultural Studies Pedagogy," Joe Parker takes seriously Foucault's mandate for scholars to take on the "common labor of people seeking to 'de-discipline' themselves."[41] His essay explores applications of de-disciplinary practices to Cultural Studies, feminist and postcolonial studies classrooms, and identifies common pitfalls at the intersection of de-disciplinary and concrete everyday practices, in ways that are useful for constituting power/knowledge relations that refuse modern disciplinary mechanisms of subjection and docility.

Chapter 4, Pegeen Reichert Powell's "Interventions at the Intersections: An Analysis of Public Writing and Student Writing," analyzes two student-produced texts to explore the potential of public writing—specifically as it might be taught in composition courses, but potentially in any university course—to facilitate an anti-disciplinary stance among students. She argues that student-authored public texts are a fruitful site in which to develop an anti-disciplinary stance, because not only do these texts and their authors seem to be working outside of the constraints of any specific discipline, but they seem to be working outside of the constraints of academia altogether. Moreover, these texts seem more likely to intervene in local political conditions than those texts that are designed to be read by solitary teachers or small groups of peers inside the classroom.

The second section of the collection, "Shifting Schemas," takes up the disciplinary and institutional challenges posed by the anti-disciplinary stance of the first section, and considers their implications in the arenas of full courses and writing programs, where disciplinary power is magnified through aggregation, and anti-disciplinarity provides an open challenge to ideologies of consistency, coherence, and efficiency. These essays share among them both a critique of the potential traps of disciplinarity inherent in curricular and institutional structures, while each suggests avenues whereby such structures might be used to write against the curriculum.

In chapter 5, "Writing is Against Discipline: Three Courses," Alan Ramón Clinton inventively combines theory with specific classroom examples to demonstrate how teachers of writing in/across the disciplines can take advantage of their simultaneously marginal and indispensable institutional locations to question the borders of disciplinarity. By exploring the history and challenges of experimental writing with students, teachers who are expected to teach them to color within the lines can demonstrate how writing can be "an unruly participant in the knowledge process."[42]

Chapter 6, David Kellogg's "The Brake of Reflection: Slowing Social Process in the Critical WID Classroom," theorizes an approach to WID courses to *slow down* the social process that Althusser calls "interpellation"; it explores how the use of reflection and reflexivity is being implemented in a WID program (at Northeastern University) that has the anomalous status of remaining within an English department; and it makes the case that viewing reflection in WID classes as helping to slow the social processes of interpellation provides a rationale for *not* dispersing WID courses around the curriculum but for maintaining them in institutional locations that value critical rhetorical perspectives (such as departments of English or rhetoric).

Chapter 7 is Catherine Gouge's essay, "Location, Location, Location: The Radical Potential of Web-Intensive Writing Programs to Challenge Disciplinary Boundaries," which asserts that Web-intensive writing programs have the potential to challenge disciplinarity at both the administrative/ programmatic and instructor/course levels. Because such programs rely to such a large extent on the staffing, support, and decision-making of individuals from a wide range of offices and centers across campus, and because the courses can be taken "anytime, anywhere" by students from a variety of major areas, the very existence of these programs challenges conventional disciplinary boundaries. However, she claims, the radical anti-disciplinary potential of web-intensive programs can only be fulfilled if the programmatic and course designs maximize opportunities for critical reflection, and challenge the ideologies of sameness and efficiency that drive institutional disciplinarity.

In chapter 8, university librarians Cathy Eisenhower and Dolsy Smith root their critique in the inherently trans-disciplinary space of the university library. Their dialogue engages the library as a site of disciplinary pressures of another sort, especially for those who labor there, in the form of demands for efficiency and standardization, emanating from an increasingly corporate model of higher education. Dissatisfied with the disciplinary conventions that define the critical article in "library literature," the authors work in an alternative, even anti-disciplinary form; they borrow the dialogic energy of a blog to seek more room to maneuver in approaching the questions that occupy them, including the possibilities for an activist pedagogy of library instruction

The third section, "Writing across the (Anti) Disciplines," imagines the place of anti-disciplinarity in writing in the disciplines and in post-disciplinary contexts. In arenas where disciplinary pressure is either explicit, through state "hostile workplace" guidelines that appear to pre-empt pedagogical and theoretical approaches, or implicit, through silent acceptance of the claims of disciplinarity, anti-disciplinary interventions carry higher material, theoretical, and pedagogical stakes for their practitioners, both teachers and students. Each context demands its own form of intervention, and the essays in this section both describe and respond to those contexts in creative ways that are intended to instigate other creative approaches to resisting the pressures of discipline and opening disciplinarity to questions of purpose and possibility.

Chapter 9, Eric G. Lorentzen's "'Only Connect': Doing Dickens, Cultural Studies, and Anti-Disciplinarity in the University Literature Classroom," reads the mandate of Virginia's "hostile workplace" guidelines as restrictive of professors' classroom practice to the areas of expertise for which they were hired, and views them as an effort to exert disciplinary control over an activist Cultural Studies pedagogy in the literature classroom. Then, by examining a range of Cultural Studies approaches taken in a course on Charles Dickens, he connects issues unearthed in Dickens' novels to similar political stakes in today's world. He concludes that such Cultural Studies methodologies and praxes result in the kind of "only connect" moments between literature and lives that a critical anti-disciplinary pedagogy should seek to embrace.

Randi Gray Kristensen argues, in chapter 10, "From *Things Fall Apart* to *Freedom Dreams*: Black Studies and Cultural Studies in the Composition Classroom," that while traditional approaches to teaching Black literature in multicultural settings have been useful, they have also been unnecessarily limiting. However, when viewed through lenses that combine Cultural Studies and composition methodologies, such texts can offer demonstrations of revision, selection, citation, and invention in their emergence from and through the disciplinary discourses of empire and colonization. They can provide important models and insights for already-enculturated university writers struggling in the overdetermined setting of academic writing to develop, articulate, and engage their own critical knowledges that challenge disciplinary convention and prescription.

Finally, in chapter 11, "Performing/Teaching/Writing: Performance Studies in the Critical Composition Classroom," Ryan Claycomb explores avenues by which we might leverage the notion of performance for a critical writing pedagogy in three particular ways: as a lens to examine, assess, and revitalize the complex performance dynamics of the writing-intensive classroom (the classroom as theatre); as an empowering tool kit for students to reconfigure their own writing practice (the student writer as performance artist); and as a body of intellectual work that serves as subject matter for critical and anti-disciplinary inquiry through writing (performance as the course text).

The essays collected in *Writing against the Curriculum* are intended to raise more questions than they answer, reinvigorate ongoing discussions about the role of writing learning and instruction at the university level, and offer theoretical frameworks, drawn from multiple dimensions of Cultural Studies and composition, as lenses through which to consider the pressures and possibilities inherent in the current moment. In a hostile academic environment that seems often devoted to the goal of composing students through a disciplinary curriculum that renders them docile, we hope that the volume will encourage the process of de-composing composition itself, making space for the unruly, the resistant, and the radical.

Notes

1. Robert McRuer, "Composing Bodies; or, De-Composition: Queer Theory, Disability Studies, and Alternative Corporealities." *JAC* 24, no. 1 (2004): 61.

2. McRuer, "Composing Bodies," 68.

3. Indeed, David Downing (following Laurence Veysey) highlights the commonality of the ideas in the very development of academic disciplines themselves, noting the roots in academic disciplines with the standards of moral piety that governed nineteenth-century education. The study that fell under the rubric of the morally disciplined was appropriate for the academic disciplines.

4. Henry Giroux, David Shumway, Paul Smith, and James Sosnoski, "The Need for Cultural Studies: Resisting Intellectuals and Oppositional Public Spheres." *Dalhousie Review* 64, no. 2 (1986): 472.

5. Giroux, et al., "The Need for Cultural Studies," 473.

6. Giroux, et al., "The Need for Cultural Studies," 473.

7. Giroux, et al., "The Need for Cultural Studies," 473.

8. Giroux, et al., "The Need for Cultural Studies," 478, emphasis original.

9. Giroux, et al., "The Need for Cultural Studies," 485.

10. Louis Menand, "The Marketplace of Ideas." *American Council of Learned Societies*, Occasional Paper No. 49. 2001. http://archives.acls.org/op/49_ Marketplace _of _ Ideas.htm.

11. Menand, "The Marketplace of Ideas."

12. Menand, "The Marketplace of Ideas."

13. Paul A. Prior, *Writing/Disciplinarity: A Sociohistorical Account of Literate Activity in the Academy* (Mahwah, NJ: Erlbaum, 1998), 287.

14. Prior, *Writing/Disciplinarity*, 277.

15. Henry A. Giroux, "Disturbing the Peace: Writing in the Cultural Studies Classroom." *College Literature* 20, no. 2 (June 1993): 15.

16. Giroux, "Disturbing the Peace," 13.

17. Giroux, "Disturbing the Peace," 24.

18. Giroux, "Disturbing the Peace," 20.

19. Kellogg, "The Brake of Reflection," 99-100.

20. Downing, "Disturbing the Peace," 29.

21. Marc Bousquet, *How the University Works* (New York: New York University Press, 2008), 158.

22. Bousquet, *How the University Works*, 3.

23. David B. Downing, "Beyond Disciplinary English: Integrating Reading and Writing by Reforming Academic Labor," in *Beyond English Inc.: Curricular Reform in a Global Economy,* ed. David B. Downing, Claude Mark Hurlbert, and Paula Mathieu. (Portsmouth, NH: Boynton/Cook, 2002), 34-35.

24. Bousquet, *How the University Works*, 168.

25. Peggy O'Neill and Angela Crow, "Introduction: Cautionary Tales about Change," in *Field of Dreams: Independent Writing Programs and the Future of Composition Studies*, ed. Peggy O'Neill, Angela Crow and Larry W. Burton (Logan, UT: Utah State University Press, 2002), 5.

26. Anne Aronson and Craig Hansen, "Writing Identity: The Independent Writing Department as a Disciplinary Center," in *Field of Dreams: Independent Writing Pro-*

grams and the Future of Composition Studies, ed. Peggy O'Neill, Angela Crow and Larry W. Burton (Logan, UT: Utah State University Press, 2002), 59.

27. Aronson and Hansen, "Writing Identity," 59.

28. David R. Russell, *Writing in the Academic Disciplines, 1870-1990: A Curricular History* (Carbondale and Edwardsville, IL: Southern Illinois University Press, 1991). 272-273.

29. Ira Shor, *Empowering Education: Critical Teaching for Social Change.* (Chicago: University of Chicago Press, 1992), 187.

30. Shor, *Empowering,* 187.

31. Russell, *Writing,* 294, emphasis original.

32. Russell, *Writing,* 311.

33. William Keep, "Rewriting Business as Usual," in *Direct from the Disciplines: Writing Across the Curriculum,* ed. Mary T. Segall and Robert A. Smart (Portsmouth, NH: Boynton/Cook, 2005), 10-11.

34. Russell, *Writing,* 313.

35. Keep, "Rewriting," 17.

36. Russell, *Writing,* 293.

37. Chris Thaiss and Terry Myers Zawacki, *Engaged Writers and Dynamic Disciplines: Research on the Academic Writing Life* (Portsmouth, NH: Boynton/Cook, 2006), 46.

38. Thaiss and Zawacki, *Engaged,* 45.

39. Jonathan Monroe, *Writing and Revising the Disciplines* (Ithaca, NY: Cornell University Press, 2002), 7.

40. Monroe, *Writing,* 8.

41. Parker, Joe, "Subjugated Knowledges and Dedisciplinarity in a Cultural Studies Pedagogy," 3.

42. Clinton, Alan Ramón. "Writing is Against Discipline: Three Courses," 14.

Part I

What Is Writing For?

Departmental disciplines operate increasingly like antagonistic nation states, with much policing of boundaries, arcane loyalty tests, and rampant intellectual protectionism. Stimulated by ever-shrinking job markets and ever-growing budget cuts, there is much anxiety about disciplinary markets and rhetorics of allegiance, mobilization, and interdisciplinary warfare are rife in large universities.

—Arjun Appadurai, *"Diversity and Disciplinarity as Cultural Artifacts,"* 33.

Chapter Two
Toward an Anti-Disciplinary Nexus: Cultural Studies, Rhetoric Studies, and Composition

Ryan Claycomb and Rachel Riedner

In the fall of 2003, the online journal *Enculturation* published a special issue (which included an earlier version of this essay) that sought to parse the nexus of Rhetoric Studies and Composition Studies—the conjunctions, disjunctions, and aporias that, for example, contributor Cynthia Haynes locates in the rhetoric/composition slash.[1] Yet lurking within and beneath several of the *Enculturation* articles lay the specter of Cultural Studies. Primarily raised as either a partner in, or rival to, rhetoric's project of invigorating Composition Studies with a real-world efficacy, we argued there that Cultural Studies must be considered with equal weight alongside these other modes of inquiry. While, in her essay, Sharon Crowley doubts the potential of Cultural Studies to effect any real political intervention by casting it as an unstable platform embedded within English Departments, Krista Ratcliffe argues that a "scholarly awareness of rhetorical theory, along with cultural studies scholarship, must be made overt."[2] We would like to extend this project even further, elevating Cultural Studies scholarship from the shadows of the rhet/comp dyad, to imagine the ways that, as a triad of modes of inquiry (not discrete disciplines), rhetoric, composition, and Cultural Studies might work in trans- or even anti-disciplinary ways to invigorate one another in service of an activist politics in the classroom and in our scholarship.

The title of Crowley's "Composition is not Rhetoric" rests upon an astute observation about the state of the field, but also upon a fairly clear insistence that rhetoric and composition remain segregated as disciplinary activities. While her primary concern is the degree to which rhetoric has been pushed to the margins of actual composition pedagogy, she is also deeply concerned that the possibilities for political intervention are compromised by this fact. Instead, she argues, most teachers who orient their first-year courses toward political intervention are not motivated by studies of rhetoric, but learn from Cultural Studies theorists, such as Stuart Hall and Raymond Williams, who are originators of, and working in, the Birmingham school methodologies of a cultural Marxist tradition. Crowley's concern with this alignment is that, in the current context of English Departments, where she locates Cultural Studies pedagogy, this commitment to intervention is "less clear and steady."[3] Making claims about current practice more than about theoretical investments, she privileges rhetoric for its "attention to intervention," arguing that this attention "differentiates it from all other practices and fields of study, including, implicitly, cultural studies,"[4] a move that fails to acknowledge a potential distinction between contemporary American Cultural Studies practice within English departments from the broader theoretical investments of a Cultural Studies that is global in scope, and materially invested in aim.

Curiously enough, in their introduction to *Disciplinarity and Dissent in Cultural Studies*, Cary Nelson and Milip Parameshwar Gaonkar make a similar claim, but instead of Rhetoric Studies, they extol Cultural Studies. They assert that, "unlike traditional disciplines, cultural studies responds consciously to immediate political problems and counts its success—its pertinent progress—partly in terms of its success at interpreting, analyzing, and intervening in local conditions."[5] Like the potentials that Crowley claims for both rhetorical scholarship and pedagogy, the theoretical tradition of Cultural Studies places value in analyzing the local (what Gramsci calls conjunctural analysis), and therefore is poised to enact what Cultural Studies emphasizes as political struggle, or intervention, into what rhetoric scholars might call the public sphere. As Ien Ang has said, "The promise of cultural studies was precisely that it would be an intellectual practice firmly located in and concerned with the major issues of the day and, as such, would provide a bridge between the academic world and the social world 'out there.'"[6] However, by alternately claiming either Cultural Studies or Rhetoric Studies as *the* primary academic site for real-world intervention, we run the risk of diminishing politicized pedagogy to an academic territorial squabble, the sort of squabble that Stephen Mailloux reminds us splintered oral rhetoric from written composition in the early decades of the twentieth century.[7] However, as we see it, these claims raise important questions about a political, scholarly, and pedagogical alliance that could be forged between scholar/teachers working at the nexus of Cultural Studies, composition, and Rhetoric Studies.

Rather than setting out Composition Studies as the site for a turf battle between Rhetoric Studies and Cultural Studies, we would suggest that doing so indulges in a sort of disciplinary thinking that limits the possibilities of both the pedagogy and the theory, rather than illuminating them and, further, limits the possibility for rhetorical action rather than facilitating it. These divisions are linked to what Nelson and Gaonkar call the "unwritten and unsigned pact post World War II disciplines made with state power . . . guaranteeing silence and irrelevance."[8] Sadly, discourse around what we do when we study and teach composition has often inured itself to these realties and internalized them—by enforcing boundaries both disciplinary and national—instead of revealing and resisting them. As Crowley suggests that composition and Rhetoric Studies are "yoked,"[9] we might do well to recognize that both rhetoricians and teachers of writing are the beasts of burden in the scenario. The interplay that these three modes of discourse, scholarship, and theory offer must be a source of strength rather than of territorial resistance. The nexus of rhetoric, composition, and Cultural Studies can create a shared theoretical and political project, one that identifies, critiques and resists the limitations of academic disciplines, which themselves are imbricated with what feminist geographer Saskia Sassen calls "methodological nationalism."[10] Thus an anti-disciplinary (and transnational) pedagogy works to break the mechanisms by which we, as academic laborers, are harnessed to academic divisions and national boundaries that we neither observe nor espouse.

Within the limited context of the American academy, this "unwritten and unsigned pact" becomes itself hegemonic, underpinning a disciplinarity that governs intellectual production. Such disciplinarity is a component of a neoliberal public pedagogy that focuses on the production of workers and consumers for the newest phase of the capitalist economy, even as such disciplinarity becomes (as Ien Ang points out) obsolete as a mode of production in the very capitalist economy for which workers are ostensibly being prepared.[11] Interdisciplinary work is valued by departments when it means they do not have to foot the entire bill for paying interdisciplinary faculty, but is rarely valued equally to traditional disciplinary inquiry in questions of tenure, promotion, and grant awards. In this way, disciplinarity reduces much intellectual labor to budgetary line items while minimizing the importance of pedagogy. At the same time, it confines intellectual labor to defined area studies without investigating relationships between these boundaries and the interests of the nation-state. This reality literally disciplines rhetoric and composition into an enforced partnership with one another and with nationalist power, even as it frequently questions the place of Cultural Studies within any academic department, and situates it erroneously within English departments (an alliance that Crowley identifies with disdain). Under the existing rationale, therefore, only rhetoric/composition may be a site for discussions of pedagogy, while those who are hired into traditional humanities disciplines do not have to deal with questions of pedagogy and certainly do not have to teach writing. What we see in this disciplinary arrangement is the separation of intellectual inquiry from the academic labor of the composition classroom, a segregation that works to diffuse dissent.

As practitioners of a Cultural Studies pedagogy with a strong emphasis on rhetoric (or vice versa) in an interdisciplinary writing program, we argue for a productive confluence of Cultural Studies and Rhetoric Studies in the contemporary composition classroom. Within the current institutional context of writing programs, we support pedagogy and scholarship that is aligned with what Lisa

Coleman, in her *Enculturation* article, calls "writing, intervention, and civic engagement."[12] Informed by a Freirian tradition in composition, our work at the nexus of Cultural Studies and Rhetoric Studies can be a point of communication. A progressive pedagogy that values intervention, activism, and agency emerges from an attention to the social and material conditions of the classroom, as well as active analysis of the social and material circumstances in which texts are produced.

This is not to say that we can simply lay a civic-minded Rhetoric Studies against a Marxist-inflected Cultural Studies and find the congruencies sufficient to guide an anti-disciplinary pedagogy. A juxtaposition of the rhetoric of "civic engagement" within rhet/comp and "activism" or "agitation" in Cultural Studies is an uneasy pairing: the "civic engagement" or "public participation" of rhetoric and composition has at times taken the nation/state as a given. Wendy Hesford and Eileen Schell argue that "composition operates in an 'isolationist discipline' where U.S. teachers of writing are focused on composition only within a nationalist paradigm—often unaware of how composition instruction is taught and engaged across the globe—and writing and rhetoric curricula are centered on U.S.-centered popular culture and history."[13]   Therefore, such an anti-disciplinary pedagogy must be informed by an "interrogation of the geo-politics of composition instruction."[14] The transnational perspective that Hesford and Schell advocate, then, is rooted in Cultural Studies methodologies, interested as it is in the connection between history and the contemporary moment, and the global circulation of power, material, and discourse from and through local contexts.

Such a transnational focus draws from the epistemologies of Cultural Studies, which sees culture as a site of activism. Culture, in this paradigm, extends beyond an analysis of textual artifacts in academic contexts to what Ien Ang contends:

> is an ongoing, plural, often conflictive process taking place in all dimensions of social activity . . . [and] is neither institutions nor texts nor behaviors but the complex interactions between all of these. In other words, culture is not only very ordinary . . . it is also fundamentally practical and pervasive to social life, as it is inherent to how the world is made to mean, and therefore how the world is run.[15]

This approach to culture as a meaning-making system find congruencies with the study of rhetoric, whose scope Mailloux has broadened to include "objects of interpretive attention, whether speech, writing, nonlinguistic practices, or human artifacts of any kind."[16] Cultural Studies might extend this even further to structures of feeling, emotion, and affects, and has existing intersections with fields such as Black Studies, Performance Studies, Queer Theory, Feminism, Postcolonial Studies, and Disability Studies. Taken together, Rhetoric Studies and Cultural Studies are both deeply invested in meaning-making as inherently wrapped up in systems of power, and potential empowerment. Each offers to the other modes of analysis as well as modes of action, both within the academy and beyond.

In this way, the roots of Cultural Studies in activist educational settings outside of traditional university settings—from Ngũgĩ wa Thiong'o's Kamiriithu Community Educational and Cultural Centre in Kenya to Appalachia's Highlander Research and Education Center in Tennessee to the Zapatistas in Chiapas, Mexico—provide models for a rhetoric of agitation that trouble such easy national and institutional boundaries. Even within an English department in the U.S. academy, we might find examples of Cultural Studies-inflected fields that use agitation as a mode of activism that unsettles the rhetorics of public participation within established frameworks. Consider Robert McRuer's aims in using queer theory and disability studies against the status quo of Composition Studies: "I am . . . hopeful that disability studies and queer theory will remain locations from which we might speak back to straight composition, with its demand for composed/docile texts, skills, and bodies" and that these discourses "provide us ways of comprehending how our very bodies are caught up in, or even produced by, straight composition."[17]

To this end, a common interest in action and empowerment, that emerges from the nexus of Cultural Studies and Rhetoric Studies in the composition classroom, can therefore be the beginning of a pedagogical project that draws from all three sites, even as we struggle to define what we even mean when we say "pedagogy." Instead of locating the burden of reflection and action exclusively within Rhetoric Studies, a Freirian tradition in Composition Studies that is allied with Cultural Studies can invigorate those efforts, a productive encounter that we struggle with below. In the field of Composition Studies, Paolo Freire and his followers in the United States have developed the idea of critical literacy as an investigation of classroom practices that challenges the knowledge (and thus the power) of the bourgeoisie. In *Empowering Education*, for example, Ira Shor cites a first year composition course he taught "which chose personal growth as its theme, and where [Shor] brought in material about corporate economic policy and discrimination. In that class, the students blamed the individual alone if he or she failed to succeed. Through dialogue, reading, and writing, the students were challenged to re-perceive the system in which they construct their fate."[18] Shor's critical pedagogy (which closely follows Freire) here is deeply concerned with introducing students to knowledge that is both transdisciplinary and activist "for the transformation of self and society,"[19] and suggests the ways that the composition classroom might become a site that engages politically and ethically with the world beyond the classroom walls.

At the nexus of Cultural Studies, Rhetoric Studies and writing (not limited to composition), then, we find ourselves reimagining pedagogy. Pedagogy becomes more than simply classroom practices, but rather a kind of world-making, enabled by rhetorical action. Rachel writes, with Kevin Mahoney, that "we conceive of rhetorical action as being concerned with both critique and the creative work of producing discursive interventions."[20] In the context of the classroom, this incorporates theory, classroom practice, and civic engagement to produce both a political stance and material change. Let us consider, then, several specific methodologies that enact such rhetorical action in an activist, anti-disciplinary composition classroom: 1) uncovering the political as it operates in and through culture and texts; 2) identifying the production of culture as contested, and contesting that production; 3) reflecting on cultural texts, artifacts, practices and affects; and 4) acting in a world of public symbols and material consequences.

Of these, the first category has tended to be the most persistent in the Anglo-American academy, with its own institutional investments in diffusing more direct-action education. In their forthcoming book, *knowing feminism? Hurricane Katrina "Refugees," Rigoberta Menchú, and Subcomandante Insurgente Marcos*, feminist scholars Kelly Cooper and Annie Lipsitz address representations of Hurricane Katrina "refugees" and of public figures Rigoberta Menchu and Subcomandante Marcos.[21] Before they engage their material and their subjects, Cooper and Lipsitz pose the following rhetorical and ethical questions: "who can speak for whom and in what contexts" or, rather, "who can speak with whom?" The process of uncovering and reflecting upon the material and historical circumstances of gendered and racialized power as it operates culturally in New Orleans, Guatemala, and Chiapas, and the interpellation of gendered power in transnational power structures, becomes the necessary context through which they engage this subject matter. Similarly, Gayatri Chakravorty Spivak's work engages the materiality of feminist political and rhetorical work, where scholars always search for modes of speaking and hearing within particular and historical contexts. This approach facilitates communication and collaboration across specific borders, including in these instances gender, race, ethnicity, and nation. Such a transnational approach, that links the local to the global, operates both through a broad scope and a more traditional rhetorical approach. As Spivak argues in "Thinking Cultural Questions in 'Pure' Literary Terms," "I find myself insisting on restoring rhetorical reading practices because I believe, in an irrational, utopian, and impractical way, that such reading can be an ethical motor that undermines the ideological field."[22] Spivak's work here is not simply following the disciplinary paths of literary studies in an English department, but is suffused with the methodologies of rhetoric, postcolonial, and subaltern studies, related sites of discourse that push the bounded assumptions of texts into their global contexts. Her insistence on a rhetorical project is conditioned by her deep investments in an anti-imperial project.

Building on a similar observation of such anti-imperial work, James Clifford says, in *Writing Culture*—a book that is concerned with ethnographic writing as "the making of texts"[23]—that "The critique of colonialism in the postwar period . . . has been reinforced by an important process of theorizing about the

limits of representation itself."[24]   He goes on to note how much post-war scholarship:

> made inescapable the systematic and situational verbal structures
> that determine all representations of reality. Finally, the return of rhe-
> toric to an important place in many fields of study . . . has made pos-
> sible a detailed anatomy of conventional expressive modes. Allied
> with semiotics and discourse analysis, the new rhetoric is concerned
> with what Kenneth Burke called "strategies for the encompassing of
> situations." It is less about how to speak well than about how to speak
> at all, and to act meaningfully in the world of public cultural sym-
> bols.[25]

Clifford, like many scholars of rhetoric, is interested in the production of culture: "culture," he argues, "is contested, temporal, and emergent. Representation
and explanation—both by insiders and outsiders—is implicated in this emergence."[26]   Writing ten years later, Ralph Cintron, in *Angel's Town*, notes that
"what interests me more is how humans 'make' and order."[27]   Working at the
intersection of anthropology, rhetoric, and Cultural Studies in a working-class
Mexican-American community in a U.S. city, Cintron, like Clifford, picks up on
how meaning-making is both invested in multiple forms of power and at the
same time struggled over:

> I came to this approach because while doing fieldwork it occurred to
> me that not only uses of language but also a wide range of artifacts
> and bodily gestures became consistently mobilized during the making
> of disputes. Those interested in the performative dimension of human
> action should find considerable compatibility with my analyses of
> public culture . . . as performances, as rhetoric gestures emerging
> from the desire to persuade others of the propriety of certain identifi-
> cations and, implicitly, of the impropriety of other identifications.[28]

For Cintron, Cultural Studies and Rhetoric Studies both consider how culture is
made and written, at the same time as they ask these same questions about their
own texts. Cultural production, then, encompasses the artifacts, texts, and affects
under analysis; the mode of analysis applied to them; and, finally, the occasion
to self-reflexively acknowledge the analysis itself as a participant in cultural
production. Cintron and Clifford both push for this self-reflexivity in their writing, locating the composing process as central to all stages of cultural production. Their work enacts the call that Ang issues for self-reflexivity as a methodology in its own right:

> We will have to demonstrate that keeping questions open is actually
> useful, that thinking more complexly and reflexively about issues is
> actually practical, if not here and now then in the longer term, in light
> of social sustainability, for example . . . what is also desperately

> needed is the capacity for people to self-reflexively invent common
> grounds within which situated social futures can be imagined and
> worked towards together with an increasingly wide range of differ-
> ently positioned others.[29]

Ang's insistence on self-reflexivity as a means to "common grounds" therefore
becomes the conduit for a pedagogy of communication across boundaries, just
as Cooper and Lipsitz argue for in their work. In the classroom, this plays out in
self-reflexivity about our teaching, as well as the writing practices we ask of our
students, creating an ethical and intellectual habitus that extends beyond individual written products.

The nexus we argue for, in other words, can be an opening to the sort of pedagogy that moves beyond writing composed documents that *observe* rhetoric as
it is constructed and culture as it is produced, and pushes toward writing as the
impetus for action. We might ask at this moment, then, what remains for texts in
this pedagogy? This question returns us to the widening scopes of both Rhetoric
and Cultural Studies. For example, for Spivak, we must approach literature with
"a sense of the rhetoricity of language" for, if not, "a species of neo-colonialist
construction of the non-Western scene is afoot."[30] Literature approached rhetorically becomes more than simply a static document for interpretation and
translation; the rupture and gap between text and interpretation becomes a site
for struggle as it gestures outside of a text to the world. As Spivak argues:

> if what happens in the literary text is the singularity of its language
> and that singularity is in its figuration, that figuration can point to the
> depth of the content by signaling that the content cannot be contained
> by the text as receptacle. To note this is not to say that the text has
> failed. It is to say that the text has succeeded in signaling beyond it-
> self. It is high praise for the book, no dispraise.[31]

This emphasis on the outward impulse of literature and other written texts at
once suggests different meanings within language, recognizes language as a site
of social struggle, critiques existing social and political orders, and gestures toward a more complete, complex, and alternative meaning. For example, as Spivak writes about Jamaica Kincaid's novel, *Lucy* (citing Hall, who in turn is citing Gramsci), "I feel that a rhetorical reading of *Lucy* can be expanded into 'the
criticism to which such an ideological complex is subjected by the first representatives of the new historical phase.'"[32] Here, even the study of literature offers
us "the power of fiction [which] is unverifiable. To learn to read fiction is to
work with this power."[33] Writing and teaching in the rhetoric/composition/ Cultural Studies nexus, then, is more than a passive observation or interpretation of
other rhetorics, but an enactment of our own—and our students' own—rhetorics
in order to effect action.

That research in Cultural Studies and Rhetoric Studies in tandem can invigorate the act of writing is, we argue, a sufficient acknowledgement. But we must not lose sight of our teaching as an act with political consequences, one that enacts, models, and encourages interventions in and beyond the community of the classroom, the institution of the university, the various local publics we inhabit, and the transnational contexts into which we are all inserted. As teachers, we must show this work within and beyond borders, both disciplinary and cultural. To begin, we can let such an acknowledgement inflect our understanding of the disciplinarity of our own work. That is, instead of haggling over which disciplinary discourse, tradition or method is better suited to activist pedagogy, we might start with the politically resistant move of working against the very disciplinary distinctions and institutional divisions that underpin this discussion. Cultural Studies, Composition Studies, Rhetoric Studies—speaking of any of them as discrete fields or overemphasizing their divergences will limit the theoretical potential and political opportunities of their interplay, while at the same time adopt a position complicit with the reduction of that intellectual work by a corporatized university.[34]

Therefore, we are calling for more than inter-disciplinarity; we are issuing a call to anti-disciplinarity in a reconsideration of Rhetoric, composition, and Cultural Studies, both to move beyond the limitation that disciplinary thinking imposes, and to leverage the theoretical, political, and pedagogical opportunities that an anti-disciplinary stance implies. These opportunities not only cut across academic boundaries, but also thematize and model the identification, contestation, and breach of discursive, cultural, and national boundaries wherever we encounter them. In the writing classroom, the four components of our pedagogical nexus—critique, contestation, self-reflexivity, and action—must take shape as both theoretical stances and particular practices. We offer, as an example of this nexus, the courses we each have taught within the First-Year Writing Program at The George Washington University (GWU), where Rachel currently teaches, and where Ryan taught for two years.[35] In the earliest years of the new writing program at GWU, when we taught there together, we (like so many writing teachers) were working under a number of administrative constraints that grew out of the fact that the administration constituted us as a program, and not as or within a department. This limited, and still limits, resources and self-determination to a degree, but also freed us from a variety of disciplinary strictures and traditions, though this freedom is increasingly subject to disciplinary/disciplining pressure. While we can talk about various administrative expediencies here, we instead prefer to talk about potentials. The program is divided into a "pre-disciplinary" first-year course (UW20), and several Writing in the Disciplines (WID) courses housed within the academic departments, of which each student must take two.

In our teaching—at GWU for Rachel and at GWU and West Virginia University (WVU) for Ryan—we have struggled against conceiving of the pre-disciplinary course as one that prepares students to enter into certain specified, disciplined modes of thinking, since this model privileges the same disciplinary discourse that we argue needs to be critiqued more rigorously and more thoroughly. We have also resisted views of writing as the production of efficient, well-composed documents that, we would argue, facilitate the university's complicity in the production of technically proficient middle-class workers for the neoliberal system. Let us offer up one example (among many detailed in this volume) of this pedagogy in practice. Take, for example, five critical activities we developed with our colleagues Robert McRuer and Carol Hayes, and that we teach alongside the long research paper. Ryan's final position paper assignment contains the following language:

> We write in part because we want to remake the world, and audiences read our work in the hopes of finding a new vision for that world. Therefore, make your vision new—stake out a territory that requires your voice, and take action to achieve that vision. Accordingly, below are five paths to help you reach beyond the boundaries that so often rein in our writing.

The description goes on to suggest 1) historicizing the debate, 2) questioning power relations, 3) employing theoretical self-reflexivity, 4) engaging in critical interventions and, finally, 5) engaging in anti-disciplinary inquiry. In his performance-centered composition courses, these practices push students to think about their own disciplinary expectations, even as they ask students to compose in spaces and ways that press beyond the boundaries of disciplines, classrooms, and academic institutions.[36]

Rachel's reading and writing assignments participate in this activist pedagogy. Writing projects in her class emerge from readings of the Zapatistas, a revolutionary group based in the mountains of Chiapas, Mexico, who, in their written communications to the outside world, contest commonsense ideologies of literacy, democracy, and power. The classroom's rhetorical approach to Zapatista writing reveals the following: the material and historical circumstances in which Zapatistas are called to write; the circulation of writing, in the Zapatista case, across and within various powerful borders; how we might engage writing that is "different" and see difference as a possibility for, rather than an obstacle to, community; and how this writing affectively destabilizes and offers the possibility for a new world, for "it is not necessary to conquer the world, it is sufficient to make it anew."[37] Writing in this classroom pushes students to rigorously investigate authorized versions of writing and of language use, and to investigate how activist writing is used to challenge these authorized versions.

In both of these composition classes, students are doing work informed by both Cultural Studies and Rhetoric Studies as they are asked to recognize boundaries of disciplines and other sites of authority from the classroom to the nation-state. As critical intervention goes into writing and research projects, students use multiple fields to think through the public and transnational dimensions of their writing, even as we encourage them to question the power relations invoked in doing so. Furthermore, by promoting an anti-disciplinary space prior, but not subordinate, to the disciplinarity that they will later be taught, we are enacting our own critical intervention against the disciplining processes of the university. Such an anti-disciplinary pedagogy is itself a political gesture, one that implicates labor structures, fields of bio-power, and the imperial investments of Anglo-American academia, just as it addresses audiences both in our classrooms, within the university, and beyond its institutional boundaries.

Notes

1. Cynthia Haynes, "Rhetoric/Slash/Composition," *Enculturation* 5, no. 1 (Fall 2003), http://enculturation.gmu.edu/5_1/haynes.html.
2. Sharon Crowley, "Composition Is Not Rhetoric," *Enculturation* 5, no. 1 (Fall 2003): http://enculturation.gmu.edu/5_1/crowley.html, and Krista Ratcliffe, "The Current State of Composition Scholar/Teachers: Is Rhetoric Gone or Just Hiding Out?" *Enculturation* 5, no. 1 (Fall 2003), http://enculturation.gmu.edu/5_1/ratcliffe.html.
3. Crowley, "Composition."
4. Crowley, "Composition."
5. Cary Nelson and Dilip Parameshwar Gaonkar, "Cultural Studies and the Politics of Disciplinarity," in *Disciplinarity and Dissent in Cultural Studies*, ed. Cary Nelson and Dilip Parameshwar Gaonkar (New York: Routledge, 1996), 6.
6. Ien Ang, "Who Needs Cultural Research?" in *Cultural Studies and Practical Politics: Theory, Coalition Building and Social Activism*, ed. Pepi Lestina (New York, Blackwell), 478.
7. Stephen Mailloux, *Disciplinary Identities* (New York: Modern Language Association, 2007).
8. Nelson and Gaonkar, "Cultural Studies," 2.
9. Crowley, "Composition."
10. Saskia Sassen, *A Sociology of Globalization* (New York: W.W. Norton, 2007), 22.
11. Ang, "Who Needs Cultural Research?" 481. For a fuller discussion of neoliberalism and universities, see Rachel Riedner and Kevin Mahoney, *Democracies to Come* (Lanham, MD: Lexington Books, 2008).
12. Lisa Coleman and Lorien Goodman, Introduction, "Rhetoric/Composition: Intersections/Impasses/Differends," *Enculturation* 5, no. 1 (Fall 2003), http://enculturation.gmu.edu/5_1/intro.html.
13. Wendy S. Hesford and Eileen E. Schell, "Introduction: Configurations of Transnationality: Locating Feminist Rhetorics," *College English* 7, no. 5 (May 2008): 464.
14. Hesford and Schell, "Introduction," 464.
15. Ang, "Who Needs Cultural Research?" 477.
16. Mailloux, *Disciplinary Identities*, 40.

17. Robert McRuer, "Composing Bodies; or De-Composition: Queer Theory, Disability Studies, and Alternative Corporealities," *JAC: Journal of Advanced Composition* 24, no. 1 (2004): 68-69.

18. Ira Shor, *Empowering Education* (Chicago: University of Chicago Press, 1992), 190.

19. Shor, *Empowering Education,* 190.

20. Riedner and Mahoney, *Democracies to Come,* 25.

21. Kelly Cooper and Annie Lipsitz, *knowing feminism? Hurricane Katrina "Refugees,"Rigoberta Menchú, and Subcomandante Insurgente Marcos.* Typescript (Lanham, MD: Lexington Books, forthcoming).

22. Gayatri Chakravorty Spivak, "Thinking Cultural Questions in 'Pure' Literary Terms," in *Without Guarantees: In Honor of Stuart Hall,* ed. Paul Gilroy, Lawrence Grossberg, and Angela McRobbie (London: Verso, 2000), 335-36.

23. James Clifford, "Introduction: Partial Truths," in *Writing Culture: The Poetics and Politics of Ethnography,* ed. James Clifford and George E. Marcus (Berkeley, CA: University of California Press, 2000), 2.

24. Clifford, "Introduction," 10.

25. Clifford, "Introduction," 10-11.

26. Clifford, "Introduction," 19.

27. Ralph Cintron. *Angel's Town: Chero Ways, Gang Life and the Rhetorics of Everyday* (New York: Beacon Press, 1998), x.

28. Cintron, *Angel's Town,* x.

29. Ang, "Who Needs Cultural Research?" 482.

30. Gayatri Chakravorty Spivak,"The Politics of Translation," in *Outside in the Teaching Machine* (New York: Routledge, 1973), 181.

31. Spivak "Thinking Cultural Questions," 350.

32. Spivak, "Thinking Cultural Questions," 354. Eric Lorentzen, in this volume, works out precisely such rhetorical reading of ideology in the work of Charles Dickens in a classroom situated within the traditional literature classroom. He argues there that such a reading and a pedagogical praxis is necessary not only to studies of Victorianism, but to breaking out of the disciplined strictures of the English departments in which many of us work, and to extending the critique that his students offer to the historically distant world of Dickens to their own politicized experience.

33. Spivak, "Thinking Cultural Questions," 353.

34. It is also important to acknowledge that universities are one site in which political and intellectual work takes place. There are other social locations where political and intellectual labor is accomplished that this response does not have time to investigate.

35. Simply tracking our narratives in relation to disciplinarity is telling. Despite his work in the trans-discipline of performance studies, Ryan was trained in English departments, and currently holds a tenure-track position in an English department with its own disciplinary controls, after teaching without the promise of tenure in the inter-disciplinary First-Year Writing Program at GWU. Ryan still occasionally teaches composition, using many of the same tactics, in the form of English 102 at West Virginia University, the second course in a composition sequence that, like GWU's, ends with a WID component. Rachel has an inter-disciplinary PhD in Human Sciences, a program that is now defunct, from GWU, with an emphasis on postcolonial theory and feminist material rhetorics. For the past five years, she has taught in the writing program at GWU, and is associated with the inter-disciplinary Women's Studies Program at GWU. While much may be written

about GWU's recent history with writing instruction, some of its problems and promise are explored compellingly in Robert McRuer's "Composing Bodies; or, Decomposition."

36. For more on performance studies as a frame for anti-disciplinary practice in composition classrooms, see Ryan Claycomb, "Performing/Teaching/Writing," later in this volume.

37. Subcomandante Marcos, "The Story of the Tiny Mouse and the Tiny Cat," in *Our Word is Our Weapon: Selected Writings*, ed. Juana Ponce de Leon (New York: Seven Stories, 2001), 309.

Chapter Three
Subjugated Knowledges and Dedisciplinarity in a Cultural Studies Pedagogy

Joe Parker

Discussions of the contested politics of academic fields that have emerged from social movements often emphasize course content while deemphasizing the ways that power circulates through specific sites in the academy. Certainly women's studies, queer studies, and the different ethnic studies fields have struggled to maintain links to the social movements that engendered them, and a concomitant focus on social change. In a more complex fashion, the same is true of postcolonial studies. Similarly, cultural studies may be understood as an academic field emerging from class-based social movements that are affiliated in complex ways with various Marxist analyses whose academic lineage is longer and differently constituted. Within and among these different fields, ongoing debates continue over their ability to remain oriented toward social justice in the face of pressures from the academy to align with knowledge protocols and modes of claiming legitimacy that are measured in terms distant from those of progressive social change.

The work of Michel Foucault offers one of the most effective ways of naming, tracking, and developing multiple modes of resistance to the mechanisms in the academy that pressure these and other fields into modern knowledge protocols. Foucault emphasized the seemingly minor but always meticulously observed small-scale ways in which those of us in the academy and in other major institutions of modernity are pressured to subject ourselves and our work to the mechanisms and apparatuses of power/knowledge. In an academic setting, we are all too familiar with demands that we subject ourselves repeatedly to the protocols of the mechanisms of what Foucault termed "the micro-physics of power" [1]: the job interview, the department meeting or memo, classroom behavioral micro-regulations, exam and paper grading criteria and hierarchies, the manuscript peer review, the teaching evaluation, the promotion and tenure review, to name just a few of many, many others. Together these mechanisms make up a "micro-economy of perpetual penalty" [2] that has been of interest to cultural studies academics and others writing about pedagogy as resistance to domination.[3] Through this micro-economy, knowledge/power relations constitute the violence of the modern. This violence is carried out through the seeming sobriety of self-surveillance and disciplinary normalization, rather than through the public spectacles of physical brutalities and the tortured body of the premodern punishment system.[4]

Foucault characterized the violent subjection of the body to these multiple, all-pervasive mechanisms as discipline, discipline forcibly regulated both by those other than the subject (the teacher, the dissertation or department chair, the Dean), but first and foremost by the subject itself through self-surveillance.[5] Disciplines are not enforced only through the mechanisms of professional associations, major journals, canonical texts, and course content, but through the micro-physics of daily interactions in the multiple quotidian sites of the academy. For Foucault, this micro-physics operates as a network of disciplinary mechanisms supported by, and working as relays within, a much larger network of disciplinary mechanisms extending across all the major institutions of modernity: the marketplace and the workplace; the heteronormative family and the state; the courtroom and the prison; the military and the medical clinic. Through discipline, the subject becomes increasingly more productive as it becomes more docile and obedient to the disciplinary regime of uninterrupted, constant coercion through careful partitions of time, space, and movement.[6] For Foucault, power is invested in the body through the highly specified modes of subjection these mechanisms carry out, thereby producing what he termed "a political technology of the body" which gives birth to a person as an object of knowledge, within an overall political economy of the body, directly involved in a political field of surveillance and discipline.[7] Through this general economy, some bodies are distributed into colleges and graduate schools as students and/or as teachers and administrators, while others find their ways to the workplace or the prison, the military, or the asylum.

Thus, power is something exercised as it traverses and is transmitted by bodies through behavior and a general economy of distribution, rather than a possession some have and others do not, so that power "exerts pressure upon them, just as they themselves, in their struggle against it, resist the grip it has on them."[8] In this conception, knowledge does not develop outside of power, but is produced by power, just as power is constituted through knowledge. This is what Foucault termed "power/knowledge": that which is usually seen as the source of knowledge, the "subject who knows, the objects to be known and the modalities of knowledge," come to be seen as the effects of power/knowledge (*pouvoir-savoir*) and its historical transformations.[9] In this sense, education is not a moment of possible modern liberation for students or scholars, since the student, as well as the teacher and researcher, are already in themselves effects of a system of subjection much more profound and pervasive than the individual.[10]

Some have read this analysis of disciplinary society as an all-encompassing caricature of passive souls, but Foucault was deeply interested in resistance to the disciplinary power/knowledge regime even as he emphasized its limits and its appropriations. Foucault argued that these "micro-powers" could not be over-thrown once and for all, but may only be disrupted through localized episodes that have power effects on the entire network in which they are caught up.[11] In the academic setting and more broadly, he argued for the refusal of disciplinary mechanisms through what he called "a common labor of people seeking to 'de-discipline' themselves,"[12] which he defined as "a different way of governing oneself through a different way of dividing up true and false."[13] Foucault's ge-nealogical method was also developed precisely as a critique in order to open up the re-emergence and insurrection of particular, local, subjugated knowledges that the modern power/knowledge regime works to disqualify.[14] Subjugated knowledges are not opposed "primarily to the contents, methods or concepts" of modern power/knowledge, but "to the effects of the centralizing powers which are linked to the institution and functioning of an organized scientific discourse within a society such as ours."[15] These two different goals for resistance to the disciplinary regime—refusing discipline and the insurrection of subjugated knowledges—have been the basis for the considerable writing about education and pedagogy that I build on in the coming sections, where they serve as my double focus.

Foucault's critique of modern society has a number of important implica-tions for developing a critical analysis of academic disciplines. His critique has been applied to particular academic disciplinary and interdisciplinary fields by a number of scholars and critics in cultural studies, feminism, and other areas.[16] At stake in these critical analyses are modern claims of the discipline fields to po-litical neutrality and of interdisciplinary fields to the reduction of inequality and the promotion of social justice.[17] Yet these arguments about education and the politics of knowledge are also caught up in larger debates over the social effects of the academy and of education more broadly, the nature and role of the intel-lectual, and the ethics and politics of epistemology and the nature of power.

If we approach cultural studies with this Foucauldian perspective, we can see some important points of intersection that are useful in the classroom. We may summarize cultural studies broadly in the terms of Simon During as "an affirmation of otherness and negation of metadiscourse"[18] that traditionally has emphasized the politics of popular culture, particularly in England and its settler colonies in North America and the Australasia. Gayatri Chakravorty Spivak, bell hooks, Rey Chow, and other women of color practicing cultural studies have extended the cultural studies notion of Otherness to include not only issues of class, but also race, gender, sexual orientation, and nation. This construction of cultural studies centers on critiques of colonization, Orientalism, and hybrid and minority discourses as they intersect with histories of racism, heteronormativi-ties, gender inequalities, and class exploitation.[19] Chow has noted, for example, that the power effects of the displacement, by poststructuralists, of the west as center has brought attention to the history of European violence under imperial-ism; attention to this violence may work to further dislodge the Eurocentrism of cultural studies and poststructuralist interpretive practices.[20] Rather than arguing that the subversive content and counter-hegemonic resistance learned in the cultural studies classroom are somehow outside of these histories and constructions of norms and Others, those in cultural studies who have drawn on Foucault have suggested that cultural studies practices must confront the political limits imposed by the disciplinary formations of modern power/knowledge.[21] These practices refuse the modernist notion that liberatory work makes possible space outside of repression and power. The argument is that the disciplinary micro-economy is active throughout society, including classrooms where Foucauldian resistance is practiced. A dedisciplinary approach to cultural studies pedagogy marks and builds on already-existing sites for resistance beyond the traditional emphases on content and form to include multiple quotidian behaviors as locations for counter-hegemonic practice. This approach to pedagogy directs those interested in cultural studies education as counter-hegemonic resistance to four areas. First, we must pay attention to the presence in the classroom of multiple mechanisms that subject both students and teachers to the modern disciplinary micro-physics of power, through quotidian repeated and meticulously observed bodily and other practices that result in both docility and productivity. These mechanisms may be redirected and their grip loosened through pedagogical techniques that encourage the failure of docility and productivity as constituted under the political and ethical limits of modernity, failures that open space for dedisciplinary modes of governing the self and dividing the true and false. Second, we must make the ways in which knowing constitutes power central to course content and practice, so that knowledge may constitute forms of power that do not replicate the social hierarchies instilled globally by modernity. Third, we must practice a pedagogy that deploys specific naming practices to render intelligible the otherwise invisible power effects of disciplinary society (such as the violence and exploitation of normative social practices), in order to interrupt the disciplinary power effects. Finally, we must acknowledge that the "subject who knows, the objects to be known and the modalities of knowledge" are effects of the disciplinary regime of power/knowledge, where the modern disciplinary regime makes its totalizing claims. So a dedisciplinary pedagogy highlights different subject positions and objects of knowledge that diverge from the terms of modernity, while deploying ways of knowing that resist the disciplinary regime—subjugated knowledges being the most central for our purposes. I take each of these areas in turn as they apply to the cultural studies classroom at the beginning level of teaching, the first and second years of college, specifically as applied to writing practices.

Failures of Docility and Productivity
in Dedisciplinary Pedagogy

From a Foucauldian perspective, the disciplinary regime coerces its subjects into subjection through a micro-economy of perpetual penalties of time, activity, behavior, gestures, speech, the body, and sexuality, what he termed "a punishable, punishing universality."[22] His analysis of this subjection suggests that it is a form of violence, violence that can only be responded to ethically through critique. This critique asks that the detailed political investment of the disciplined body be interrupted temporarily and partially through classroom practices. Such practices first bring the multiple intersecting systems of subjection and coercion to critical awareness, and then work with the students to perform bodily behaviors that refuse self-subjection, a refusal which is paramount for Foucauldian notions of agency. This practice may also be extended from the coercion of students to the subjection of instructors caught in the same net of power/knowledge.

The proliferation of sites for interrupting disciplinary practices in the Foucauldian cultural studies classroom may seem unwieldy at first, but they may be used selectively where appropriate for different topics and courses. Alternatively, such sites for interrupting disciplinary subjection may be used in a targeted fashion to resist tendencies of particular practices to fall into forms of power/knowledge relations that are readily appropriated back into the power/knowledge regime. Bodily practices, time schedules, and speech all constitute what Foucault termed "minor techniques of multiple and intersecting observations."[23] The possibility of diverging from these practices may at first seem trivial (or what Foucault terms micropolitical), but as students and the instructor experiment with diverging even slightly from these practices, a profound unease often finds its way into the educational space. Habits of raising only one hand rather than two in order to speak, legible penmanship, and the carefully observed physical docility of quietly seated note-taking students are generally valued in a positive way as productive behaviors. Yet Foucault compared proper penmanship in early modern French education to the bodily training of the military recruit in early modern armies as examples of the bodily docility required of the modern subject. In my experience in the Foucauldian classroom, when readings, lecture, or discussion mark productive practices that seem positive under modernity as practices of coerced subjection and docility, students often become defensive, as their modern self-concepts as free individuals are put at risk. Yet students are often highly motivated by modern presumptions to freedom to refuse docility, even as they continue to operate under the sign of modern freedom, so the refusal of docility is still often of interest. On such occasions, I point to examples of well-respected challenges to modern docility, such as bell hooks's adoption of a failure of proper punctuation in her own self-naming, refusing proper linguistic practice even as her books reach wide audiences and her critiques spread well beyond the limits of the academy.

When a class adopts practices that seem to displace the instructor's authority (circular seating, discussion replacing lectures, speaking without raising the hand) or to diffuse authority (students calling on each other, community members selecting class materials), a Foucauldian analysis suggests that the classroom remains a site for disciplinary regulations and self-surveillance.[24] These critiques may provoke some to reject these pedagogical practices, yet peer pressures and the familiarity of the "orderly" classroom make it very difficult to diverge even in a small, temporary way from the disciplinary regime. This often induces internal conflicts and provokes modernist questioning of how any freedom may be possible in an educational setting. When this is compounded in discussion of how behaviors are organized into a graded system of gratification and punishment that distributes all behavior in the field of observation, including examination performance, surveillance, and other ways,[25] students may become discouraged about possibilities for resistance. Here, discussions of agency and the limited freedom emphasized in Foucault's later writings become central to classroom practice.

Yet the behavioral divergence from the disciplinary regime in a classroom or other institutional setting does not disrupt the power/knowledge network of multiple mechanisms for subjection that form the network of power/knowledge that stretches across multiple institutions, including the state. Self-surveillance and instructor observation and regulation of classroom attendance and behaviors are part of a series of other "innumerable petty mechanisms . . . for] progressive objectification and . . . partitioning of individual behavior,"[26] including hierarchical distribution through the examination, records of attendance and lateness, seating for visibility, monitoring of cheating and plagiarism, and grading and tracking.[27] Students receive much more from these objectifying and distribution mechanisms than grades and college degrees, for these mechanisms constitute the individual status of students (linked to the measurements, gaps, and marks that characterize their case) even as students are homogenized in the uniformity of their subjection to the modern disciplinary regime. In this sense, the disciplinary regime constitutes students (and instructors) as effects and objects of power and knowledge.[28] Consequently, this perspective finds the greatest individualization where the power is more anonymous and more effective through comparative measures with the norm. In this way, the anonymous constitution of the individual does not reduce specific features but inserts them into a field of compulsory objectification. Individuals are therefore located in a comparative economy that calculates the gaps between individuals and that is useful for bodily distribution in an economy of subjection.[29]

There are multiple ways to work against the multifaceted enforcement of this hierarchy of student individuation. Because students are often so interested in grades, it is possible to refuse disciplinary hierarchical differentiation by giving all students the same grade. Yet students long-accustomed to grade-based measures of achievement may be driven to expect the highest grade possible, so in an instance where I explored this possibility, the students, after long discussion, agreed that they should all receive a high grade. As you may expect, the resulting high average grade for the class drew the attention of my department chair at the time, since as an instructor, I am also caught up in the net of disciplinary power relations. We encountered similar pressures in various sorts of student peer evaluation, where it is difficult to find students who are not ready to evaluate their peers as generously as they hope to be evaluated and ultimately graded. The refusal of the hierarchical effects of the classroom may be seen as an argument for the rejection of grading, as has been and still is practiced in a few institutions. Yet I would suggest that more effective pedagogical work takes place with students who are confronting these hierarchizing mechanisms in the classroom as they will beyond the academy. Of course, we can create social spaces where learning occurs without grading and other normalizing mechanisms, and perhaps even where self-surveillance may take a temporary holiday in the classroom and the research arena.

One of the most difficult aspects of the disciplinary regime to dislodge is the persistent emphasis on productivity as a goal, and writing may become a central mechanism for troubling these modern practices of productivity-as-docility. Diverging from an emphasis on student productivity may arouse profound feelings of being unprofessional for instructors, or encouraging inefficiency and even sloth in teachers and students. Often, these deeply felt responses indicate the high stakes of such divergences within the disciplinary regime, and we must work with them actively in the classroom setting, by naming them explicitly, and opening time for students to work with them in the classroom and in other writing and reflection work. Since most of the many mechanisms for instructor surveillance of students depend heavily on student productivity, finding ways to validate failures of productivity (refusing to attend class, not writing assignments, failing to read texts, not participating in discussions) become moments that are very disruptive of the disciplinary regime at work in the classroom, even as they are extremely important and potentially fruitful pedagogically. Tying these moments of failures of productivity to an emphasis on bodily behaviors (dance, emphatic gestures, emotionally demonstrative actions, disruptive passivities, bodily civil disobediences, etc.)[30] that are generally antithetical to good citizenship may be particularly effective at creating forms of production that interrupt docility and take students beyond the constricted physical limits of discipline. When applied to writing, such failures at modern productivity may become sites for resistance to subjection to the disciplinary regime. Self-reflexive writing is one such pedagogical technique, as long as it is centered in interruptions of self-surveillance, rather than encouraging students to express their creativity or individualized internal experiences in modern fashion.

Jennifer Gore has suggested working beyond the limits of teacher surveillance as a way to weaken the grip of the disciplinary regime.[31] One weakness of her suggested approach is that students carry the deeply ingrained and multiply reinforced habits of self-surveillance with them on these projects. My attempts to carry this idea into practice have also consistently found that the projects students carried out were often readily appropriated back into modernist conceptions of student freedom and activist conceptions. As a response, I have taken to introducing students to critiques of modern conceptions of social change and alternative models taken from poststructuralist, feminist, Foucauldian, postcolonial studies, and cultural studies social theory.

Gayatri Chakravorty Spivak has developed a set of practices that interrupt the presumptions of radical activism within the terms and political limits of modernity in many of her essays. In an essay specifically on human rights work, for example, she argues for educational practices linking work in western universities with education beyond the limits of the western university system, practices that replace the misguided claims in the global north to right wrongs of the world with work that opens education up to the agency of the subaltern Other activated through democratic structures.[32] By linking her work in the western university system with work in elementary schools where the teacher learns from below, from the children and the subaltern,[33] she displaces the educational effects of children's subjections to docility, modern forms of resistance, modern forms of class apartheid, and nationalist identitarianism.[34] These practices open up room to activate the episteme and ethical practices of subaltern groups through the uncoercive rearrangement of desires, operating in terms divergent from those of modern education but aligned with democratic reflexes.[35] In this model, the terms of learning, authority, expertise, and Otherness are fundamentally rearranged, so that the teacher learns from the students (or from subaltern materials brought into the classroom when the students are not subalterns) rather than teaching in pedagogies that locate universalist knowledge in the instructor.

There is clear congruence here with the work of Paolo Freire in the displacement of the teacher as a source of knowledge, but Spivak also asserts solidarities with the "Freedom Schools" of the American South and the Gopathshala in Bangladesh, the educational writing of W. E. B. DuBois and of Antonio Gramsci on teaching southerners, and other educators who have worked in subaltern education.[36] This pedagogy also suggests an important response to the central problem for a dedisciplinary pedagogy: the decentralized character of power in a Foucauldian analysis and the resulting confusion about where to direct resistance and organizing. If power is constituted through the event of knowing and all of those in the classroom are caught up in the disciplinary regime, no obvious utopian social order may serve as a model for pedagogical relations. Spivak's pedagogy, which emphasizes democratic reflexes grounded in an encounter with the agency of the global south, displaces the first world university and the experts it legitimates, including herself and virtually all other faculty, from the position of pure radical resistance in a binary opposition to the student. This may be compared to the efforts in cultural studies with the founding of the Open University and, more recently, in adult education all over the European Union, to reconfigure pedagogical relations in the classroom of instructor and student, where adult and working class students bring expertise beyond that of the instructor.[37] Pedagogical approaches that emphasize the politics of location likewise delimit the knowledge of the instructor and the texts within the specific limits of race, class, sexuality, gender, and nation, rather than making universalist claims, which produces openings for more variegated power relations between students, teachers, and course materials. bell hooks's notion of "talking back" is another way to work to invigorate student knowledges and invite them to talk as equals in a setting where there is so little equality, holding their own against the grain of so many mechanisms and experiences in which they are forced to subject themselves to the disciplinary regime.[38] Writing assignments that invite students to explore their own expertise and authority beyond that of the university and the instructor, or that track and critique the limitations of universalist knowledge claims, can help students hone their skills at enacting these refusals of the disciplinary regime.

Constituting Knowledge/Power Relations
Other than Those of Modernity

Foucauldian conceptions of power/knowledge suggest that power is constituted through the act of knowing, just as knowledge is constituted through power relations. This opens up a suggestive area for pedagogical reflection on renegotiating the limits of the cultural studies classroom based on critical interrogation of the limits and politics of the field. The limits of cultural studies, particularly in its relations to the Others of a Euro-U.S.-centered modernity, are outlined in Spivak's critique of cultural studies. In her call for the supplementation of cultural studies (and area studies) by comparative literature, she is critical of cultural studies as "monolingual, presentist, narcissistic, not practiced enough in close reading even to understand that the mother tongue is actively divided."[39] Rather than this monolingual, presentist practice, Spivak asks cultural studies to take up an approach to "culturally diversified ethical systems diachronically, through the history of multicultural empires, without foregone conclusions."[40] On this point, Spivak agrees with Rey Chow's argument for an emphasis in cultural studies on critiques of Orientalist constitutions of empire, and the subalterns, hybrids, and minorities that may otherwise be erased through modern modes of knowledge and of epistemic violence.[41] The critique and rejection of erasures, aporias, and epistemic violence draws on Foucault's critique of the violence of modern forms of power/knowledge, violence through repeated, forcible subjections that are naturalized under modernity to the point that we identify with this violence and defend it. How may classroom education do something other than reproduce such modern power/knowledge relations?

Cultural studies pedagogy in this frame stretches beyond the inherited limits of the monolingual English-language classroom, or even colonizing, language-centered, comparativist practices, to find ways to bring materials in the languages of the global south, particularly colonized and subaltern groups, into the classroom. The traditional centrality of counter-hegemonic popular cultural practices in cultural studies may be readily adapted to this need for non-English language materials. There are many possibilities in this area, such as using visual culture from colonized and subaltern groups, working with local diaspora communities in the metropole from indigenous populations or other colonized groups as students in classrooms, as partners in field work and web-based collaborations, and as supervisors and advisors in developing these materials where they are not readily available.

Spivak and Chow's insistence on the historicized analysis of popular cultural practices suggests another pillar for the cultural studies pedagogy that maintains its center on the interrogation of the presumptions of gendered, racialized, and class-stratified colonial histories. One danger of presentist cultural analysis is to define culture in terms of the free choices of the individual artist or artistic collaborative. Persistent attention to the ways in which racialized and gendered histories of colonization constrict the range of available cultural practices and strategies of resistance can have surprisingly suggestive implications for representation and solidarities in classroom practices. Carrying out cross-border site visits in a cultural studies class on communities, for example, has allowed my students to uncover collaborations of Latino artists with indigenous squatter communities. By observing how indigenous populations, often operating without full literacy, take advantage of the porosity for U.S. citizens of the colonizing border to work in collaboration to build community centers rich in scarce legal, economic, and cultural resources, students may be exposed to the agency of those whose languages they do not understand. By framing student understanding of this agency in terms historicized both by oral indigenous narratives through interpreters and by readings critiquing normalizing "multicultural empires," the classroom stages contestations between modern knowledges and their violent effects.

Spivak also demands that classroom pedagogy reconfigure the relation of self to Other, thereby transforming the power relations of self-same and Other into new forms. Spivak calls this pedagogy "an institutional calculus recoding or instrumentalizing undecidability," where the Other of any presumed collectivity (nation, gender, etc.) is rendered undecidable by "really letting yourself be imagined (experience that impossibility) without guarantees, by and in another culture, perhaps. Teleopoiesis." [42] Through this approach "alterity remains underived from us; it is not our dialectical negation, it contains us as much as it flings us away." [43] This can be accomplished by giving attention, in materials we teach, to events "stag[ing] more surprising and unexpected maneuvers toward collectivity," and by teaching in a way that begs "the question of collectivity, asking again and again "How many are we? Who are they?" as a way of teaching the "recognition of ceaselessly shifting collectivities." [44] This opens up interpretation of specific cultural texts and objects to the multiple solidarities that local marginalized or subaltern communities have found fruitful in their construction of cultural politics. The task for cultural studies pedagogies is to reject unthinking collectivities, such as nation or gender, colonized or colonizer, and instead to allow the classroom to become a site for the recognition of alliances unthinkable within the modern grid of intelligibility.

This pedagogical work may be readily carried out in writing assignments. In-class short and free writing assignments are an important way to intervene in the unthinking "we" cathected by course readings, by students during discussion, and by the instructor herself in unreflective constructions of self/Other binaries. By calling attention to the normalized constitution of questions of "we" and "they," students may flex their newly found teleopoietic muscles, imagining unexpected alliances (northern underemployed populations with urban southerners; urban first world Chicanas with rural subalterns) and rendering legible unanticipated oppositions within the classroom and beyond. Entire assignments may be constructed around exercises in critical self-reflection on the subtly racialized and class-stratified politics of the first person subject, eternally present even if often erased, allowing students to recognize undecidability in sites of contradictions (simultaneous privilege and subordination; nation of origin and of citizenship) and ambivalences (multiracial identities; sexualities under question). Most important from this perspective is writing that tracks and intervenes in the tendency in interpretation to inscribe normalized Others installed through epistemic violence, and radically reconfigure self/Other relations from the teleopoietically imagined perspective of the erased Others of that same violence.

Attention to the Politics of Naming and Intelligibility

In a dedisciplinary pedagogy, the moment when central objects of knowledge are named and identified, often early in the course of the term or course sections, is profoundly important in the politics of knowledge. Spivak explored the politics of Foucauldian power/knowledge to find that as we know, through language, we are inevitably working with a catachresis or misfit, a naming that occludes as it discloses.[45] To summarize Spivak's reading of Foucault rather dogmatically, every success of rendering something intelligible is an objectification, not only for the object of knowledge, but also for the knowing subject, an objectification that subjects the knowing subject to the political and ethical terms of modernity through language. Spivak's proposal for resisting this subjectification cum objectification is to assiduously work with an awareness of the limits of knowing, to make the problems and occlusions and erasures of the object of knowledge apparent and, ultimately, to be critical of every success at rendering something intelligible.[46] In the classroom, this problematizing of every act of knowing may become a central pedagogical goal, rendering what seems obvious more troubling and less familiar while giving central place to a certain indeterminacy of meaning and power/knowledge relations. This indeterminacy destabilizes the fundamental lineaments and power effects of disciplinary power/knowledge, making the classroom a space for rendering intelligible knowing subjects and objects of knowledge impossible under the binarisms (colonizer/colonized, masculine/feminine, student/prisoner) of the modern interpretive grid, as I discuss in my final section. In other words, attention to the politics of naming and intelligibility allows the classroom to become a site for the insurrection of subjugated knowledges, with classroom writing an important site for this attention.

bell hooks likewise objects to the naming of structural domination in ways that may render it innocuous for members of dominant groups through the substitution of ethnicity for race, of difference or the Other for oppression, of hegemony for exploitation.[47] Inherited bad habits in the classroom may domesticate topics otherwise disruptive to racist or exploitative social practices, making them intelligible under the terms of universalist humanism. As a result, it may come to seem that all of us have ethnicity while whites can escape discussions of race, or that we are all different (under modern liberal individualism) rather than some of us are exploited while others are oppressors. Rey Chow also emphasizes histories of racist practices and exploitation that can confront the theoretical claims to subversion and resistance of poststructuralist and cultural studies theorists.[48]

Possible applications of the politics of naming and intelligibility may be seen in Foucault's own naming practices. Foucault's response to problems with the politics of the innocuous term "knowledge," for example, led him to render it with the neologism "power/knowledge." This inconvenient innovation names the power aspect so readily overlooked by academics and others in modernity who produce knowledge: prison policy critiques; school grades; the corporate prospectus; the psychoanalytic session; government ministry reports; public health studies; the court case; and many others. Foucault provides us with many examples of terms that we may substitute for those in common parlance both in academic settings and in colloquial usage. Foucault developed general terms to replace innocuous words such as economies of subjectification (for society), self-surveillance (for identity), technologies of the body (for behavior), or compulsory objectification (for knowledge). The term "regime" may be simply added to terms that might otherwise sound appealing, such as truth (truth regime) or discourse (discursive regime) or discipline (disciplinary regime). This practice is particularly useful even when working within a Marxist or Gramscian frame, as hooks pointed out, so that we may come to render key terms like "structure" or "production" with the Foucauldian "mechanisms of subjection."

We may develop a similar critique of a number of common disciplinary terms for widespread social and cultural practices that render violence unintelligible. The specific vocabulary that must be reconsidered depends on the discipline of the classroom, of the textbook or journal article under discussion, and of the primary document in the archive or the field setting. Yet each must be interrogated for ease of appropriation in order to interrupt domestication to the extent possible. Social scientists and historians in assigned readings who lapse into descriptive summaries of "social order," for example, may be interrupted as classroom discussion centers on using terms introduced in a major methodological reading from early in the semester by substituting a term such as "power/knowledge regime." Humanities discussions of modern individualist proliferations of "interpretation" as manifestations of free will may be redirected to critical analyses of speech and other uses of language as sites for subjection into the modern grid of intelligibility. Claims to objectivity and the political neutrality of knowledge pervade nearly every academic field, and may be interrogated in various ways: through questions about complicity with colonialism (likewise found in most fields), or through cross-cultural analyses of how seemingly objectivist categories produce aporias that silence and exclude. Modernist presumptions of free speech or egalitarian practices in the classroom can be interrogated with readings and discussion of the classroom as a site for docility, either explicitly with readings[49] or implicitly after an early introduction of critiques of modernity.

In terms of concrete practice, writing assignments might take, as one objective, translation from standardized vocabulary that normalizes inequality and violence into terms and phrases that refuse and critique that normalization, as in the paragraph above. I also begin most introductory classes with a warning that students will encounter many terms that seem neutral but are not, in order to return, again and again, to this reinscribing of putatively neutral terms into a more critical vocabulary when they come up in the readings, and I end the semester with a study guide of reinterpreted "Neutral Terms" as students prepare for the final exam.

In my own teaching on the historicized Others of the masculinized west, I have found that sometimes the simple translation of key terms must be supplemented with the above techniques. For example, when teaching late medieval Japanese culture, students are comfortable with the term "shogun" because of the popularity of samurai movies and other aspects of U.S. popular culture. Some teachers might feel that this term requires translation, but the usual translation as "Barbarian-Subduing Generalissimo" makes little sense to students when they have been trained to see the "shogun" as a head of state that glorifies military violence. A translation with a more appropriate term from political science, something akin to "military dictator," consolidates the premodern kingdom of Japan as identical with the modern nation-state, while also erasing the origins of the office in Japanese history as an office for the maintenance, defense, and military expansion of the people of Yamato (those who claim to be Japanese), with the northern and eastern indigenous peoples named as "barbarians." It is the subjection of these indigenous groups and the expansion of the Yamato people into their territory that makes the coherent entity of past centuries known to our students as Japan possible, yet this violent history must be articulated explicitly in order to identify some of the aporias generated by the term "shogun" or "Japan." Only when such a historical analysis is carried out will questions about the perspectives of those who have been forcibly consolidated into the modern nation-state become possible, opening up room for subjugated knowledges.

Yet effective naming and intelligibility are themselves fundamental criteria for grading and other evaluation, both written and oral, so they present particular challenges for designing assignments and evaluating classroom performance. An important preliminary response to this problem is to recognize that subjection to language through writing and speaking is fundamentally an event of ordering,[50] an ordering that is perhaps unavoidably complicit with social inequalities and the foundational violences of the society in which that order is normative. As Nikki Sullivan has suggested, in an overview of queer theory, "naming something constitutes a form of closure, or of assimilation,"[51] where assimilation is not a welcoming gesture of successful integration of queer into the heteronormative, but the moment where, by definition, the queer comes under threat through the inscription of social norms. Rey Chow argues a similar point in her attack on those antitheory moralists who approach language as instrumental, as something to be rendered clear and transparent for effective communication in the case of the humanities (but not in the sciences or math or such trade professions as medicine or law). If we are to challenge the Eurocentrism of the Western logos and problematize the politics of the production of meaning and value, Chow suggests we must approach language as a type of labor that restores "an originary difference" and acknowledges the implicit ideological and theoretical assumptions of the clear language that claims to be "natural."[52]

In this cultural studies approach to teaching writing, the simplicity, clarity, and persuasiveness of the perfectly legible sentence and perfectly reasonable common sense argument are pleasures and delusions we "must learn to forgo."[53] Teaching written and oral use of language in a setting influenced by poststructuralist politics and critique takes place through a "profound distrust of literal, naturalized meanings; a persistent refusal or deferral of reference, a determined unmasking of any use of language that seems devoid of semiotic self-consciousness."[54] In this way, the cultural studies classroom may become a site for the practice of "acts of subversion of an unbearable regime (Western logocentrism and its many 'ideological aberrations,' to use a phrase from [Paul] de Man)," even as it teaches speaking and writing that both "wants to be of the masses yet ends up speaking and writing in such ways that few of the masses will ever understand."[55] In a certain sense, then, Chow suggests that the cultural studies classroom becomes a site for training in comfort and skill at what she terms this "permanent contradiction," perhaps the opposite of how many teach writing as skill at the erasure of contradiction.

For that reason, dedisciplinary pedagogies must take up as one fundamental and necessary practice the disordering, the critical interrogation, the self-reflexive deconstruction of the author or speaker's order and reason, genre and gesture, self and Other.[56] To this end, Robert McRuer has argued for an approach to composition that emphasizes practices of what he calls "decomposition," that clear linguistic space for unruly, disorderly cultural and social practices.[57] In designing assignments and evaluating their performance, the measure of a successful assignment shifts from established notions of clarity and consistency, persuasion and precision, to the successful practice of the critical and the disorderly, understood as a refusal of what McRuer terms "the current corporeality." Classroom performance and written work might then be evaluated in terms of its success at whether the topic has been made queer or crip, whether implicit norms or ideologies or power/knowledge politics have been successfully decomposed and, ultimately, whether order and composure have been effectively lost.[58] D. Diane Davis develops a comparably reformulated pedagogy of excription and laughter that proliferates sense to allow for illicit styles, impurities of argumentation and truth and, ultimately, unreason (Foucault's *déraison*) within the limits of "good writing."[59]

By refusing domestication of the knowing subject and her Others, dedisciplinary power/knowledge relations in the classroom shift from demonstrating mastery of oneself and one's subject matter towards a site for critique shaped as a practice of a particular refusal of intelligibility, of objectification, and of sub-jectification. This refusal renders visible the occlusions and violences that acts of knowing and writing and speaking install and attempt to normalize, making visible the political and ethical specificity of the subject and her Others, rather than making possible "the unquestioned transparent ethical subject—the white male heterosexual Christian man of property."[60] In this frame, evaluation centers on the examination of a legible ethics and politics, of "the ways in which the subject 'subjects' itself through 'ability to know' (*pouvoir-savoir*),"[61] a subjec-tion that is a "success" only when it refuses to conceal or bracket problems with the thing named and with the act of naming itself, the act of constituting reality and its limits, ethics, and politics. Effective writing becomes that which refuses the naturalized meanings and direct references enforced by Western logocen-trism in order to explicitly practice subversion of its unbearable regime. Such "success" is displayed not through proximity to normalization, but through what McRuer calls queering and cripping the object of knowledge, the subject, and ultimately power/knowledge relations themselves.

Recognizing Subjects and Objects of Knowledge that Refuse the Disciplinary Regime

As the power effects of disciplinary knowledge/power relations are rendered visible, the classroom may become a site for the insurrection of subjugated knowledges that are under siege in the modern truth regime. An example of this practice is seen when bell hooks begins one response to cultural studies with a saying that recognizes as authoritative a person and a statement that would be unintelligible under the disciplinary regime and is suggestive for pedagogy. A favorite saying of her mother's mother, Sarah Oldham—"If you play with a puppy he'll lick you in the mouth"—forms the basis for a critique of white scho-lars who assume familiarity without recognizing that their work is made possible by a history and cultural context of white supremacy.[62] The subject hooks rec-ognizes is one close to her but far from most of the hallways in academe: the southern black rural woman in the 1950s. The object of knowledge hooks rec-ognizes looms large for many in the academy who study race: the many subtle ways in which difference is domesticated and racism made more palatable.

hooks's critique of the speed by which cultural studies gained legitimacy in the academy, that was and in many ways still is denied to Black Studies and third world studies, is a warning to those working in fields dominated by white academics, particularly white men. She suggests that this rapid success may be-tray an ease with which the subjects of cultural studies are more readily appro-priated into white supremacist and colonizing academic practices and the mod-ern truth regime more generally.[63] As a warning to whites, her grandmother's saying also serves as a warning to people of color in cultural studies and beyond, who may forget the need for distance and wariness against being surprised when the visitor in your house takes liberties and treats you with contempt, viz. the hope that easy bonding with whites across racial boundaries is feasible. By introducing her mother's mother's saying into her writing about the academy, hooks clears room to discuss racism, even in a white-dominated field such as cultural studies, and also to engage with forms of intellectual discourse that were and are not traditionally welcome in the academy, such as her own grandmother's. hooks elaborates specific implications of this statement for cultural studies classrooms, focusing on the cultural studies classroom as a place for white students to grapple with race and domination even as it puts the professor at risk of collaboration with racist structures.[64] This is part of a more general argument about cultural studies as a practice that critically interrogates the location from which writing occurs and the role of the educator as potentially supporting colonization and domination.[65]

The concrete practices suggested by hooks are those she carries out herself in this essay: introduction of knowledges and speaking subjects generally excluded from the academy, what we might call subjugated knowledges; and work in the medium of colloquial materials and dialect that rarely, if ever, make their way through the modern machinery of academic publication and into the classroom. Her quoting of her mother's mother, rather than turning to academic press publications and other acceptable documentation, extends the reach of her truth practices beyond the limits of the modern truth regime. Her references to her mother's mother as "grandmamma Aunt Sarah" and "baba"[66] uses colloquialisms rather than the official language of the scientific kinship system of the modern truth regime, gesturing toward the familiar even as she refuses the attempts of the disciplinary regime to regulate her language in discussing the familiar and personal. Yet hooks does not allow the personal and the local to distract her from the rigorous intellectual points she makes about racist social structures and the role of education in supporting domination and colonization.

When hooks interrogates these structures by sharing the local strategies of her mother's mother with those of us who were not able to hear Sarah Oldham's warnings, she draws on the extensive experience of her baba in dealing with racism, while generating an anti-racist practice that is almost as difficult to domesticate as her mother's mother was and is. By bringing the anti-racist practices of her mother's mother into the classroom, her students and readers can taste the effects of their own presumptions to familiarity across the boundaries of difference, and may learn to recoil from these presumptions, even as we might recoil from the friendliness of the slobbering dogs that we all know and that some of us are. This self-critique is necessary both for white faculty and students in a white supremacist society, and for the women and men of color who risk complicity with racist practices and their multiple means of appropriation and domestication, and suggests the central importance of self-reflexive analysis and critique in a cultural studies pedagogy.

While hooks' warning has clear implications for teachers and authors in cultural studies, it can readily be applied as well to rethinking student writing. Many of our students have expertise in non-standard English that they often are

unlearning in the writing classroom, but hooks's deployment of her own colloquial skills, as well as those of her mother's mother, suggests a different focus
for the writing classroom. Rather than teaching written language as univocal,
hooks's practice asks us to consider teaching writing as a site for multivocality,
where those students' heritages are accorded a respect equivalent to that of standard English. The writing teacher may design assignments that encourage code-
switching from standard English to vernacular forms, and experimentation with
ways in which the vernacular may displace the standard language form at key
moments in building persuasive arguments through logics and colloquialisms
that refuse normalization. Students who do not have an expertise in non-standard
English, or who lack strong connections to subjugated knowledges, may seem to
be at a disadvantage in learning this practice, and they will have to work harder
at these assignments in a reversal of the usual advantage of students more familiar with standard English in the writing classroom. Students may also be asked
to reflect on folk knowledges of the sort that hooks deploys in building their
own critiques of racialized, unequally gendered, or class elitist aspects of the
academy, or in addressing other topics relevant to the course subject matter.
Advanced work of this sort would entail assignments that draw on folk wisdom
and other forms of subjugated knowledges that reverse and displace the legitimacy of the ways in which academic objects of knowledge and course topics are
constituted, modeled on course readings, lectures, and discussions that do the
same.

hooks's introduction of her mother's mother in the classroom is also an example of the revitalization of subjugated knowledges that Foucault argued was
central to resistance to the centralized regulatory mechanisms of modern pow-
er/knowledge. As a local knowledge that would be ranked very low on the modern hierarchy of reliable knowledges, Sarah Oldham's local wisdom is marginal
to modern power/knowledge, even as it interrogates its racialized politics. Just
as Foucault wrote his histories to bring attention to the knowledges of delin-
quents, psychiatric patients, and "of the nurse, of the doctor—parallel and marginal as they are to the knowledge of medicine,"[67] hooks brings into the feminist
cultural studies classroom knowledge that would otherwise be refused entry into
the hallways of academe, as Spivak[68] and other cultural studies practitioners
have done as well. Foucault suggested that awareness of these subjugated knowledges is fruitful, not because it may be rendered into general commonsense
knowledge of modern hegemonies, but rather because it is a local, popular, particular knowledge, "a differential knowledge incapable of unanimity and which
owes its force only to the harshness with which it is opposed by everything
around it."[69] Focus on subjugated knowledges asks us to rethink the myth of the
"silent Other" that ignores the presence of already-formed oppositional voices.[70]
But the more general point of pedagogies that support the introduction and vi-
talization of subjugated knowledges is that they refuse the claim to universality
and the logic of modern commonsense, the logic of hegemony.

Cultural studies pedagogical practices have a clear affinity with popular culture that may readily be seen as the re-emergence of these local popular knowl-

edges, but not all such differential knowledges are counter-hegemonic. As Rey Chow has argued, selection of case studies and field sites, classroom videos and texts must be interrogated as to their position in relation to a confrontation with the significance of race, and rejected if they carry out the "persistent denial of racial inequalities" or practice the "reification of culture."[71] Here it is useful to distinguish between two overlapping but contradictory conceptions of the "popular." First is the popular that meets with success in the circuits of advanced capitalist consumer society, the popular that may appropriate critiques of race or erase it altogether, as it may with other forms of Othering. Second is the popular that Foucault emphasized, that is localized and site-specific, refusing claims on the universal or unanimity, surrounded not by consumers eager to hand over cash for its commodified form but by the "harshness with which it is opposed by everything around it."[72] Cultural studies pedagogy must be ever-vigilant for the appropriations of an exploitative society, as Rey Chow reminds us, and refuse those appropriations as it makes the "dogged turn towards the other"[73] that remains at the center of a dedisciplinary pedagogy for cultural studies.

Conclusion

The simultaneous focus in a cultural studies pedagogy, on resistance to disciplinary mechanisms and the insurrection of subjugated knowledges, demands that we pay attention to physical bodies as they encounter bodies of knowledge. As students are expected to subject themselves bodily and intellectually to the classroom disciplinary regime, so the scholarship and teaching of the teacher is expected to subject herself to the disciplinary regime articulated through departmental, field, and publication mechanisms. Where possible, the partial refusal of this subjection is the goal of dedisciplinary pedagogy for cultural studies. This allows for new embodied practices and new subject positions in the classroom for teachers and students, as it allows for new objects of knowledge, new logics and ethical practices, new uses of and limits on language and, ultimately, new power/knowledge relations for faculty in their publications and syllabi and for students in their writing and oral performance.

This is one way that interdisciplinary fields like cultural studies can begin to proliferate sites for releasing the stranglehold of multiple disciplinary mechanisms on our students and ourselves. Through work at multiple sites, the subjugated knowledges that have been disqualified by modern power/knowledge may be visible and revivified in the spaces of modernity: our classrooms and research archives, field sites and homes. In a certain sense, then, dedisciplinary pedagogies are training for comfort with being indecorous, illegitimate, immodest, illegible, illicit, and even indecent or improper, at ease in working against these and all the other prohibitions that protect the social hierarchies and disciplinary order of the modern. Successful students and teachers in dedisciplinary classrooms will have learned to be indefeasible, illimitable, and even irascible when it comes to interrogating, displacing, decomposing, queering, cripping, and interrupting the unbearable regime of modern disciplinary practices.

Rendering intelligible these pervasive gatekeeping and regulatory mechanisms opens the door to new curricular content and research topics, new practices in writing and speech of naming and exposing violences and contradictions. Just as the turn towards class issues and then gender at Birmingham, and then towards adult education at the Open University and elsewhere in Europe, the U.S., and Australasia changed classroom content, this pedagogy recenters course content in ways that refuse Eurocentrisms and the logics and politicized limits of modernity. A Foucauldian approach to cultural studies may weaken the exclusive emphasis on Marxism as the only center for left or progressive practice, but the shift to a multi-centered approach to pedagogy that began many years ago with feminist participants at Birmingham must be accompanied as always by careful attention to the multiple, intersecting power issues I have emphasized here. This may seem to some like a high price to pay for the inclusion of subjects many see as marginal, like bell hooks's baba or illiterate rural subalterns, yet it is a necessary price if cultural studies wishes to face its Others in its journals and its classrooms. The writing practices found in such a cultural studies classroom may not be recognizable as good, clear, persuasive writing to those still effectively subjected to the occlusions and violences that the acts by good modern citizens of knowing and writing and speaking install and attempt to normalize. Yet such practices may allow us to confront the complicities of our departments and our own writing in inscribing and enforcing such subjection, complicities that may be interrogated and disordered at any time through our subversion, decomposition, and agency.

Notes

1. Michel Foucault, *Discipline and Punish: The Birth of the Prison*, trans. Alan Sheridan (New York: Vintage Books, 1995 [1975]), 26, 139-41, 170-73.

2. Foucault, *Discipline*, 181.

3. Rey Chow, "Introduction: Leading Questions," *Writing Diaspora: Tactics of Intervention in Contemporary Cultural Studies* (Bloomington: Indiana University Press, 1993), 15-17; Joyce E. Canaan, "Examining the Examination: Tracing the Effects of Pedagogic Authority on Cultural Studies Lecturers and Students," in *A Question of Discipline: Pedagogy, Power, and the Teaching of Cultural Studies*, ed. Joyce E. Canaan and Debbie Epstein (Boulder, CO: Westview Press, 1997), 157-77; Deborah Lynn Steinberg, "All Roads Lead to . . . Problems with Discipline," in *A Question of Discipline*, 192-204; R. Perlstein, "'Funny Doctor, I don't *feel* antidisciplined': Cultural Studies as Disciplinary Habitus (or, Reading *Cultural Studies*)," *parallax: a journal of metadiscursive theory and cultural practices* 1 (1995): 131-41.

4. Foucault, *Discipline*, 14-16.

5. Foucault, *Discipline*, 200-219.

6. Foucault, *Discipline*, 137-8.

7. Foucault, *Discipline*, 24-25.

8. Foucault, *Discipline*, 27.

9. Foucault, *Discipline*, 27-28.

10. Foucault, *Discipline*, 30.

11. Foucault, *Discipline*, 27.

12. Michel Foucault, "La Poussière et le Nouage," in *L'Impossible Prison: Recherches sur le Système Pénitentiaire au XIXe Siècle Réunies par Michelle Perrot*, ed. Michelle Perrot (Paris: Éditions du Seuil, 1980) 39, qtd. in Jan Goldstein, *Foucault and the Writing of History* (Cambridge, MA: Blackwell, 1994), 3.

13. Michel Foucault, "Questions of Method," in *The Foucault Effect: Studies in Governmentality*, ed. Graham Burchell, Colin Gordon, and Peter Miller (Chicago: The University of Chicago Press, 1991), 82.

14. Michel Foucault, "Two Lectures," in *Power/Knowledge: Selected Interviews and Other Writings, 1970-1977*, ed. Colin Gordon (New York: Pantheon, 1980), 81-85.

15. Foucault, "Two Lectures," 84.

16. Ellen Messer-Davidow, David Shumway, and David Sylvan, *Knowledges: Historical and Critical Studies in Disciplinarity* (Charlottesville: University of Virginia Press, 1993); David R. Shumway and Ellen Messer-Davidow, "Disciplinarity: An Introduction," *Poetics Today* 12.2 (1991): 201-25; Ellen Messer-Davidow, *Disciplining Feminism: From Social Activism to Academic Discourse* (Durham: Duke University Press, 2002); Vincent Leitch, "Postmodern Interdisciplinarity," *Theory Matters* (New York: Routledge, 2003), 165-71; Jennifer Gore, *The Struggle for Pedagogies: Critical and Feminist Discourses as Regimes of Truth* (New York: Routledge, 1993).

17. I discuss these debates in more detail with my co-author, Ranu Samantrai, in "Interdisciplinarity and Social Justice: An Introduction," in *Interdisciplinarity and Social Justice: Revisioning Academic Accountability*, ed. Ranu Samantrai, Joe Parker, and Mary Romero (Albany: State University of New York Press, forthcoming).

18. Simon During, "Introduction," *The Cultural Studies Reader*, ed. Simon During (New York: Routledge, 1993), 16, qtd. in Rey Chow, "Theory, Area Studies, Cultural Studies: Issues of Pedagogy in Multiculturalism," in *A Question of Discipline*, 14.

19. Rey Chow, "Theory," 11-14; bell hooks, "Culture to Culture: Ethnography and Cultural Studies as Critical Intervention," in *Yearning: race, gender, and cultural politics* (Boston: South End Press, 1990), 123-34; Gayatri Chakravorty Spivak, "Scattered Speculations on the Question of Culture Studies," *Outside in the Teaching Machine* (New York: Routledge, 1993), 255-84.

20. Chow, "Theory," 15.

21. Joyce E. Canaan and Debbie Epstein, "Questions of Discipline/Disciplining Cultural Studies," in *A Question of Discipline*, 4; Perlstein; Canaan; Spivak, "Explanation and Culture: Marginalia," in *The Spivak Reader*, ed. Donna Landry and Gerald MacLean (New York: Routledge, 1996), 29-52.

22. Foucault, *Discipline*, 178, 181.

23. Foucault, *Discipline*, 170.

24. Mimi Orner, "Interrupting the Calls for Student Voice in 'Liberatory' Education: A Feminist Poststructuralist Perspective," in *Feminisms and Critical Pedagogy*, ed. Carmen Luke and Jennifer Gore (New York: Routledge, 1992), 83-87; Jennifer Gore, "Disciplining Bodies: On the Continuity of Power Relations in Pedagogy," in *Foucault's Challenge: Discourse, Knowledge and Power in Education*, ed. Thomas Poplkewitz and Marie Brennan (New York: Teachers College, Columbia University, 1998), 231-51.

25. Foucault, *Discipline*, 170-94.

26. Foucault, *Discipline*, 173.

27. Foucault, *Discipline*, 170-94.

28. Foucault, *Discipline*, 194.

29. Foucault, *Discipline*, 190.

30. I am indebted to Lindon Barrett for comments that suggested this analysis.

31. Gore, *The Struggle for Pedagogies*, 140-56.

32. Spivak, "Righting Wrongs," in *Human Rights, Human Wrongs: The Oxford Amnesty Lectures 2001*, ed. Nicholas Owen (New York: Oxford University Press, 2003), 173, 194, 217-20, 226.

33. Spivak, "Righting Wrongs," 201, 208, 217.

34. Spivak, "Righting Wrongs," 183, 226.

35. Spivak, "Righting Wrongs," 173, 217-21.

36. Spivak, "Righting Wrongs," 195, 215; "Thinking Academic Freedom in Gendered Post-Coloniality," in *The Anthropology of Politics: A Reader in Ethnography, Theory, and Critique*, ed. Joan Vincent (Blackwell), n. 11, p. 458-59; http://www.arts.cornell.edu/sochum/sct/html/courses.html#spivak (accessed 1-20-07). Spivak notes in her essay on academic freedom that her argument "is not just a fancy way of talking about community involvement for the college teacher. . . . It means investigating the details of rural literacy in the post-colonial state."

37. Ramón Flecha and Victòria dels Àngels Garcia, "Mirrors, Paintings, and Romances," in *A Question of Discipline*, 131-56.

38. bell hooks, "Talking Back," in *Talking Back: thinking feminist, thinking black*, South End Press, 1989, p. 5-9.

39. Gayatri Spivak, *Death of a Discipline*, The Wellek Library Lectures in Critical Theory (New York: Columbia University Press, 2003), 20.

40. Spivak, *Death*, 12-13.

41. Chow, "Theory," 11-14; Spivak, "Subaltern Studies: Deconstructing Historiography," in *The Spivak Reader*, ed. Donna Landry and Gerald Maclean (New York: Routledge, 1996), 219; Spivak, "Can the Subaltern Speak?" *Marxism and the Interpretation of Culture*, ed. Cary Nelson and Larry Grossberg (Urbana: University of Illinois Press, 1988), 280-81.

42. Spivak, *Death*, 52.

43. Spivak, *Death*, 73.

44. Spivak, *Death*, 56, 70, 102.

45. Gayatri Spivak, "More on Power/Knowledge," in *Outside in the Teaching Machine* (New York: Routledge, 1993), 29.

46. Spivak, "Power/Knowledge," 25, 28, 39.

47. hooks, "Critical Interrogation: Talking Race, Resisting Racism," in *Yearning*, 51-52.

48. Chow, "Theory," 15.

49. Gore, "Disciplining Bodies"; Foucault, *Discipline*, 170-94.

50. Kenneth Burke, *A Rhetoric of Motives*, 1950, ctd. Robert McRuer, *Crip Theory: Cultural Signs of Queerness and Disability* (New York: New York University Press, 2006), 146.

51. Nikki Sullivan, *An Introduction to Queer Theory* (New York: New York University Press, 2003), 46.

52. Rey Chow, "The Resistance of Theory; or, The Worth of Agony," in *Just Being Difficult? Academic Writing in the Public Arena*, ed. Jonathan Culler and Kevin Lamb, Cultural Memory in the Present (Stanford: Stanford University Press, 2003), 98.

53. Chow, "Theory," 99.

54. Chow, "Theory," 98-99.

55. Chow, "Theory," 99.

56. McRuer, 146-70; Ian Barnard, "Anti-ethnography?" *Composition Studies*, 34, no. 1 (Spring, 2006): 95-107.

57. McRuer, *Crip*, 146-47, 158-59, 238, n. 12.

58. McRuer, *Crip*, 158, 237, n. 5; Barnard, 99-104.

59. D. Diane Davis, *Breaking Up [at] Totality: A Rhetoric of Laughter*, Rhetorical Philosophy and Theory Series (Carbondale: Southern Illinois University Press, 2000), 6-15, 209-53.

60. Foucault, "Power/Knowledge," 39.

61. Foucault, "Power/Knowledge," 39.

62. hooks, "Culture to Culture," 123-4.

63. hooks, "Culture to Culture," 124.

64. hooks, "Culture to Culture," 130-31.

65. hooks, "Culture to Culture," 125.

66. hooks, "Culture to Culture," 123.

67. Foucault, "Two Lectures," 82.

68. "'Draupadi' by Mahasweta Devi, translated with a Foreword by Gayatri Chakravorti Spivak," *Critical Inquiry*, 8, no. 2 (Winter, 1981): 381-402; "Righting Wrongs"; *Imaginary Maps: Three Stories by Mahasweta Devi*, trans. and intro. by Gayatri Chakravorty Spivak (New York: Routledge, 1995).

69. Foucault, "Two Lectures," 82.

70. Ellsworth, Elizabeth, "Why Doesn't This Feel Empowering? Working Through the Repressive Mythos of Critical Pedagogy," in *Feminisms and Critical Pedagogy*, 100-105.

71. Chow, "Theory," 16.

72. Foucault, "Two Lectures," 82.

73. Chow, "Theory," 15.

Chapter Four
Interventions at the Intersections: An Analysis of Public Writing and Student Writing

Pegeen Reichert Powell

Student-authored public texts—or texts designed to circulate outside of the classroom—appear to be a fruitful site in which to develop an anti-disciplinary stance, because not only do these texts and their authors seem to be working outside of the constraints of any specific discipline, but they seem to be working outside of the constraints of academia altogether. Moreover, these texts seem to be more likely to intervene in local political conditions than those texts that are designed to be read by solitary teachers or small groups of peers inside the classroom. In this chapter, I analyze two student-produced texts to explore the potential of public writing—specifically as it might be taught in composition courses, but potentially in any university course—to facilitate an anti-disciplinary stance among students.

My analysis of the two examples of student-produced public writing complicates assertions of automatic political intervention, however. I will argue that rather than privileging public writing over academic writing as part of an anti-disciplinary project, we may be best served by recognizing the ways that all texts—disciplinary, interdisciplinary, anti-disciplinary, academic, and public—intersect with other texts, with other discourses and genres, and with other people and events. First, I will describe the production and circulation of the two examples of student texts in order to assess the efficacy of teaching public writing as part of a larger anti-disciplinary project. Then, I will provide a more detailed analysis of these texts in order to model and argue for an approach to reading and producing texts that highlights the intersections among texts, discourses, and politics.

Founders' Day for Farmworkers and a Panel Discussion on Gay Marriage

Both texts that I study here were produced by undergraduates at Duke University. While there are some remarkable similarities between the texts themselves (more about this later), the contexts of production and distribution of the texts were different.[1] The first was produced by a group of student activists, Duke Students Against Sweatshops, in October, 2002, and distributed to readers during Founders' Day festivities, an occasion of great pomp at Duke, similar to convocation or graduation. The second text was produced by a group of students in a first-year writing seminar that I taught during the spring of 2004, and distributed to readers at a panel discussion that they had organized on the topic of gay marriage.

Since the fall of 1999, Duke Students Against Sweatshops (hereafter SAS) had been working to persuade Duke to support a boycott of the Mt. Olive Pickle Company. At issue were the living and working conditions of the farmworkers who harvest produce processed by Mt. Olive. The boycott was organized by the Farm Labor Organizing Committee (FLOC) and was much bigger than SAS, but Duke is a visible institution in North Carolina, so Duke's endorsement would have both practical and symbolic ramifications.[2]

Duke did endorse the boycott in March 2002 and, in a verbal agreement with student activists, the administration pledged not to change policy during the summer while students were away. They were true to their word only in the very strictest sense. In August 2002, when students were moving in and buying books, before the activists had a chance to meet or establish a phone list, President Nan Keohane called SAS into her office. She had in her hand a press release, dated and time-stamped for the exact time of that meeting, announcing that Duke would rescind the boycott. Administrators had been in "consultation" with Mt. Olive executives over the summer, and the decision was made without any communication with students. SAS tried over the next few weeks to negotiate with administration—they submitted petitions, held forums, and wrote letters to the editor, all to no avail.

Then the occasion for a significant political action presented itself: Founders' Day 2002 was the day before the Board of Trustees meeting, and the local organizer of the Mt. Olive boycott was working to include the boycott on the Trustees' agenda. Founders' Day, a tradition at Duke since 1901, celebrates wealthy benefactors and important alumni (often one and the same). It is quite a grand affair, attended by trustees, administration, alumni, faculty, and select students. Not attending, but still an important presence this year, were the farmworkers, many of whom migrate from state to state, season to season, but who were still in North Carolina at this point. Members of SAS, dressed up for the day, with only the color red in ties or skirts to signal their solidarity with the farmworkers, stood in front of the people who were handing out the official Founders' Day brochures, and passed out their own brochure—"Founders' Day for Farmworkers: A reflection on Duke University's Heritage"—to everyone who entered the chapel, including President Keohane.

Despite the creativity and perseverance of SAS, Duke never endorsed the boycott again. When the boycott was eventually lifted by FLOC in 2006, Chris Paul, then president of SAS and an important resource for my research, was quoted in Duke's student newspaper: "What's fair to say is that Duke didn't play any role at all in the final resolution of the boycott."[3]

The second text I am studying here was produced by a small group of students in a first-year writing seminar that I taught, titled "I read the news today, oh boy!: Popular Debates and Public Writing." In the seminar, through a series of reading and writing assignments, we considered the problems inherent in the dichotomy between academic and public—as sites, as roles, as types of writing—and I challenged them to recognize their responsibility as intellectuals to participate in important public debates, as well as the difficulties of doing so. Bruce Horner argues for seeing the "classroom as a specific site both located in and acting on the social" and for "recognizing and exploiting the specific material resources and conditions associated with the 'academy' generally, and the composition classroom in particular: in many institutions, time, paper, library resources, the gathering for a period of several months of a relatively small number of students and faculty and the range and depth of knowledge and experience these bring to the classroom, the opportunity for frequent writing and the reading of that writing . . . ," and so forth.[4] One of the goals of my course was to teach students to understand their privilege, due to their access to these resources.

A major project in the class was to identify a current public debate that the entire class would study, using the academic resources at our disposal. First they had to browse news media for several weeks and, through listserv and in-class discussions in which individuals argued for various topics/debates, decide as a class which one we would take up. (I was teaching three sections, and all three sections had to agree on the same topic.) The students decided to pursue the topic of gay marriage, which was widely discussed in mainstream news media in spring 2004, when the seminar was held.

The assignment for the final project read, in part, as follows:

> You are an academic. And because of the reading and writing you've done about gay marriage, you are participating in a very current, many would say very important, public deliberation. Your assignment for project three is to produce a text that reflects that participation.
>
> This assignment raises many questions that must be answered before you begin—and during—the process of producing this text:
> - What is your responsibility as a member of a body politic to "form judgments and influence the judgments of others on public issues" (Halloran 263)?
> - Can you, *will* you, participate more *publicly* in this deliberation?
> - If so, how will you construct a "responsive public" (Wells 329)? (Who will be the "others" whose judgments you intend to influence?)

- What kind of text might you produce that will enter the more popular venues of public deliberation about gay marriage?
- If you can't, or *won't*, participate more publicly, why not?
- And what kind of text will you produce?
- You've enjoyed access to a premier research library—what kinds of arguments about gay marriage can you make now that you couldn't have made before we began this project?
- How will you incorporate the variety of sources you've read about this issue?[5]

Ultimately, the assignment asked the students to think about the circulation of writing.[6] In which directions and by what means and in what forms would the arguments and ideas in the academic and popular texts they've read as part of the course move, now that they themselves were producing texts? Some students decided to produce traditional academic essays, with a thesis and traditional scholarly support. The text that I'm studying here, however, was produced by a small group of students who wanted to "go public" with their research. They decided to organize what they referred to as "a panel discussion" on gay marriage, held in an auditorium on Duke's campus, in the evening of April 19, 2004. They invited representatives from a variety of student groups to speak— Newman Catholic Student Center, Duke Conservative Union, Duke Law Democrats, the Alliance of Queer Undergraduates at Duke, and the Duke Undergrad chapter of the ACLU—and then opened up the discussion to attendees. They advertised the event through typical means (flyers, a blurb in the student newspaper, and word of mouth in the dorms), secured the venue, and hosted the well-attended event. The text I'm studying is the brochure they distributed that evening to everyone who attended.

Public Writing: A Success Story?

I consider the SAS brochure to be a point of reference for thinking about the success of the brochure that was distributed at the gay marriage panel. The SAS brochure seems to be truly *public*, in the best sense of the word: it seems to be what composition teachers wish for students in our classrooms to be able to produce. As Susan Wells says in "Rogue Cops and Health Care: What Do We Want from Public Writing," most composition teachers feel a "desire for efficacious public writing," a desire she describes as "urgent."[7] Christian R. Weisser argues that compositionists "have turned toward public writing for a number of reasons. Most important, such an approach gives student writing real significance; public writing often allows students to produce meaningful discourse that has the potential to change their lives and the lives of others."[8] (One might argue that these are some of the same motivations for anti-disciplinarity.) The SAS brochure clearly had the "potential to change . . . the lives of others," most notably the lives of the farmworkers. If the action had been successful, and Duke had once again endorsed the boycott, such a move may well have hastened the improvements that Mt. Olive eventually made in the working conditions of the migrant laborers. Even though the activists did not meet this most immediate—and admittedly most important—goal, it would be difficult to argue that their brochure was not "meaningful discourse."

Moreover, an important element of the SAS brochure was the ability of the activists to identify—or as Wells might say, *construct*—their audience: "All speakers and writers who aspire to intervene in society face the task of constructing a responsive public."[9] Nancy Welch extends this point: "Ordinary people *make* rhetorical space through concerted, often protracted struggle for visibility, voice, and impact against powerful interests that seek to deny visibility, voice, and impact. People take and make space in acts that are simultaneously verbal and physical."[10] SAS distributed their brochure to the attendees of the Founders' Day festivities, building their audience out of people who otherwise would never have chosen to read their text. Their tactical physical position, just ahead of the people handing out the "real" Founders' Day programs, effectively made a space for the activists and, by extension the farmworkers, in festivities that they were never invited to.

The SAS brochure, then, might be considered a success as an example of public writing. To the extent that the gay marriage brochure is similar, we might also consider the writing my students produced to be successful. The gay marriage panel was designed to change people's lives, too—the lives of their audience as they considered new (to them) arguments about gay marriage; indirectly, the lives of gay couples whose decisions to marry would be affected by the votes of people like those attending the panel; and the lives of my students themselves, as they entered into public life, some of them for the first time. As Emily Znamierowski, one of the students involved in the panel, says in her written reflection on the event, "I learned so much not only from the event itself, but by working with my five classmates and going through the planning and advertising process of hosting such an event."[11]

Moreover, the students who put together the gay marriage panel, like those involved with the SAS action, were aware that audiences for such meaningful discourse do not come ready-made. Marco Salmen, another participant in the gay marriage project, considers this problem in the proposal he wrote before embarking on the final project:

> I have found it surprisingly difficult to find an opportunity for my involvement in the ongoing public deliberation about gay marriage, besides the occasional locker room debate. In acknowledging Susan Wells' assertion that all speakers must construct a "responsive public" (329), I have found it tough to locate an exact public who will hear and consider my judgments. . . .
> While I may be unsuited to address a national audience, I feel that I am in an appropriate position as to address a much smaller, cohesive audience: first-year students of Duke University. I believe that Wells' responsive public can indeed be created out of the freshmen of Duke University and I will attempt to do so along with Hali Cooperman-Dix, Lindsay Bressler, Jessica Stone, Mark

Sembler, and Emily Z. Although the issue of gay marriage has been thrust to the forefront on the national scene, it is eerily absent from our college campus.

If, as Wells says, "the classroom itself can be seen as a version of the public sphere: as a model of the public, or a concentrated version of the public," then certainly the students who put together the panel created a "version of the public" even just by extending their discussion of gay marriage to other undergraduates at Duke.[12] The effort that the students put into advertising the event, to bringing together their audience from various places on campus, suggests that they understood to some extent the complicated nature of public writing. Marco says,

> We have specifically chosen the date and time to ensure the largest possible turnout but we will also engage in significant advertising. We will use traditional measures such as flyers on campus and under-door leafleting, but we also hope that a well timed letter to the editor will spur increased excitement about the issue as a whole and result in a large audience for our panel discussion.

(The letter to the editor was never printed, to the tremendous disappointment of the group; however, as Welch says, "there's also rewarding learning that takes place when we and our students consider the myriad ways in which our attempts to make voices heard are *foiled*."[13])

In the most important ways, then, the SAS brochure and the gay marriage brochure were similarly successful attempts at public writing: both groups produced a text designed to change lives and both groups engaged in efforts to construct a "responsive public." And there are a number of other ways these two texts are similar. Both were written collaboratively, and both were distributed by hand, in face-to-face interaction with their audiences. Perhaps most striking to me as I began this project were the similarities in the textual features. Both groups used a tri-fold brochure format, with, among other items, a title and the date on the front panel. In the inside of the brochure, both used a bulleted list of arguments or questions in the center panel, and a timeline of significant events in the right panel. On the back of the brochure, in the center panel, both groups included a list of other relevant organizations and contact information.

Perhaps the most significant *difference* between the two texts is that the SAS brochure was not written for a class at all—it originated entirely outside of the mechanisms of an instructor's course and assignment design, deadlines, and grading. The fact that my students, working within these mechanisms, produced a text that so closely paralleled this other non-academic text may suggest that my pedagogy achieved many of the goals of teaching students to produce public writing. However, while I do not think that the students' experience in my class was unsuccessful, several qualifications need to be made to the argument that it was a truly non-academic text.

First, the context in which it was distributed—the panel itself—very closely mirrors the academic panel. "Experts" were brought in to speak on a single issue, and audience members were instructed, in the brochure and in written instructions at the panel itself, to abide by an "ethic of civility."[14] It was a very orderly event: for the most part, the audience waited in line to speak, one at a time, into a microphone, and the panelists remained composed, even in the face of obviously polarizing positions. And like most academic panels, not all speakers stayed within the time limit they were allotted. In "Living Room: Teaching Public Writing in a Post-Publicity Era," Welch explores a history of working class activism and popular art, seeking alternative models of teaching public writing; she says, in what seems to be a direct indictment of my students' project, "I find myself very far not only from 'Once More to the Lake' but also from the academic conference or debate, our usual stand-ins for the idea of public rhetoric."[15]

Admittedly the brochure itself does not resemble an academic text per se (this is not to say that academic institutions do not produce brochures—the admissions brochure is an important case in point). However, it is worth considering how the brochure entered into what critical discourse analyst Norman Fairclough terms an "intertextual chain" : a "series of types of texts which are transformationally related to each other in the sense that each member of the series is transformed into one or more of the others in regular or predictable ways."[16] The gay marriage brochure entered into an intertextual chain that is very much located in the academy. The students had to write annotated bibliographies, position papers, exploratory essays, project proposals/abstracts, and follow-up reflection papers. The brochure they produced fell near the end of this chain, and clearly demonstrates connections to these other texts, most notably in the "Important Questions Embedded in the Gay Marriage Debate" in the inside center panel, where students asked questions that arose out of their research and earlier attempts at formulating positions. The brochure was discussed explicitly in several of the group members' proposals for the project, and thus it was a very predictable text in this intertextual chain. The significance of these connections to the other, more academic texts, will be discussed in more detail later, but here it is enough to say that this example of "public" writing might not, automatically, be considered non-academic.

Nor can it really be considered the product of an anti-disciplinary stance. Disciplinary thinking runs all through the text. My assigning students to read Halloran and Wells, for example, locates the gay marriage project in the context of rhetoric. Although rhetoric has the potential for facilitating an anti-disciplinary stance, especially, as Ryan Claycomb and Rachel Riedner suggest, as part of a "triad of modes of inquiry" with composition and cultural studies, rhetoric is still, nonetheless, subject to its own disciplinary vocabulary and methodology.[17] And my students both designed the brochure and panel, and reflected on it, through this disciplinary lens. For example, Emily says in her reflection on the project, "It was . . . interesting to see how the concepts and theories we learned about (i.e. kairos, ethos, pathos etc.) were employed in spoken language by the panelists."

Rhetoric was not the only discipline that the students drew from. Their research covered many disciplinary perspectives: law, theology, political science, social science, psychology, history, and many more. We see these disciplines in some of the questions they ask in the inside center panel. For example, it is easy to guess that this question came from political science: "Is a constitutional amendment an appropriate method for resolving this issue"; and this question surely came from psychology: "Does same-sex parenting have harmful social and psychological effects on children?" The timeline on the inside left panel is a simplistic version of history. If anything, I would call what my students did multi-disciplinary. The topic of gay marriage—perhaps more than any other topic the students could have chosen—gave us the opportunity to do truly anti-disciplinary work: Ellen Messer-Davidow, David R. Shumway, and David J. Sylvan note, in their Introduction to *Knowledges: Historical and Critical Studies in Disciplinarity*, that "gay studies is not (yet) a discipline."[18] While my students did read articles from this not (yet) a discipline, I do not think I provided enough guidance to turn their reading into anti- (or non-) disciplinary thinking. Moreover, Messer-Davidow, Shumway, and Sylvan admit that although gay studies may not be a discipline, "its practitioners are disciplined by other disciplines."[19] In other words, even if we had limited our research to gay studies, the disciplinary thinking that still informs scholars in gay studies would surely have leaked into my students' project.

So if the gay marriage brochure is not a purely non-academic or non-disciplinary text, then can we call it public? And if the SAS brochure shares some of these academic and disciplinary features—and it does—then must we also call into question the publicity of that text? This latter question strikes me as absurd: it does not seem productive, or even fair, to ask whether the Founders' Day for Farmworkers brochure is non-academic or anti-disciplinary enough. Clearly, these are not the best questions to ask in light of the more important goals for that text, namely, improving the working conditions of migrant farm laborers. Rather, what my comparison and analysis of these two texts indicates is the instability of the oppositions between public and academic, disciplinary and anti-disciplinary, or simply put, between inside and outside.

An Analysis of Intertextuality

Jean Ferguson Carr, in "Rereading the Academy as Worldly Text," argues that "Once we become alert to the social distortions of seeing 'inside' and 'outside' as ready dichotomies, we can trace the worldly aspects of the most recalcitrant and unreflexive materials."[20] And it is to this project of "tracing the worldly aspects" of the brochures that I turn now. The methodology that informs this project is critical discourse analysis, and specifically the analysis of intertextuality. Drawing on Bakhtin and Kristeva, Fairclough defines intertextuality as "the property texts have of being full of snatches of other texts, which may be explicitly demarcated or merged in, and which the text may assimilate, contradict, ironically echo, and so forth."[21] What is significant here is that this is a property that all texts share, and so we may study "the most recalcitrant and unreflexive materials" that Carr refers to (including, possibly, the gay marriage brochure), as well as more dynamic texts like the SAS brochure. This way of reading—and ultimately, of writing and teaching—texts, I argue, provides an alternative, yet complementary, approach to developing an anti-disciplinary stance.

In the first half of this chapter, I use the SAS brochure as a point of reference to determine the extent to which I might consider the gay marriage brochure a success as non-academic and anti-disciplinary writing. This comparison brought me full circle, so that the similarities between the two texts actually raised the question of whether or not the SAS brochure was itself public enough. Of course, this question, as I say above, is absurd, and the absurdity indicates that we need to be asking different questions.

In this part of the chapter, I again use the SAS brochure as a point of reference, this time, however, not to determine the publicity of the two texts, but their creativity. By creativity, I mean, following Fairclough, the extent to which texts demonstrate the potential for social change. Fairclough explains that one can see texts "historically as transforming the past—existing conventions and prior texts—into the present." He continues, "This may happen in relatively conventional and normative ways: discourse types tend to turn particular ways of drawing upon conventions and texts into routines, and to naturalize them. However, this may happen creatively, with new configurations of elements of orders of discourse, and new modes of manifest intertextuality."[22] To identify the creative elements of the SAS brochure is to name those moments in which this text intersects with other texts and discourses in ways that open up the possibilities for change—change in discourse practices and in social structures. These are the possibilities that an anti-disciplinarity stance is striving for.

Perhaps what is most significant in terms of the creativity of the SAS brochure is the decision the students made about the genre itself: a tri-fold brochure, distributed in face-to-face interaction with the intended audience. In this respect, the text does not explicitly refer to other texts, but draws on their generic conventions, an example of "constitutive intertextuality." Fairclough explains that an analysis of constitutive intertextuality focuses us on "the configuration of discourse conventions that go into its production."[23] What is important here is not the genre of the brochure itself, but how the SAS brochure "refers to" that genre through the particular "configuration of discourse conventions": the tri-fold, the images, the "for more information" on the back. Drawing on Bakhtin, Fairclough says "texts may not only draw upon such conventions in a relatively straightforward way, but may also 'reaccentuate' them by, for example, using them ironically, parodically, or reverently, or may 'mix' them in various ways."[24] While the brochure is clearly *a brochure*, at the same time, it is also a parody of a brochure, playfully mimicking the conventions of that genre to achieve the authors' own (quite serious) ends. Some of the students involved in making this brochure had been to a Founders' Day ceremony before, and they knew they had a captive audience, but an audience who needed to be pretending to be listening to speeches and singing hymns—hence their decisions about bulleted lists and timelines, rather than extended blocks of prose. Moreover, they knew that audience members would willingly, almost unthinkingly, accept a brochure from a dressed-up student as they entered the ceremony, where they would not accept another genre—a more typical activist leaflet from a group of protesters, for example.

One of the most specific ways we can identify the brochure as a parody is the activists' decision about font on the front cover. In selecting the italicized script, the authors deliberately drew on the discourses of tradition and pomp of the occasion, rather than signal an alignment with another, perhaps a radical political, discourse. (For example, a font like Impact would not have achieved the same effect.) John Trimbur insists on the importance of paying attention to typography in analyses like these: "From a typographical perspective . . . the visual design of writing figures prominently as the material form in which the message is delivered. That is, typography offers a way to think of writing not just in terms of the moment of composing but also in terms of its circulation, as messages take on cultural value and worldly force, moving through the Marxian dialectic of production, distribution, exchange, and consumption.[25] In other words, the font on the front cover of the SAS brochure must be understood in the context of the "worldly force" of the message of the brochure, not just as an isolated decision made in front of the computer. The activists were parodying the event, subtly mocking the "real" Founders' Day brochure and, at the same time, achieving their own ends of delivering the message they were politically committed to.

We see these moments of parody in other elements of the text, too. The rose, for example, can be read as a reference to the sophistication and beauty of Founders' Day (as most of the audience members would read it), but also as an historically leftist symbol, in this case, a signal of the activists' solidarity with the farmworkers (as the activists themselves would read it). The dual signification of this image is in some ways, then, an inside joke on a genre that we would rarely consider comical. Likewise, the image of Mt. Olive pickles in the center inside panel is a parody along the lines of Ad Busters, and thus references these other leftist discourses.[26] The parody of the Mt. Olive logo in that image achieves an even more powerful effect when contrasted with the image of the farmworkers on the back left panel. This moment of visual gravity among the other parodic images is another indication that this is not a "straight" brochure, but a deliberate mix of registers and modes to achieve the activists' goal of drawing attention to the boycott.

There are other moments of intertextuality that are worth noting. The bulleted list in the inside left panel is an example of what Fairclough refers to as manifest intertextuality. Fairclough explains that "in manifest intertextuality, other texts are explicitly present in the text under analysis. . . . Note, however, that a text may 'incorporate' another text without the latter being explicitly cued: one can respond to another text in the way one words one's own text, for example."[27] When I asked Chris Paul, one of the producers of the text, where they got "The Facts" listed in the brochure, he said some of them were borrowed from the Mt. Olive web site and others were taken from a collection of texts SAS members were in the process of writing—reports, letters-to-the-editor, press releases—portions of which get continually revised and integrated into new texts. This continuous re-use of other texts indicates the dynamic nature of their work. Moreover, the lack of "explicit cues" in their text to indicate which pieces they "borrowed" from the Mt. Olive web site is an important example of the power dynamics at play. They do not feel it necessary, nor particularly useful, to acknowledge the authority of Mt. Olive, suggesting that they are obtaining their authority from other sources—from a history of leftist resistance, from the principles of direct action and, probably most keenly, from a real sense of justice.

Not just how they refer to other texts, but how they refer to other people is important. I asked Chris Paul why the authors referred to Duke in various ways throughout the brochure: as Duke, as the administration, as President Keohane, and so on. He explained the marriage of writing and activist principles at work: they had learned always to name an individual decision maker, rather than an entity that individuals can hide behind. So in the items on the brochure that involve unpopular decisions they refer specifically to Keohane, then-President of Duke University. In the fourth bullet in the inside middle panel, they refer to "President Keohane's proposed solution," rather than, for example, "The University's proposed solution," and in the August 2002 entry in the timeline, on the inside right panel, they state "President Keohane rescinds Duke's endorsement of the boycott." More favorable actions, though, are named as "Duke," for example, "Duke has set a precedent for supporting the struggles of workers" in the last bullet in the inside middle panel, and "Duke publicly and fully endorses the Mt. Olive boycott" in the March 2002 entry in the timeline. In this way, all readers can identify with these positive moves. "Duke administrators" in June 2002 was chosen to suggest individuals acting, but acting under their official titles, as a way to connote conspiracy and secret dealings.

The activists' keen awareness of these decisions points to one of the reasons this approach to studying the intersections of texts with the social and political worlds around them might be useful to compositionists and others working toward the goals of anti-disciplinarity: it is a teachable methodology. Teaching students to become aware of these intersections in theirs and others' texts opens up moments in the production of texts where authors need to negotiate the various forces that impinge on them and their writing. These are moments where decisions—writerly and political—need to be made. Fairclough argues that

> the concept of intertextuality points to the productivity of texts, to how texts can transform prior texts and restructure existing conventions (genres, discourses) to generate new ones. One can . . . conceptualize intertextual processes and processes of contesting and restructuring orders of discourse as processes of hegemonic struggle in the sphere of discourse, which have effects upon, as well as being affected by, hegemonic struggle in the wider sense.[28]

What Fairclough is suggesting is that producers of texts—like these activists working against the formidable power of both the Mt. Olive Corporation and Duke University—can enter into this hegemonic struggle through the decisions they make about genre, font, citation practices, visual elements, and other manipulation of discourse conventions. But, as Fairclough insists, and the SAS brochure illustrates, "this productivity is not in practice available to people as a limitless space for textual innovation and play: it is socially limited and constrained, and conditional upon relations of power."[29] We see these constraints not only in the larger failure of the action to persuade Duke to endorse the boycott again, but also in the activists decision to produce a brochure, rather than a leaflet, to use a fancy font, to dress up to distribute the text, and so on.

Nevertheless, the elements of parody and the mix of registers and modes make the SAS brochure a fine example of creativity, in the politically charged meaning of the word, and this is where the contrast with the gay marriage brochure is most significant. While the brochure my students produced to distribute at the panel on gay marriage is a good example of public writing (with all the relevant qualifications duly noted above) and, arguably, a successful introduction to the practices of rhetoric and composition, it is not necessarily a creative text.

The genre of brochure in the case of the gay marriage panel is much more predictable—we are used to receiving brochures at public events, to guide our behavior and inform us of what is going on. In fact, the activists working on the SAS brochure relied on this predictability to ensure that their actively resistant piece of discourse would be accepted and read at the Founders' Day festivities. The students who organized the gay marriage panel, on the other hand, were not trying to ironically or parodically "reaccentuate" that genre, but simply produced a text in the form that best fit their purposes. One way to consider the differences in the SAS brochure and the gay marriage brochure is through John Swales' definition of genre, which places "the primary determinant of genre-membership on shared purpose rather than on similarities of form."[30] While clearly the two texts share similarities of form, which enables me to refer to both of them as *brochures*, they just as clearly do not share purposes. The SAS brochure was designed to disrupt an event, to insert a leftist political agenda into an otherwise conservative occasion, to achieve goals that the University was actively resisting. The form the SAS text took was the result of deliberate decisions about how to achieve these purposes and, as I detail above, was an ironic or parodic version of that form. By contrast, the gay marriage brochure did share its primary purpose with other texts in the genre of brochure: it was designed to inform audience members about the nature and logistics of this particular event (the panel) and provide them with a written record of information they may find useful later. According to Swales' definition, then, the SAS brochure is not really a brochure at all. Of course, what matters is that it *refers* to that genre in significant ways. What a methodology and a pedagogy focused on intertextuality offers is a means to identify those textual opportunities when authors might insert their own purposes into the text, even within the constraints of relations of power (including generic constraints).

We see the lack of creativity in the brochure's citation practices as well. The descriptions of the panelists on the back left panel integrate quotes that are "'manifestly' marked or cued by features on the surface of the text," in this case, quotation marks and footnotes.[31] Likewise, the entire inside left panel is "borrowed" from a Duke University website, and the students—as well they should—cited the source in predictable, normative ways. These practices contrast with the refusal of the activists to mark in any way their borrowings from the Mt. Olive web site. It is over-simplistic to suggest that manifest intertextuality that is explicitly cued in the text is less creative than instances that are not explicitly cued. However, the quotation marks and footnotes in the gay marriage brochure do come from rather conservative impulses: first, the impulse to observe intellectual property rights and avoid plagiarism in the context of an academic assignment and, second, the impulse to indicate that the producers of this text are relying on sources with greater authority than they possess on their own. This is not to say that in the name of political creativity, I should have encouraged my students to plagiarize. However, I am admitting here that I do not think, in this course at least, that I taught my students to take full advantage of those opportunities for creativity that present themselves as we refer to other texts, both constitutively and manifestly.

Conclusion: Interventions at the Intersections

My analysis demonstrates that intertextuality is, in many respects, easily recognizable and involves those writing features that belong to no discipline, and yet are constrained in all disciplines: citation practices, genre conventions, fonts, visual design.

Upon reflection, I believe my failure to fully enact the pedagogy I am arguing for here was the result of my own privileging of public writing in this course. Personally and professionally, I was at a crossroads when I taught that course in Spring 2004: my family was moving several states away at the end of the semester, and I was trying to decide whether to look for work in the academy in our new home state or pursue other avenues. My own commitment to activist projects was a big factor in my decision making process. In that course, I raised the question with my students that I, myself, was struggling with: can we do meaningful work, and achieve *real* change, from inside the classroom? This is a question that I think motivates much work on anti-disciplinarity. But I realize now that the very formulation of the question posed barriers to the solution. First of all, it assumed a distinction between public and academic, or outside and inside, a distinction that is blurry at best, as my analysis suggests, and usually unproductive. Second, I assumed that there was something *real* outside, as opposed to . . . what? The false work we do in the classroom? The fictional work? An imitation?

It is not that the SAS brochure is more real than the gay marriage brochure, or any other text that students produce in the classroom. All texts are real. The exam a student takes in a history class is very real and, in the context of credit hours, tuition, diplomas, that one exam can have real, material consequences. As Carr claims, "there are reciprocal problems with identifying only certain practices as 'real' and thereby producing the academy as an artificial 'ivory tower' divorced from (or secured from) authentic experience. In the effort to celebrate the extracurriculum's 'reality,' it is risky to free the academy from its obligations and connections, its worldliness."[32] What matters is that the SAS brochure is simply more creative. It intersects with other texts in ways that open up the potential for shifts in power relations in ways that the gay marriage brochure does not.

The students in my course organized a panel that reflected the multiple positions in the gay marriage debate, rather than, for example, turning it into a less productive "pro/con" debate; moreover, while most in the group were in favor of officially recognizing gay relationships, they had various positions on the politics of marriage itself (both heterosexual and homosexual), and at least one began the semester vehemently opposed to gay marriage due to religious convictions. However, the brochure they distributed that evening, as a straightforward example of that genre, did not betray any of this dissent. If there were any missed opportunities in my course, it was in my failure to help them identify ways to produce a text that intersected with other texts in more creative ways. I might have encouraged them to explore opportunities for making those disagreements, which were central to the purpose of the panel anyway, more apparent in the form of the text itself. I could have asked them questions like these: What might a "brochure" look like when the producers of such a text do not agree about the politics of gay marriage? How might power relations constrain their design choices: given the dominance of heterosexism in our culture at large, and the instances of homophobia on Duke's campus itself, what does it mean to give equal space in the text to all the positions in the debate? And what about the power relations in the university: if the brochure does not look like a "brochure," how might that affect their grade in the class? How might these power relations affect their citation practices: should all positions, all voices, be manifestly cued in the same way? How could design elements such as font, page layout, or images be used to communicate the dissent that characterized the group organizing the panel?

The students' explicit appeal to "civility" in the text is reflected in the cohesion of the brochure *qua* brochure. My failure to introduce the idea of "creativity" at those moments when their text intersected with other texts may have restrained the debate itself: perhaps a louder, messier, angrier panel discussion would have been possible if the brochure itself was less self-contained. However, a louder, messier, angrier panel discussion was not what my students intended at the time. They achieved exactly what they wanted to achieve: they brought together a variety of positions into one room and allowed the arguments to unfold, much like they would have in a well-organized, well-researched, well-*disciplined* academic essay. Therefore, privileging public writing in the name of achieving an anti-disciplinary stance was not as productive in this course as privileging a kind of writing that takes creative advantage of the intersections could have been. The goal is to teach students to become aware of such intersections in theirs and others' texts in order to open up moments in the production of texts where they, as authors, are able to negotiate disciplinary, generic, political, and ideological forces that impinge on them and their writing.

These are moments where decisions—writerly and political—need to be made, and moments with the most potential to intervene in the political world around us. By privileging public writing in our pedagogies, we fail sometimes to recognize the possibilities for challenging students' received notions of academic and disciplinary practices; moreover, we as teachers can fail to recognize all literacies—academic, public, and "private"—as possibilities for intervening in local problems. In the end, privileging public writing in the name of achieving an anti-disciplinary stance is not as productive as privileging a kind of writing that motivates the intersections in creative, potentially radical, ways. If it is the isolation from other ways of thinking and from local politics that motivates the project of anti-disciplinarity, then a methodology and pedagogy that focuses on intersections should prove useful.

Notes

1. See Appendix for full text of brochures.

2. In the interest of full disclosure: in 2000-2001, independent of the Duke Students Against Sweatshops, but as part of FLOC's campaign, I visited restaurants in Durham, NC, requesting that they support the boycott by refusing to serve Mt. Olive products.

3. Kelly Rohrs, "Mt. Olive Boycott Ends after 5 Years," *The Chronicle Online*, http://www.dukechronicle.com/media/storage/paper884/news/2004/09/16/News/Mt.Olive .Boycott.Ends.After.5.Years-1471088.shtml?norewrite200605091308 (accessed December 14, 2006).

4. Bruce Horner, *Terms of Work for Composition: A Materialist Critique* (Albany: State University of New York Press, 2000), 115-16.

5. The parenthetical references to Halloran and Wells were included in the assignment. These were required reading for the course. The full bibliographic information is as follows:

Michael S. Halloran, "Rhetoric in the American College Curriculum," *Pre/Text* 3 (1982): 245-69.

Susan Wells, "Rogue Cops and Health Care: What Do We Want from Public Writing?" *College Composition and Communication* 47 (1996): 325-41.

6. John Trimbur. "Composition and the Circulation of Writing." *College Composition and Communication* 52 (2000): 188-219.

7. Wells, "Rogue Cops," 326.

8. Christian R. Weisser, *Moving Beyond Academic Discourse: Composition Studies and the Public Sphere* (Carbondale: Southern Illinois University Press, 2002), 91-92.

9. Wells, "Rogue Cops," 329.

10. Nancy Welch. "Living Room: Teaching Public Writing in a Post-Publicity Era." *College Composition and Communication* 56 (2005): 477.

11. Quotes from student writing are used with their permission. They also chose to be identified by their given name, rather than by pseudonym.

12. Wells, "Rogue Cops," 338.

13. Welch, "Living Room," 476.

14. See inside left panel of the gay marriage brochure, available in the appendix.

15. Welch, "Living Room," 478.

16. Norman Fairclough, *Discourse and Social Change* (Cambridge, UK: Polity Press, 1992), 130.

17. Ryan Claycomb and Rachel Riedner. "Cultural Studies, Rhetorical Studies, and Composition: Towards an Anti-Disciplinary Nexus," *Enculturation* 5, no. 2 (2004), http://enculturation.gmu.edu/5_2/claycomb-riedner.html (accessed November 16, 2006).

18. Ellen Messer-Davidow, David R. Shumway, and David J. Sylvan, "Introduction: Disciplinary Ways of Knowing," in *Knowledges: Historical and Critical Studies in Disciplinarity*, ed. Ellen Messer-Davidow, David R. Shumway, and David J. Sylvan (Charlottesville: University Press of Virginia, 1992), 19.

19. Messer-Davidow, Shumway, and Sylvan, *Knowledges*, 19.

20. Jean Ferguson Carr. "Rereading the Academy as Worldly Text." *College Composition and Communication* 45 (1994): 96.

21. Fairclough, *Discourse*, 84.

22. Fairclough, *Discourse*, 85.

23. Fairclough, *Discourse*, 104.

24. Fairclough, *Discourse*, 103.

25. John Trimbur, "Delivering the Message: Typography and the Materiality of Writing," in *Rhetoric and Composition as Intellectual Work*, ed. Gary A. Olson (Carbondale: Southern Illinois University Press, 2002), 192.

26. http://www.adbusters.org/home/ (accessed January 2, 2007).

27. Fairclough, *Discourse*, 104.

28. Fairclough, *Discourse*, 102-3.

29. Fairclough, *Discourse*, 103.

30. John M. Swales, *Genre Analysis: English in Academic and Research Settings* (Cambridge, UK: Cambridge University Press, 1990), 46.

31. Fairclough, *Discourse*, 104.

32. Carr, "Rereading the Academy," 96.

Part II

Shifting Schemas

Any successful curricular integration of reading and writing would require getting beyond the dominance of the whole disciplinary apparatus of the modern university. As ambitious as that project sounds, it helps to recognize that curricular innovations linking cultural, rhetorical, and composition studies are moving in that direction already. Unfortunately, disciplinary practices still serve to measure success and failure in our profession in ways that often prohibit or defeat the kinds of innovations toward which many of us would like to work.

—David Downing, *"Beyond Disciplinary English: Integrating Reading and Writing by Reforming Academic Labor,"* 24.

Chapter Five
Writing Is Against Discipline:
Three Courses

Alan Ramón Clinton

Writing Across and In the Disciplines courses are the social result, more than anything else, of the shift from a literate to a digital age. It is understandable that professors and administrators, having grown up in the waning age of print, would be
chagrined at the writing styles produced by students raised in the age of electronic
proliferation. Students in various disciplines, lacking the literate training of their
forebears, play catch-up in order to be able to approximate the genre conventions of
academic writing. Ironically, they are urged to develop skills in what Robert Ray—
and others in so many words—has called "a particularly retrograde subspecialty" of
writing.[1] This retrograde quality stems from the university's, and Western culture's,
consistent denial of writing as anything other than a container of pre-existing information. The idea that knowledge or "truth" can somehow exist outside of a material
form, a consequence of logocentrism, not only gives students the wrong idea about
how knowledge is actually produced in disciplines, but it also prevents them from
exploiting various technologies of writing as means of invention. The courses I have
developed as a Postdoctoral Teaching Associate in Northeastern University's new
Advanced Writing in the Disciplines program are designed to help students view
writing as a means of gaining knowledge, a technology of invention. In this essay, I
would like to discuss how I foreground the inventive possibilities of writing in three
courses: Advanced Writing in the Arts and Sciences, Advanced Writing in the Humanities, and Advanced Writing in the Sciences. The interconnections and variations in each course serve to show how writing against the disciplines involves acknowledging and exploiting the fact that writing itself is against discipline.

I. The Virtues of Proliferation

The first thing that one might notice about the course titles cited above is that, quite
frankly, they are not very discipline specific. The Sciences? The Humanities? The

75

Arts *and* the Sciences? Good grief! How can one even hope to be a Rosetta Stone with such towers of Babel? Is there something called "research" that connects these disparate ventures? Can writing professors hope to somehow convince students that they are the rhetorical guides who can ferry all disciplines from unwritten knowledge to written knowledge regardless of its content?

The worst thing an instructor can do in this situation is, I think, to pretend to somehow unify all these discourses, which would require a false and transparent claim of mastery. Instead, I foreground the proliferation of knowledge from day one, requiring that students introduce themselves by declaring, among other information, their majors. I point out the impossibility of any instructor mastering all their disciplines, and instead declare that the course will be about writing their way out of their disciplines. Why would they want to do this? That is how one comes up with truly new ideas and, at some point, they must move beyond repetition of knowledge to the creation of knowledge. I am there to help them think about ways in which they can do that. One of the main ways, I tell them, involves collaborative work with people who know different things than they know. I concretize this point by the second class period when I assemble students into their collaborative groups for the semester and reveal that my justification for doing so was to ensure that each group of four students (whom I do not yet know personally) contains at least two, and preferably three, different disciplines.

Although students work in groups throughout the semester, disciplinary proliferation pays off most in the third paper (students write four papers that represent different approaches to a "knowledge problem"[2] of interest to them), which I call "Interdisciplinary Explorations":

> One of the main features of "The Postmodern Condition,"[3] a state whose effects we are currently experiencing, involves an increasing awareness of the potential interrelatedness between various traditions (both authorized and unauthorized) of knowledge. This interrelatedness was anticipated by historical avant-garde movements such as Surrealism, particularly in their experiments with collage and collaboration, which is why I have attempted to incorporate some "Surrealist" elements into the classroom, both as subject matter and as writing practice. My belief in the creative function of collage and "ideas on the level of language"[4] has also motivated the organization of groups and group work in terms of disciplines (majors) that are unalike, with effects that simulate on a social level the "Exquisite Corpse" game coined by the Surrealists.

> To take advantage of these conditions, paper #3 will ask you to look at your knowledge problem from the perspective of one of your group members' disciplines. How would his or her discipline approach your problem or, for that matter, "change the subject"? Are there methodologies or metaphors in the discipline which can be transposed onto your own knowledge problem, thereby adding to the interventions you have made in paper #2?

In order to make this assignment productive, each group member will have to pull his or her share of the weight. So, rather than first thinking about which group member you will borrow from, begin by thinking about what information you can provide to someone seeking your aid. By the next class period, come to class with several copies (enough for me and each of your group members) of a one page "guide" to potential collaborators. This guide should identify at least one founding and/or leading text in your discipline and give a brief description of its contribution to "the field." You need not have read this text yourself—you only need to be "aware" of it and its importance. Second, you will want to look back over your first two essays and identify sections (by essay and page #) where you feel that specific "elements" of your discipline can be readily identified or inferred. Provide those references in list form at the end of your text description. Next class we will further explore how one might make use of these documents for the "interdisciplinary" paper.

Although I do not absolutely require it, this assignment clearly encourages students to understand interdisciplinarity in terms of the relationship between writing and proliferation. First of all, the illusion of disciplinary coverage is shattered by the fact that members are required to suggest only one "text" from their discipline to others, and they do not even have to have read it! Perhaps this part of the assignment may encourage the children of textbooks and Wikipedia to read a "primary" text from their respective fields, but it is not required. Instead, students are required to read one of the suggested "primary" texts from someone else's field. Obviously, they cannot hope to gain a complete understanding of these other fields or even of the texts they read. They lack the expertise that would even allow one the illusion of such an understanding. Rather, their status as amateurs (in the Barthesian sense of being both lovers and beginners) is foregrounded. That is, they are encouraged to dip into a text that looks interesting to them and make what they can of it, to collide with it (montage) or rip an idea from its original context (collage). Furthermore, the implication that all disciplines operate according to guiding metaphors gives them the method for how to "make what they can of" these texts. They alter their own disciplinary approaches by importing metaphors more common (perhaps barely visible) in another discipline.

For instance, Carrie Tropeano, a communications student in my Advanced Writing in the Arts and Sciences course, used the metaphor of "natural selection" from Darwin's *Origin of Species*[5] as a potential explanation of why certain television shows of a given genus/genre survive and certain ones do not. She proposed that the answer to this question might parallel Darwin's theory that the survival of a given species (television show) depends on the relationship between specific "traits" or variations and a particular environment (the viewing public and its attendant ideologies). To further parallel Darwin's scientific formulation, Tropeano chose television's most blatant form of "progeny," the sit-com spin-off. As a way of testing this metaphor *cum* methodology, Tropeano compared one spin-off that survived (*Frasier*) with one that did not (*Joey*). Both shows focused on a single male character (from which they derived their name) previously featured in a long-running, successful situation comedy (*Cheers* and *Friends* respectively). Furthermore, both shows "involved the characters locating to a new city (Frasier in Seattle and Joey in LA) and pursuing a career in the entertainment industry (Frasier with his own radio talk show, and Joey with his acting career)." Despite these similarities, Tropeano posited, one show represented a "favorable mutation" and the other an "unfavorable mutation." "Looking at both *Frasier* and *Joey* as a form of mutation," Tropeano devilishly begins, "allows one to understand that it was Frasier's strength of character, both intelligence and wit, that allowed him to survive in his new environment." Playfully oscillating between treating *Frasier* and *Joey* as shows (species) and as "individuals" who must survive, Tropeano points out, "Joey, on the other hand, who is notoriously dim-witted, could not function without the strength of his fellow 'Friends' to keep his character in line."

The playful nature of Tropeano's study shows how, as Gregory Ulmer has noted, "the discovery process . . . works with the poetic devices of analogy—with the association of elements previously unrelated (as in the surprise editing of the joke)."[6] One student in my Advanced Writing in the Sciences course, in fact, based her interdisciplinary paper on an actual joke, or at least what I presented as a joke: "Do snails think?" Reflecting on the role of the joke in her process of discovery, Maggy Hunter, a marine biology major who has become something of an expert on sea snails, sees the joke as an opportunity to pursue more traditional, if previously unconsidered, areas of scientific inquiry:

> My original assumption was that snails were incapable of thought, and my personal knowledge on thought was not very refined either. I began to explore in what different contexts thought was classified; I began to challenge my original assumptions. Breaking thought down to processes and reactions, I used neuroscience as the bridge fusing the two ideas. I found that both sea snail functions and human thought are controlled by the transmission of information through a series of chemicals, synapses and receptor sites. In essence, the very different species of humans and snails are detecting and reacting; they are capable of reactionary thought, chemical thought. But this recent discovery through my own thought processes does not leave me satisfied. I know from experience, research, and my own communication that no one has discovered which chemicals and receptors are involved in a snail's detection and reaction to predators, wave action, anything. I want to know what chemical is forcing this snail [*L. obtusata*] into its reactionary waves of shell thickening, predator detection, and "unconscious thought." With snails, as with Freud, "unconscious thought" is thought "gone postal," where messages are sent from one site to another without the mediation of a transcendental consciousness.

The realization that invention (most) often takes the form of playful post directs my motivation for using Surrealist games in preparation for the interdisciplinary paper and the anti-disciplinary classroom. For my Advanced Writing in the Arts and Sciences course, I have adapted the following games from Alastair Brotchie's pocketsized compendium *Surrealist Games*: 1) To what are mutual attractions due?; 2) Analogy Cards; 3) One into Another.[7]

The first game introduces the concept that language games can form the basis of research; the second game incorporates this concept directly into students' chosen knowledge problems; the third game addresses this concept to the question of disciplinary proliferation. "To what are mutual attractions due?" is the first sentence in an excerpt of automatic writing Brotchie includes from André Breton's and Philippe Soupault's 1919 *Magnetic Fields*:

> To what are mutual attractions due? There are some jealousies more touching than others. I willingly wander in such baffling darkness as that of a rivalry between a woman and a book. The finger on the side of the forehead is not the barrel of a revolver. I believe that although we paid heed to each other's thinking, the automatic "Of nothing" that is our proudest denial did not once need to be uttered during the whole wedding-spree. Lower than the stars there is nothing to stare at. No matter what train you may be traveling in, it is dangerous to lean out of the carriage-door window. The stations were plainly distributed about a bay. The sea that to the human eye is never so beautiful as the sky did not leave us. In the depths of our eyes disappeared neat reckonings bearing on the future like those of prison walls.[8]

"Pretend that each of the sentences recorded," I tell students, "is the answer an oracle has given you to the initial question, and that you will never be happy in love unless you interpret the answer properly." I then assign each group two of the sentences and give them time to come up with a "translation." Since this exercise is an oral one, I will give a written simulation as to how it might proceed, which is partly based on how it has proceeded. The "answers" I have produced, while the products of hermeneutic inventiveness, are deliberately unspecific with respect to disciplinary knowledge. "Mutual attraction" is a popular concept that everyone engages in one way or another, and I have addressed it as such.

> 1) *There are some jealousies more touching than others. I willingly wander in such baffling darkness as that of the rivalry between a woman and a book.*
> Mutual attractions, which we normally consider to be positive emotions, are actually based upon what we normally consider to be a negative one: jealousy. In fact, jealousy motivates our entire relationship to the world; we view the world in terms of things that we want and do not want others to have. Mutual attraction, or "love," is merely the apotheosis of this relationship to the world, the happy accident of two individuals wanting one another exclusively. Love, however, is not the end of a story as it so often is in Hollywood films, but the beginning of one, not an

illumination but a "baffling darkness" to be negotiated willingly. Hence, what sustains love is a certain mystery, a mystery producing a narrative we read as much as a situation we live, an undecidable "rivalry between a woman and a book."

2) *The finger on the side of the forehead is not the barrel of a revolver. I believe that although we paid heed to each other's thinking, the automatic "Of nothing" that is our proudest denial did not once need to be uttered during the whole wedding-spree.*

The disturbing reference to "the barrel of a revolver" and a "wedding-spree" suggests that mutual attraction, or love, has a certain violent, even deadly quality to it. When two people wed, do they die in a way, lose whatever autonomy they once had? Auto-nomy reminds us of that curious phrase, "automatic 'Of nothing' that is our proudest denial." Perhaps the phrase implies the spontaneous nature of love, how it seems to come out of nowhere, but is that just an illusion, an "automatic" cliché. The fact that it takes the form of a denial rather than an affirmation is also disturbing, suggesting that "denial" in the psychological sense may be at work, which of course we all know (from Psych 101) often affirms rather than negates the existence of something. What does love, as currently conceived, deny? Maybe it is a denial of the imperfections of the human mind, and the "finger on the side of the forehead" is both the sign of thinking as well as a revolver we would like to deny, the mind's undeniable presence and consequent potential to undermine the spontaneity of mutual attraction. In such a state, we can only "pay heed" to one another without ever perfectly coinciding, which may be a blessing in disguise, as it leaves a remainder of auto-nomy in every relationship.

3) *Lower than the stars there is nothing to stare at. No matter what train you may be traveling in, it is dangerous to lean out of the carriage-door window.*

For mutual attraction to be successful, a certain abandon is necessary. Do not bother trying "to settle" or avoid "danger." Every mutual attraction is about sticking one's head out of the train in order to "stare at the stars," thus risking the possibility of decapitation. But, if there is only one mode of travel in the game of love, what does it mean when it is a train? Although we are exhorted to settle only for the heavens, for "true" love, does our earthly position on a train suggest that we are always "abandoned" in love, that love is doomed to failure?

4) *The stations were plainly distributed about a bay. The sea that to the human eye is never so beautiful as the sky did not leave us.*

When it comes to mutual attraction, we should appreciate what is "available" to us. We can rely on it, although we may only recognize this in retrospect, as the sentences are written in the past tense. Perhaps after the chaos of love, there is some pleasure in noting that it did, after all, have meaning. It had a pattern, if not a transcendent meaning, about "a bay" rather than "the bay."

5) *In the depths of our eyes disappeared neat reckonings bearing on the future like those of prison walls.*

Mutual attraction is an escape from the prison of ourselves, but it is also an escape from predictability. The interpenetration of gazes is a collision that involves an encounter with the other, and neither party can predict either the thoughts and actions of that other or how those phenomena will interact with one's own being. That is the contract we sign with our eyes, although we sign it on bottomless paper.

As one can tell from the above simulation, this exercise is crucial in getting students to practice "playing seriously" with language, allowing its constraints to set one on an unpredictable chain of association. It also shows how such association can be used to generate more traditional analytic formulations—in this case analyses about the nature of love. I always introduce this particular game in relation to Breton's dialectical statement about Surrealism in the first manifesto: "If the depths of our mind contain within it strange forces capable of augmenting those on the surface . . . there is every reason to seize them—first to seize them, then, if need be, to submit them to the control of our reason."[9] Thus, the purpose of Surrealist games in the context of (anti)disciplinary research is to supplement traditional modes of inquiry rather than do away with them.

"Analogy Cards," as I adapt the game, helps individual students view their knowledge problems according to this particular dialectic. The game, as Brotchie points out, originally functioned to create dreamlike passports for people of interest to the Surrealists, such as Sigmund Freud. I give the game a disciplinary focus by having the class help create a passport for a particular student's knowledge problem. As with all of the Surrealist games, I encourage students to take such group exercises and later use them as a means of invention for their own knowledge problems. Below are the characteristics of the passport, along with the Surrealist substitutions, that Brotchie provides:

Photograph: an animal
Father and Mother: born of the union of
Place of Birth: a geographical location
Date of Birth: an historical event [I substitute contemporary event here]
Nationality: a civilization or culture
Profession: pastime
Domicile: a painting [I substitute a movie here]
Height: a vegetable
Hair: a color
Appearance: a romantic or legendary hero
Eyes: a mineral
Complexion: a meteorological phenomenon
Nose: a perfume [I substitute scent]
Distinguishing Characteristics: sexual preference
Religion: conception of the world [I merely ask, what religion or philosophy is it]
Fingerprint: unique signature [its emblem, logo, or "tag"].[10]

While initially students are both puzzled and intrigued by the proposition of treating their knowledge problem as "an entity" with specific characteristics, they soon find that the real value of the exercise, for them, lies on the right side of the column. It is not so important that their knowledge problem have a "nose" as it is that "Nose" becomes the occasion for connecting their knowledge problem, metaphorically or metonymically, to a particular scent. To add further intrigue to the game and emphasize its purpose as a means of rhetorical invention, I often have the rest of the class substitute particulars for the right side of the column. Subsequently and, according to Breton's dialectic, it becomes the job of the entire class to "help" the individual student explain how the metaphors generated either "fit" or extend the boundaries of his or her knowledge problem.

"One into Another," adapted to academic disciplines, makes use of an imposed metaphor with respect to students' interdisciplinary groups. First, however, here is Brotchie's explanation of the original game:

> One player withdraws from the room, and chooses for himself an object (or a person, an idea, etc.). While he is absent the rest of the players also choose an object. When the first player returns he is told what object they have chosen. He must now describe his own object in terms of the properties of the object chosen by the others, making the comparison more and more obvious as he proceeds, until they are able to guess its identity. The first player should begin with a sentence such as "I am an (object)."[11]

In my version, the objects are already decided (knowledge problems and majors), but their combinations are not. Rather than the goal of guessing the correct object, a randomly chosen member of the group must connect his or her knowledge problem (originating in one major), to a different discipline in the group, also randomly chosen. Consequently, the group must work together from their combined expertise and amateur statuses in order to answer the question for a group member, "My knowledge problem is a good example of [foreign discipline]."

In my Advanced Writing in the Sciences course, the main preparation for the interdisciplinary paper takes the form of a paradigmatic example from an individual whom Ulmer designates as an "heir" to the Surrealist tradition, Jacques Derrida. While the late "founder" of deconstruction may seem an unlikely candidate as an example for writing in the sciences, his book *Glas*, in fact, raids the discipline of botany for metaphors to help describe his science of rhetoric. Since Derrida often works with painstakingly developed metaphors, particularly in *Glas*, the three-page excerpt included in Comley, Scholes, and Ulmer's *Textbook* actually provides for an illuminating discussion of just how Derrida invents and "transplants" metaphors from one discipline to another. The following paragraph represents a short inventory of issues simulating a condensed lecture/discussion related to the excerpt.

First of all, it is important to note that Derrida has chosen botany as his imported discipline based on the coincidence that the last name of the author he is studying, Genet, means "broomflower" in French. "Genet" is thus a pun designating a proper name and a common noun, a figure known as "antonomasia." Antonomasia is one example of the "research pun" which links disciplines based upon the chance materialities of language. The pun, then, produces unpredictable information precisely because it represents, as Ulmer notes in his first book (which happens to be about Derrida) *Applied Grammatology*, the "bridge of least [conceptual] motivation" between disciplines.[12] It can therefore become the basis for a more extended exploration of disciplines one had not previously considered connecting to one another. Thus, Derrida does not stop at noting the coincidence that Genet has a botanical meaning, but in fact uses concepts from botany as a means of conceptual invention:

> So this flower name would be a cryptogram or a cryptonym. It is not proper because it is common. On the other hand . . . it is not proper because it leads back to the nether realms, to the marshes, verily to the depths of the sea. Above the sea, with heavy sides but carried by it, the galley. In the depths of the sea, algae. Alga is a cryptogam, one of those plants that hide their sexual organs. Like ferns, which in general multiply themselves through the dispersion of spores. Whether one remarks them or not on the surface, the text is full of them. The "ferns" of the "Man Condemned to Death" are "rigid." Certain brackens unfold their fronds several meters below the ground. Cryptogams are evidently not flowers.[13]

Derrida's botanical connection of flowers to algae allows him to discuss how, in his new theory of reading, one finds certain motifs (such as Genet's name) in unlikely places, as if they had been disseminated like pollen and/or hidden in the ground or ocean like pollen/algal spores. Although one may be tempted to view this method as a misuse of science for the purposes of literature and/or philosophy, remember Paul Feyerabend's suggestion that, even in the sciences, "conceptual change" tends to come about as a result of new metaphors rather than vice versa.[14] The use of research puns, of which this excerpt provides just one example, becomes a means of generating metaphors that one had not previously considered.

II

While students in the sciences often exhibit an initial resistance to the idea that "writing games" can serve the function of interdisciplinary innovation, a resistance that can be countered with examples from science itself, my "Advanced Writing in the Humanities" students are generally more open to the joys of antidisciplinary gaming. Furthermore, they are generally more willing to entertain the incorporation of science in their writing than science students are (at least initially) willing to allow their own practices to be similarly "contaminated." Thus, I present my interdis-

ciplinary assignment to humanities students in terms of a "scientific" structuring of
the entire course. First, I tell them that I am not sure what the "humanities" are, but
feel that they should be less interested in upholding a tradition than experimenting
with the future, like science. Furthermore, the humanities' closest equivalent to science's pure research, Robert Ray claims, is the historical avant-garde.[15] In other
words, the avant-garde is interested in forming new concepts by various experiments, and can be ransacked for models to replicate, transplant, or modify. This
proposition not only motivates my choice of textbook, *Art in Theory: 1900-2000*,
but how I select and use texts from this copious anthology in order to stimulate the
students' interdisciplinary assignment:

> Following Robert Ray's claims about the avant-garde and science, the justification
> of the interdisciplinary paper is as follows: 1) It focuses on readings coming from
> the twentieth-century artistic avant-garde and related theoretical formulations. 2) It
> takes steps to help broaden the potential solutions or types of interventions you
> come up with by the very heterogeneity of the readings (further ensured by the
> random algorithm, inspired by John Cage, I devised in order to "choose" them). It
> is because we do not want to limit your interventions in advance that I am requir-
> ing you to choose a quote from one of the readings each day which, in some way,
> you think could be related to your knowledge problem. It will give you practice in
> this type of associative thinking as well as provide you with potential material for
> the paper.
>
> Another justification lies in the avant-garde's open espousal (if not outright
> invention) of interdisciplinary research as we know it today. Many of the most in-
> ventive answers to questions in a given discipline may come by bringing in the aid
> of another discipline, even if this translation makes either the former or latter
> somewhat unrecognizable to traditionalists.
>
> What you should be reading:
> 1) The assignments on the syllabus, as the interdisciplinary paper will ask you
> to address your knowledge problem from the perspective of at least one of the es-
> says from *Art in Theory*.
> 2) As you have time and inspiration, work more "directly" related to your
> discipline or knowledge problem in particular.
> 3) New avenues of research suggested by the readings from *Art in Theory* it-
> self.
> 4) Things that, in conversation with me, I suggest might be helpful.

One of the most important elements of the assignment is the admission that, after selecting a theoretically appropriate text, I used a random method to choose the
readings, one based on Cage's even more random method of designing course syllabi by generating random call numbers from the library. In doing so, I resign my
own position as "master of knowledge" and become a participant of the game, even
as I reassert some of that authority initially by giving students ideas about how they
might use various artist's statements, manifestos, and contemporary art theory to
generate language games and engines of invention that twist the students' initial
disciplines and related knowledge problems. Also, by emphasizing that the goal of

the assignment and related reading practices is to produce heterogeneous ideas, I assure students that someone like an art history major (with a specific topic) has no particular advantage over a psychology or sociology major. To give readers an idea of the kind of thinking I was trying to encourage, I will list some of the readings and "philosophical investigations" they provoked as in-class exercises and paper topics.

1) from Sigmund Freud, "On Dreams":[16]
Given Freud's observation that dream logic and its attendant elisions/repressions occur in everyday life, are there certain elements of your knowledge problem which could be illuminated by viewing them in Freud's specialized definitions of condensation, displacement, false continuity, and motive?

2) from Otto Weininger, *Sex and Character*:[17]
While Otto Weininger's claim that "The decision must be made between Judaism and Christianity" strikes one as indefensible today, in fact many issues are framed in terms of false oppositions in which a choice "must be made" between one or another. What oppositions are struck in your discipline and knowledge problem, by you or others? Are there other ways of framing the issue?

3) from Hans Prinzhorn, *Artistry of the Mentally Ill*:[18]
There is a sense of injustice in Prinzhorn's observation that "most children possess an original configurative urge which develops freely in a suitable environment, but which disappears rapidly as the rationalism of schooling turns an instinctual, playful creature into a knowing and purposeful one." Do you see areas in your knowledge problem or discipline where a more playful or creative approach would be helpful? Characterize the type of play you suggest and what its potential effects to the system might entail.

4) from Marinetti, "The Foundation and Manifesto of Futurism":[19]
What does your problem sound like?
Take something in your discipline not normally considered beautiful, and point out its beauty according to new rules.
Are there techniques/beliefs/preconceptions in your approach/discipline that you should or could, as an experiment, do away with?

5) from Jacques Riviere, "Present Tendencies in Painting":[20]
"The elimination of perspective leads quite naturally to this simple rule: the object must always be presented from the most revealing angle."—If you had to represent your knowledge problem in one visual image, what would it be and why?
For Riviere, air or depth, which is often regarded as "pure emptiness," must be both regarded and depicted as a thing in its own right. Is there some element in your discipline/knowledge problem which is presently considered a "nonthing," an absence, which would benefit from being included into the discussion?

6) from Corbusier and Ozenfant, "Purism":[21]

"The work of art is an artificial object which permits the creator to place the spectator in the state he wishes."—Is there a designated "creator" and "spectator" in your knowledge problem? What would happen if those roles were reversed?

7) from Francis Picabia, "Thank you, Francis!":[22]

"There is no such thing as a moral problem; morality like modesty is one of the greatest stupidities."—Take a commonly accepted maxim or belief from your discipline and invert it. Then attempt to explain why the new version is the correct one.

8) from Kasimir Malevich, "Non-Objective Art and Suprematism":[23]

Change the traditional goals of your discipline, as Malevich does when he says that art is not about beauty but about knowledge. Is there an element of your project that is open to mysticism?

9) from "Statement of the Editors of *Vesch*":[24]

What larger aspects of the social structure need to change in order to properly deal with your knowledge problem?

What role can amateurs play in the situation?

Can you think of any unlikely allies?

10) from Bertolt Brecht, "Popularity and Realism":[25]

How is realism defined in your discipline? Could it be defined differently, for different ends? Would this require new modes of representation?

11) from Jackson Pollock, "Answers to a Questionnaire":[26]

Name a famous figure in your field and contradict his or her major "theories."

12) from Michel Tapié, *An Other Art*:[27]

Consider a "mistake" related to your problem as if it were a solution.

13) from John Cage, "On Robert Rauschenberg, Artist, and his Work":[28]

Import a tool/object into your discipline/approach that seems "out of place"—such as Rauschenberg does with newsprint.

Taking a cue from Cage's style, write in a manner that "simulates" the structure of your knowledge problem rather than merely discussing it in "traditional discourse."

What would this simulation look like?

14) from Michael Fried, *Three American Painters*:[29]

In suggesting a more collaborative role between artists and critics in a shared project, Fried seems to be calling for a change in art's traditional division of labor. Does your knowledge problem or discipline presuppose a division of labor? In what ways and to what effect would changes in the division affect the questions you are dealing with?

In a nod to Fried's own self-critical attitude, question the meanings of key words or catch-phrases that tend to recur in your research or your own writing.

For Fried, Manet's greatness lies in his recognition of his problematic relationship to reality and his exploration of the limitations of painting itself. Discuss your knowledge problem based upon your own problematic relationship to it or to the limitations of the "medium" your discipline uses to discuss it.

15) from Michael Fried, "Art and Objecthood":[30]

Create an unlikely/surprising opposition either within your knowledge problem or with respect to something outside it, just as Fried opposes art and theater.

If your knowledge problem was a religion or philosophy, what would it be and why?

16) from Robert Morris, "Notes on Sculpture 4: Beyond Objects":[31]

In what ways is your knowledge problem "defused" or "repressed" by your discipline or the culture at large rather than directly addressed?

17) from Hélio Oiticica, "Appearance of the Supra-Sensorial":[32]

Use old words in new ways or invent words to designate/create a new concept for use in your writing.

What is considered "insane" in your discipline or knowledge problem and why?

18) from Art & Language, "Letter to a Canadian Curator":[33]

Suggest some guerilla tactics or other strategies of infiltration in order to subvert the power structures limiting your discipline or knowledge problem.

19) from Krzysztof Wodiczko, "Public Projection":[34]

What is intoxicating or seductive about your knowledge problem or discipline?
What seems permanent, yet undesirable about the situation?

20) from Victor Burgin, "The Absence of Presence":[35]

What does your discipline disavow and why?

21) Interview with Jeff Wall:[36]

Think of something in your discipline that is now considered obsolete, passé, or out of style, and then apply it to your knowledge problem with renewed optimism.

What are the most utopian or dystopian results you can envision with respect to the situation?

III. Conclusion: What Is a Knowledge Problem?

In each of these three courses, my insistence that students pick a "knowledge problem" rather than a "topic" is an immediate provocation on the level of language that prepares them to think about how, as the title of this essay suggests, writing is against discipline. The limitations of the word "topic" are extensively discussed by philosophers and rhetoricians alike, and those limitations not only go back to its roots in the Greek *topos* or "place" but extend to the present in its very familiarity. For students, a topic is something that already exists, already has an identity and an attendant methodology that bounds it. A "knowledge problem," on the other hand, to the extent that students identify it with a rupture in their "field" (also a spatial metaphor, of course), even if their understanding is as simple as thinking of this problem as an "unanswered question," demands that they envision their field as being, at least for the moment, either limited, characterized by conflict, or both. On the one hand, "disciplining" a conflict requires eliminating particular options, thereby limiting a field's scope of inquiry. On the other hand, the very expansionist rhetoric that disciplines (particularly the sciences) often employ undermines any sense that they can remain "stable" modes of inquiry.

Going beyond this initial alienation of language, the term "knowledge problem" forces students to think of disciplinary questions in terms of crises, however large or small. Any time a member of a discipline asks an earnest question, he or she may encounter a problem of knowledge, a situation in which the discipline as currently defined is inadequate. This passive formulation of the problem is, of course, Thomas Kuhn's thesis concerning how "scientific revolutions" occur.[37] Others, from disciplines as diverse as physics and the plastic arts, actively try to create these crises or knowledge problems by interrogating the means of knowledge production themselves, not only interrogating these means but playing with them, inventing with them. I am of the belief that teachers of writing in/across the disciplines are, or at least should be, uniquely situated to aid in this more active means of questioning disciplinarity precisely because they seem to occupy an ill-defined, and yet seemingly indispensable, place within the emerging schemas of the university. Charged with the meager task of teaching students to translate disciplinary knowledge into writing, they can employ the history and emerging futures of experimental writing to help students create disciplinary knowledge. To the extent that students are encouraged to think of writing as an unruly participant in the knowledge process, they are prepared to write against *the* disciplines and write *toward* new disciplines, the ones that are always emerging and the ones that could emerge.

Notes

1. Robert B. Ray, *How a Film Theory Got Lost and Other Mysteries in Cultural Studies* (Bloomington, IN: Indiana University Press, 2001), 73.
2. For the time being the reader may consider a "knowledge problem" in his or her own sense or, otherwise, as being a general question the student wants to explore that somehow relates to his or her discipline. For a more extended discussion of how a knowledge problem represents the very potential of anti-disciplinarity, see section three of this paper, "Conclusion: What is a Knowledge Problem?"
3. Jean-François Lyotard, *The Postmodern Condition: A Report on Knowledge*, trans. Geoff Benington and Brian Massumi (Minneapolis, MN: University of Minnesota, 1999).
4. Roland Barthes, *Roland Barthes*, trans. Richard Howard (Berkeley, CA: University of California Press, 1994), 85.
5. Charles Darwin, *Origin of Species* (New York: Gramercy Books, 1995).
6. Gregory Ulmer, *Teletheory* (New York: Routledge, 1989), 172.
7. Alastair Brotchie, ed., *Surrealist Games* (Boston: Shambhala, 1995).
8. Brotchie, *Surrealist Games*, 17.
9. André Breton, *Manifestoes of Surrealism*, trans. Richard Seaver and Helen R. Lane (Ann Arbor, MI: University of Michigan, 1969), 10.
10. Brotchie, *Surrealist Games*, 88.
11. Brotchie, *Surrealist Games*, 31.

12. Gregory Ulmer, *Applied Grammatology* (Baltimore, MD: Johns Hopkins University Press, 1985), 309.
13. Qtd. in *Textbook*, ed. Robert Scholes, Nancy R. Comley, and Gregory L. Ulmer, (New York: Saint Martins, 1995), 260.
14. Paul Feyerabend, *Against Method* (London: New Left Books, 1978), 203.
15. Ray, *How a Film Theory*, 75.
16. Charles Harrison and Paul Wood, eds., *Art in Theory: 1900-2000* (Oxford: Blackwell, 2003), 21–28.
17. Harrison and Wood, *Art in Theory*, 28–30.
18. Harrison and Wood, *Art in Theory*, 121–24.
19. Harrison and Wood, *Art in Theory*, 146–49.
20. Harrison and Wood, *Art in Theory*, 190–94.
21. Harrison and Wood, *Art in Theory*, 239–42.
22. Harrison and Wood, *Art in Theory*, 274–75.
23. Harrison and Wood, *Art in Theory*, 292–93.
24. Harrison and Wood, *Art in Theory*, 344–45.
25. Harrison and Wood, *Art in Theory*, 499–502.
26. Harrison and Wood, *Art in Theory*, 569–70.
27. Harrison and Wood, *Art in Theory*, 629–31.
28. Harrison and Wood, *Art in Theory*, 734–37.
29. Harrison and Wood, *Art in Theory*, 787–93.
30. Harrison and Wood, *Art in Theory*, 835–46.
31. Harrison and Wood, *Art in Theory*, 881-85.
32. Harrison and Wood, *Art in Theory*, 913–15.
33. Harrison and Wood, *Art in Theory*, 1039-41.
34. Harrison and Wood, *Art in Theory*, 1065–68.
35. Harrison and Wood, *Art in Theory*, 1068–72.
36. Harrison and Wood, *Art in Theory*, 1158–61.
37. Thomas Kuhn, *The Structure of Scientific Revolutions* (Chicago: University of Chicago Press, 1970).

Chapter Six
The Brake of Reflection:
Slowing Social Process in the Critical
WID Classroom

David Kellogg

If, as Michael Carter has recently argued, "writing in the disciplines is founded on an integrative relationship between writing and knowing," it is worth asking what kind of knowledge is produced.[1] The traditional answer is, of course, disciplinary knowledge—not, Carter stresses, knowledge *of* a discipline, but "procedural knowledge, writing as a way of knowing *in* a discipline."[2] This may be the most important insight of the writing in the disciplines (WID) movement to date: that the social and epistemological significance of differences among disciplinary writing practices suggests that the trans-disciplinary ambitions of writing across the curriculum (WAC) are ultimately quixotic. As a consequence of this insight, WID administration has led to a number of programmatic innovations, many of which have challenged the traditional role(s) for English departments in sponsoring and administering writing instruction in American higher education. Indeed, Carter argues (from the perspective of an English professor) that bridging the gap between content knowledge and procedural knowledge "is not a problem that can be solved by reference to *our own discipline's understanding* of the relationship between writing and knowing."[3] In such a context, the notion of a WID program housed in an English department seems a contradiction in terms.

Such developments have quite rightly led to a heightened awareness about the broadly held stakes of writing instruction and the collective responsibility of university faculty for bringing writing into the classroom. Yet these same developments have come with a price: in particular, they seem to lend support to the reductive assumptions of cultural, political, and financial authorities that the only reasonable goal of writing instruction is to provide practical training for employment in, and subjugation by, the workplace. There is, however, another important kind of knowledge implicated in writing: knowledge of the self in the contexts of its becoming. This kind of self-knowledge, the dynamic reflexivity at the heart of critical pedagogy, is not often given priority in models of disciplinary knowledge commonly associated with WID. If we are committed to creating the opportunity for the cultivation of this knowledge in writing classes, WID pedagogy may seem to conform rather too easily to social demands for practical return.

In what follows, I hope to do three things. First, I theorize how notions of reflection and reflexivity might help forestall the reduction of WID practice to wholly pragmatic ends. Second, I explore how reflection and reflexivity are being implemented in a WID program (at Northeastern University) that retains the anomalous status of remaining within an English department. And third, I argue that reflection in such a program serves to slow the social processes of subject formation and interpellation and opens a space for critical engagement that is unlikely to be created by WID programs housed in the disciplines (which are designed to accelerate those very processes). This version of a critical WID pedagogy acknowledges the knowledge-constructing conventions of disciplinary frames but holds that such conventions must be interrogated as much as learned. When conceived as a *brake* on social formation rather than as a *means* to it, reflection provides a rationale for maintaining WID courses in institutional locations that value critical rhetorical perspectives (such as departments of English or rhetoric).

I

In the fourth chapter of *Working Theory: Critical Composition Studies for Students and Teachers*, Judith A. Goleman explores "the capacity students have to reproduce in the present the very theme writing they would claim to see through."[4] To illustrate this capacity, Goleman introduces a student essay by "Susan M.," who critiques the constraints of an earlier writing assignment using Richard Ohmann's essay "Freshman English and Administered Thought." In seeing her earlier writing through the critical lens Ohmann offers, Susan M. finds that she once chose topics with no internal motivation: "Everything I wrote about had to interest the teacher. It made no difference if the topic interested me."[5] The narrative of growth and enlightenment in Susan M.'s essay will be familiar to teachers who have asked students to reflect on previous writing practices and products: a critical stance quickly becomes a dismissal of earlier efforts, now seen as products of an immature mind or (here) of a constrained institutional environment. Just as familiar is the product of this growth: the new, presumably transformed writing does not depart from the mode of engagement that constrained the student's earlier work. As Goleman puts it, in this essay Susan M. "dutifully receives and assembles Ohmann's work in relation to her own," and Ohmann becomes a new master text to rehearse in her own writing rather than a catalyst for an altered subjectivity.[6]

From this reading of Susan M.'s retrospective critique, Goleman argues more generally against "the assumption that historical knowledge of academic forms will alter one's subjectivity and affect one's present situation." Goleman presciently saw in 1995 that this assumption, common among composition scholars even now, "is an idealism and must be rethought." Indeed, Goleman notes, this view "tend[s] toward reification in pedagogical contexts" and "threatens to become the key concept of a new, authoritative discourse."[7] I take this rethinking of idealisms to be central to Goleman's project in *Working Theory*, which Goleman defines as enacting "the application of postmodern theory to the teaching of composition."[8] It is that, of course, but only in the same sense that Frederic Jameson's *Marxism and Form* is an introduction to Marxist literary criticism, which is to say, not very much.[9] In fact, like *Marxism and Form*, Goleman's project is much more transformative than its title implies. Composition graduate students who picked up *Working Theory* hoping for a quick comp-friendly survey of postmodern theory encountered, instead, a rich intervention in the very theories it introduced. This intervention makes the book both more difficult and more valuable. In Goleman's transformational project, theorists from Bakhtin to Fish are "worked" (to use Goleman's insistent term) not for their own sake but to illustrate a common problematic: the limits of critical writing as a mode of becoming, or, to put it another way, the tendency for dialectical thinking to settle into a static, taken-for-granted sense of having arrived.

Goleman stresses this point repeatedly, and in a wide variety of contexts. For example, in a passage that carefully elaborates Bakhtin's concept of "internally persuasive discourse," Goleman argues that "a pedagogy directed toward the cultivation of internally persuasive discourse is not the same thing as a pedagogy directed against authoritative discourse."[10] At first glance, either pedagogy seems acceptable—certainly either is better than one directed *toward* authoritative discourse. But then she goes on: "In the former, we direct ourselves toward knowledge of the language relations we are in; in the latter, we would seek to divest them out of hand. As such, the second pedagogy would constitute another authoritative discourse, directed toward the affirmation or rejection of students' language relations."[11] Goleman's critique here (and throughout *Working Theory*), while basically sympathetic, uses theory in an effort to rescue critical pedagogy from its own tendency to reify ideology as a thing to be resisted rather than a condition of subjectivity itself. It is this approach to ideology that makes *Working Theory* one of the most politically subtle texts in composition theory.

Goleman's postmodern view of ideology and authority allies her with thinkers such as Michel Foucault and Louis Althusser. Early in *Working Theory*, Goleman engages Althusser through Jameson, noting that ideological overdetermination implies that "ideology cannot exist as a thing in itself; rather, it exists only in its own specific effects as the practice of representation."[12] Armed with this notion of ideology as effect and ideological analysis as a "responsive hermeneutic," Goleman squeezes the blood of agency from the stone of Althusserian Marxism:

> [C]ritical individuals are dialecticians—continually re-seeing their subjectivity
> and acting on what they see as it evolves and is transformed by circumstance.
> With this in mind, it could be said that Althusser's discovery of structural effec-
> tivity implies a material theory of human agency that can be named critical ef-
> fectivity. The concept of critical effectivity presupposes that knowledge of
> one's subjectivity cannot be learned in the fixed or static manner of a "history
> lesson" but rather must be understood over and over again in its effects.[13]

Critical effectivity in this passage involves a kind of reflection ("re-seeing")
that, like ideology itself, is not a thing or even an event so much as a constantly
shifting and unfolding process. Much of *Working Theory* focuses on moments
like these, moments when critical effectivity breaks down and a possible understanding (of teacher as well as student) becomes fixed and static. I see the interpretive passages in *Working Theory* as building toward what Goleman calls a
"counterhegemonic writing project" by allowing these moments to inhabit the
fullness of their contradictions. Goleman's own continuing contradictions in the
book are, she declares in her conclusion, "an unavoidable symptom" of her project's scope and, more positively, a consequence of her dialectic and dialogic
practice.[14]

In constructing critical effectivity as a form of agency, Goleman must deal
with agency's seeming absence in Althusser's famous essay on ideological state
apparatuses (ISAs).[15] We may recall that Althusser coins the term *ISA* to distinguish certain institutions from repressive state apparatuses (RSAs). RSAs (such
as the police, the court system, and the prison) function by violence or the threat
of violence; ISAs on the other hand (such as the family, the political system, and
the school) function "*by ideology.*"[16] The analysis is more complex than this, as
Althusser adduces a role both for ideology in RSAs and for repression in ISAs.
Further, as Goleman is keenly aware, Althusser has been critiqued by advocates
of critical pedagogy for minimizing resistance.[17] It is in part against such a reduction of Althusser to a static system that Goleman employs his work in the
service of agency.

In any event, Goleman's focus on ISAs makes sense, given the clear role
played by educative institutions in cultural reproduction and Goleman's suggestion that a critical pedagogy should include itself "as one of the objects of
study."[18] Yet nowhere does Goleman discuss the crucially important concept of
interpellation, which for Althusser is the process by which individuals are constituted as subjects (in part by means of ISAs). This omission is surprising. For,
as the continual practice of misrecognition by the subject of him- or herself,
interpellation serves as critical effectivity's functional opposite. If critical effectivity is a process of individuals "continually re-seeing their subjectivity and
acting on what they see," interpellation is the occlusion of that capacity. As Althusser puts it in a well-known passage:

> [I]deology "acts" or "functions" in such a way that it "recruits" subjects among
> the individuals (it recruits them all), or "transforms" the individuals into sub-
> jects (it transforms them all) by that very precise operation which I have called

interpellation or hailing, and which can be imagined along the lines of the most commonplace everyday police (or other) hailing: "Hey, you there!"[19]

Critical effectivity, then, can be understood as a kind of counter-interpellation. Yet the relationship between the two processes is by no means symmetrical. Critical effectivity is cultivated by individuals, fleetingly and late; interpellation begins before birth and is reinforced by all manner of social institutions, including ISAs. In their role as ISAs, schools do not initiate this hailing so much as exploit its ongoing activity by ejecting students at various points into class positions which students then (mis)recognize as their own proper role.[20]

We need not (as in fact I do not) accept the Althusserian model in its totality to appreciate how the opposition between interpellation and critical effectivity describes a perennial difference of opinion about the proper role of writing instruction in American colleges and universities. This is the difference between institution and individual, between repression and liberation, between being invented by the university and inventing it for oneself.[21] But this difference is not reducible to any of the standard oppositions of composition studies: neither to Bartholomae's brief equivocation over the agent of invention, nor to Peter Elbow's distinction between academics and writers, nor to Pat Bizzell's uneasy linkage of "academic discourse and critical consciousness."[22] Examples like these—and they could be multiplied—suggest the following, additional asymmetry: over the past forty years, composition has generally declared itself (in contradictory ways, to be sure) on the side of students. Presented with a choice between critical effectivity and interpellation, no self-respecting composition scholar would willingly side with the latter.

Yet this is precisely where we find university administrators, labor market intermediaries,[23] and other public advocates for literacy education as a component of civil society. As the National Commission on Writing argued in its 2004 report "Writing: A Ticket to Work . . . or a Ticket Out":

Writing is a "threshold skill" for salaried employment and promotion. It is particularly important in services and in finance, insurance, and real estate (FIRE), growing employment sectors that are likely to generate the most new jobs in the coming decade. In a nutshell, the survey confirms our conviction that individual opportunity in the United States depends critically on the ability to present one's thoughts coherently, cogently, and persuasively on paper.[24]

To put it in Althusserian terms, if you want to be hailed as a Realtor®, you had better learn to write well—including, one imagines, how to deploy the crucial trademark symbol. Of course, the Commission report was issued during the expansion of the real estate bubble, so the key literacy genre for the twenty-first-century job seeker (a person we might call the interpellant) may be the scannable resume.

Small wonder, then, that students also tend to take the side of interpellation. This is more or less what Russel Durst finds in his *Collision Course: Conflict, Negotiation, and Learning in College Composition*.[25] Durst's book studies how student expectations and hopes for writing instruction at the University of Cincinnati differed from the critical literacy goals of its writing program. Durst comes to see that "entering students' assumptions about writing, and their aims for what they hope to learn in first-year composition, appear strongly opposed" to the goals of a composition program grounded in critical literacy.[26] Rather, he notes, these students have "aspirations [that] are overwhelmingly pragmatic and utilitarian, far more focused on attaining practical skills and achieving career goals than on critiquing current society or developing reflective capabilities."[27] Such attitudes are hardly surprising. Durst, however, does not dismiss these values as the expected outcomes of an ideological development that is already quite advanced. He draws quite a different lesson: "Rather than condemn instrumentalism in students . . . we need to find ways to make sense of and come to terms with [it] and, ultimately, to develop means of making better use of it in the classroom."[28] The approach Durst develops, which he calls *reflective instrumentalism*, honors students' vocational goals but "adds a reflective dimension" that, Durst hopes, "provides numerous opportunities for students to question and begin to develop critical perspectives."[29]

Durst's explanation of reflective instrumentalism itself is rather thin; the bulk of *Collision Course* is devoted to analyzing the problem rather than offering a solution. In the final chapter, Durst briefly outlines a first-year composition course focusing on education in which students investigate their intended major through, among other things, departmental self-descriptions, field observations, and interviews with professionals. In performing and writing up research of this type, Durst suggests, "students should learn that a major is more than a set of courses leading to certification and employment, that it constitutes a body of knowledge and a set of problem-solving strategies, that it promotes particular ways of thinking and acting, that it has a history, and that it performs certain functions in the larger society."[30] Education-themed writing classes are not uncommon in current writing pedagogy, but the class Durst describes does allow students to customize their investigation in ways that suit their interests and intentions—avoiding, one hopes, the motivational problem faced by Goleman's student Susan M.

We might question how reflective this course really is; at least one scholar has recently questioned "whether Durst was really investigating the effects of a true critical pedagogy."[31] For that matter, how instrumental is it? Nothing in Durst's book suggests that his students learn to *compose* practical documents in the manner, say, of a technical or professional writing class. Perhaps this is too much to ask for a first-year composition course, but other solutions are possible. Consider the difference between Durst's approach and that of Bruce McComiskey, whose "social process" pedagogy addresses the same challenge from a slightly different tack, using a "heuristic for rhetorical inquiry based on the cycle of cultural production, contextual distribution, and critical consumption."[32] There is not space here to examine this pedagogy at length, but it is worth noting that, like Durst, McComiskey begins by declaring his dissatisfaction with critical pedagogy, although, he says, while "I found new energy in the social process theories we applied to composition in [Jim Berlin's] graduate classes, I missed the pragmatic power I used to feel from teaching the writing process."[33] Unlike Durst, however, McComiskey asks his students to compose pragmatic documents (such as letters to specific audiences) that intervene at various points of a particular production/distribution/consumption cycle; these documents are then examined critically within the course itself, and in writing by the students who wrote them. A student who wants to intervene in, for example, the distribution cycle of an advertisement may write a letter to the editors of a magazine in which the ad appears. At this point, however, the student has initiated a new cycle by producing (and perhaps distributing) a new document. So what needs to be analyzed now is not merely the distribution stage of the advertisement but the production stage of the student's intervention. Assignments in social process pedagogy are typically sequenced in this recursive manner: not drafts leading to a final product but practical documents combined in various ways with analytical and academic texts that put those practical documents under interpretive pressure. This organization cultivates, it is hoped, a kind of reflective practice.

It is worth pausing here to define our terms. What do we mean by reflection? In *Turns of Thought: Teaching Composition as Reflexive Practice*, Donna Qualley offers a useful distinction:

> Reflexivity is not the same thing as reflection, although they are often part of the same recursive and hermeneutical process. When we reflect, we fix our thoughts on a subject; we carefully consider it, meditate upon it. Self-reflection assumes that individuals can access the contents of their own mind *independently of others*. Reflexivity, on the other hand, does not originate in the self but always occurs in response to a person's critical engagement with an "other."[34]

If *reflection* generally represents a mental activity, *reflexivity*, as suggested by Qualley's invocation of the dialectic, represents a dynamic and open stance toward the self and the other. In writing instruction, reflection is further complicated by the genres of the *reflection* (or *response*) *paper*, which vary widely from informal responses to particular activities to comprehensive evaluations of an entire course.[35]

Qualley's distinction suggests that when we, as writing teachers, refer to the things written reflection makes possible, we often mean something like reflectivity. This distinction also implicitly offers four ways reflection and reflexivity might be observed in composition courses.

Non-reflexive reflection. This is common in writing classes that include reflection papers, especially those sponsoring end-of-term reflective papers that collapse inevitably into simple narratives of progress or conversion. Examples are many and familiar, including Susan M.'s paper discussed earlier.

Reflexive reflection. This is the kind of reflection teachers covet but rarely receive. Unlike non-reflexive reflection, reflexive reflection gives an impression of a student having changed in the process rather than going through the motions or engaging in tacit negotiation for a higher grade.

Reflexive non-reflection. Reflexivity without reflection can be hard to recognize because, unlike reflection, reflexivity is not identified with a particular genre. But we should learn to recognize such moments because they point toward an encounter with an other that is not necessarily expected or sought—the encounter that may be more "authentic" or destabilizing (in a positive sense). We can see such moments in some student texts that struggle and break down in ways suggestive of a difficult encounter with an Other. Such "failures" in student writing can be evaluated positively as we see how new meanings generated by this encounter seem to escape the student's ability to capture them. Indeed, reflexive non-reflection may name the very kind of openness that a writing class focusing on discovery and invention hopes to foster.

Non-reflexive non-reflection. This is the default position of student writing: the unchallenged, unchallenging paper. This is the student argument that rehearses known positions, that may succeed on superficial grounds such as correctness and length, and that showcases held knowledge rather than creates new knowledge.

As a concept, reflection is widely embraced by contemporary writing teachers. Yet if we fail to distinguish between the *activity* of reflection and the *stance* of reflexivity, we may be less able to evaluate the failures and successes of reflective writing. For example, in a brief case scenario for WAC teachers, Kathleen Blake Yancey offers the story of Rick. Rick is a new political science professor who added a reflective component to an assignment as a way to clear up some uncertainty about what to expect. His rationale? "He wasn't at all sure what he'd find in this reflection, but he didn't see that it could hurt."[36] The main assignment asked students to examine how a particular social force "worked [a country] toward coherence" or "worked to fragment the country." In the accompanying reflection, students were asked to take attitudes of belief and doubt toward the assignment, predict how it would be received, and describe what was learned that would not be apparent by the assignment.[37]

Yancey contrasts the work of two students. The first student's paper "told the story of Denmark in exactly the terms . . . specified," and the reflection described the student's interest in Denmark in personal terms. Reading this assignment and reflection together confirmed for Rick the value of personal motivation and "made [Rick] think that perhaps . . . he had underestimated the students' abilities."[38] This optimism was short-lived, as the second response was incoherent and fragmented—not an essay at all but "a response to the questions." The second student's reflection also follows the form of the assignment precisely, repeating key terms of the prompt questions in italics:

> I am trying to *believe* that this is the best paper I've never written, but it's too short. I know that. I don't know how much the shortness will affect my grade.
> I *doubt* that this paper is any good because I don't think it's long enough. I couldn't seem to understand what you meant by coherence and fragmentation,

and I couldn't check the textbook because I haven't bought it yet. I can buy it next week when I get paid.

I predict you will be disappointed in this paper. I am too.

You can see everything I learned in this assignment. I put everything I learned into the paper, and it's still too short. Can you help me?[39]

Everything about the scenario suggests that the first paper succeeds while the second fails. The student reflections work to confirm this view of success and failure, for Rick and for Yancey. In fact, the discussion questions provided by Yancey all refer to "this student"—presumably the second, problematic student whose work needs to be explained and repaired.[40]

But the first reflection, as described in the scenario, has the feel of a carefully crafted performance. I do not question the authenticity of the student's interest in Denmark or her desire to travel there. I do, however, think that, much like her picture of Denmark, the student's reflection "cohered in significant ways" and that both texts "told the story . . . in exactly the terms [Rick] had specified."[41] The extraordinary coherence of the reflection, in other words, suggests that reflexivity—which leads inevitably toward contradiction—is absent. Like many "successful" student reflection papers, this is reflection without reflexivity.

Neither the second paper nor its accompanying reflection could be called successful. The reflection does, however, contain the seed of reflexivity: an openness to change, which is prompted by an awareness of the contradictory positions the writer occupies (as student and consumer of textbooks). We find these seeds in the very features of the text that mark it as failing. Three of the four paragraphs refer to the work's inadequacy in terms of its length. *It is as though the student were asking the teacher to help him grow.* There is, of course, an element of performance in this as well, as the writer crafts the reflection to mitigate the inevitable bad grade on the paper. Yet the student seems to be experiencing the class as a genuine encounter with a number of others (the teacher, the task, the textbook) which have not yet been fully negotiated. With his flailing, fragmentary reflection, this student may be nearer to achieving critical effectivity than the first student's highly polished success. The first student moves swiftly and steadily along the path to being interpellated; the second student stops, stalls, and *hails the teacher* ("Can you help me?"). Reflection has slowed down the process of interpellation, and created a space where critical effectivity may be possible.

II

Northeastern University is a diverse private research institution in Boston, Massachusetts. Its approximately 15,000 undergraduate students study in six colleges: arts and sciences, engineering, health professions, computer and information sciences, business, and criminal justice. It also offers more than 125 graduate degrees.

Like the University of Cincinnati (the subject of Durst's study), Northeastern has long been identified with its extensive cooperative education program.[42] Historically, co-op at Northeastern allowed students to pay for college and gain valuable work experience while earning a degree. So universal was co-op that an additional year (the third or "middler" year between the sophomore and junior years) was added to the standard four-year undergraduate calendar. Over the last three decades, Northeastern has invested heavily in its academic programs and has engaged in an intensive, and largely successful, campaign to improve its academic ranking. During this period it transformed from a commuter school largely serving the local working class into a highly selective residential university drawing students from around the world. Understandably, these changes have affected the role of co-op in a Northeastern education, which is not as universal as it once was. Students in the College of Arts and Sciences, for example, may now satisfy their experiential education requirement by avenues such as study abroad.

I mention this transformation because advanced writing at Northeastern was founded on a connection with co-op. What was called the Middler Year Writing Requirement (MYWR) arose in the 1980s in response to the pragmatic demands of co-op employers who wanted students to write in professional settings. MYWR was imagined as a class where students would use their co-op experience to solve problems in the workplace through writing. Typically, MYWR students identified a problem they encountered while on co-op and proposed a solution in a fairly long (5,000–6,000 word) recommendation report. This report would be written for the audience prepared to solve the problem (usually the former co-op employer or supervisor) and accompanied by a letter of transmittal. Six versions of MYWR were developed for the various Northeastern colleges. They were all taught within the English department, however; they all had the same basic structure (a series of small practical assignments—memo, annotated bibliography, proposal, letter of transmittal, and so forth—culminating in a researched recommendation report and a comprehensive portfolio); and they all used the same custom-published textbook.[43] The assignments were more or less similar from course to course; what changed were the topics and the constituencies.

What is now called Advanced Writing in the Disciplines (AWD) at Northeastern is still taught almost entirely by faculty and graduate students in the English department,[44] and like its predecessor, it remains a universal graduation requirement. All Northeastern undergraduates must complete AWD with a grade of C or higher to graduate. It cannot be satisfied by transfer credit and is almost never waived. But AWD today differs considerably from MYWR. To the previous six courses, AWD has added six more, allowing students in the arts and sciences to take courses specific to their interests in the humanities, the social sciences, the sciences, pre-law, education, and literature. AWD no longer assumes a co-op connection and no longer focuses on the long recommendation report. A uniform syllabus has been replaced by a set of courses addressing the diverse needs of students in different fields; in these courses, students compose several papers in a variety of genres and for a variety of audiences. In AWD courses, students highlight the role of writing in the construction and dissemination of disciplinary knowledge; they both produce workplace texts and inquire about the role of those texts in producing subjects of their field.

AWD's new diversity is unified in two ways. First, the following statement is central to all AWD courses:

AWD Learning Goals
A student who successfully completes the AWD requirement at Northeastern should have demonstrated:

1. A strong understanding of the uses of writing in his/her academic discipline and/or career path
2. Critical understanding of and facility in the discourse of a field
3. Successful use of appropriate citation conventions
4. An understanding of the importance of audience and context with respect to writing style and arrangement
5. Confidence and facility with the processes of revision
6. The production of 5,000+ words of polished, revised writing
7. Written reflection on his or her own writing processes and texts and their role in his or her own practice of critical reasoning

The Learning Goals (LG) statement is designed to bring all AWD offerings under a fairly broad conceptual umbrella emphasizing diversity among fields. It does not describe assignments or activities and leaves particular ways of meeting the goals up to individual classes (and students, on whom the burden of "demonstrating" the goals ultimately falls).

Second, every successful AWD student produces a reflective portfolio. Here the AWD program closely follows the approach developed by Edward White in his 2005 article, "The Scoring of Writing Portfolios: Phase 2."[45] In this article, White seeks to move portfolio scoring forward by "connect[ing] the power of the reflective letter to the actual scoring of portfolios."[46] "This method," White argues,

> requires the development of two new documents as part of the assessment: first, a set of goals set by faculty for the particular course, program, or purpose for which the portfolio is submitted; and, second, a reflective letter to readers composed by the student, an argument showing that those goals have been met (or, perhaps, not met), using the portfolio contents as evidence. Although these do not appear at first to be particularly novel developments, when used together they completely change the nature of portfolio assessment, and for the better in every sense.[47]

(In AWD, the first document is, of course, the LG statement.) White's approach to portfolio assessment seeks to resolve a set of questions that have long dogged

portfolio grading, such as how holistic scoring methods can square with the demands of portfolio assessment and whether graders of portfolios are in actuality
grading individual papers for a second time. Here the grade is assigned to a *new*
reflective essay (White's "reflective letter") that makes an argumentative case
for the value of the student's *already submitted* work.

The AWD reflective portfolio comprises three elements: the reflective essay
itself; the polished and revised documents that represent the major unit papers of
the class; and a section of supporting materials that may include anything from
rough drafts and peer reviews to material used in research. To assist in this process, students use *The AWD Toolkit*, a custom-published textbook that includes
labeled notebook dividers for assembling the portfolio itself.[48] Students often
(though not always) compose their reflective essays by going through the LG
statement one goal at a time, citing the work contained in the other sections of
their portfolio. To demonstrate having met Goal 6, for example, students sometimes provide a word count of their final versions in a table, along with a justification for calling that work "polished" and "revised."

As for the assignments themselves, some general patterns still hold within
the diversity of AWD offerings. One relatively common pattern consists of four
units. In the first unit, students analyze a document in their field as the artifact of
a discourse community and compose a paper in which that analysis becomes a
means of introducing their classmates to the writer's discipline. From this beginning, students write papers for professional, public, and academic audiences
in their field. These three papers—for example, an instructional document (professional audience), an opinion column (public audience), and a literature review
(academic audience)—are often focused on a single topic.

Over a semester, four such unit papers will typically add up to well over
5,000 words of revised writing. In fact, students write much more than this.
Each unit paper is the culmination of an assignment sequence involving many
types of writing to distinct audiences in multiple genres. Consider a class in
writing for the health professions where students are asked to create a health
education document for the public writing unit. Different students will develop
different kinds of documents depending on factors that include major (nursing,
pharmacy, and so forth) and interests (pain, geriatric health, mental health, and
so forth). A pharmacy student with an interest in depression might compose a
guide to anti-depressant drug interactions for psychiatric patients. A nursing
student with an interest in addiction might compose a needle hygiene protocol
for intravenous drug users.

The resulting unit paper, when revised, may be only 1,000 words or so, but
it is typically nested in a set of other documents. These might include the following:

- A **context memo** proposing the document itself, explaining its rationale,
  discussing how it might be used, and describing the needs of its intended
  audience. The context memo resembles a short proposal written for the
  teacher and classmates. The context memo is designed to give peers suffi-

cient information to review the draft competently. It assumes that the intended audience of the document might differ from the actual audience of the classroom, and that the difference between these two audiences needs carefully to be negotiated.

- A **rough draft** of the document. The rough draft is given to two peers and is accompanied by the context memo.
- Two **peer reviews** written by two other members of the class. Peer review in AWD is modeled on peer review in academic scholarship, where papers are sent out to two peers who compose substantial written responses (as compared to marginal notes). Papers are sent for peer review along with a context memo or other supportive document. Peer reviews are written as a memo to the teacher and include a *summary* of the draft (ensuring that the paper is understood), a section devoted to *major critiques*, and a section devoted to *minor critiques*. Treating peer review as a genre of writing keeps the focus on the major rhetorical issues as compared to surface concerns.
- A **response letter** to the instructor describing in detail how the paper was revised in response to the peer reviews. Response letters discuss what revisions were made, why, and what reviewer suggestions, if any, were not followed. Response letters may be quite detailed: *Reviewer A suggested . . . and I responded b. . . . Reviewer B was concerned that . . . but I believe the reviewer misunderstood my point because. . . .* The response letter is turned in with the final draft and addressed to the instructor.
- A **unit reflection**, sometimes composed in class on the due date, explaining how this assignment has moved the student toward completing the learning goals.

This is one possible configuration; there are others. The salient point is that the writing process always unfolds socially, in response to various interlocutors, including the class itself, and that the assignment sequences in AWD seek to acknowledge that sociality in a variety of ways. In this example, students are given a chance to articulate and explain their formal writing, and their revisions of that writing, to different audiences in relatively low-stakes contexts.[49] The hope is that the students will take the process of peer review fairly seriously, and that the rhetorical choices may be made for the sake of the project rather than as a way of second-guessing the teacher's authoritative reading. In the process, genres such as the letter and the memo are "taught" as rhetorical responses to particular social needs of classroom practice.

Over the last two decades, the WID movement has sought to create reasonable versions of what it takes to be academic discourse in the classroom. But its promise has, in my view, been realized inconsistently, with different institutional locations exhibiting different types of failure. Discipline-specific WID classrooms tend to get overwhelmed by the subject-forming agenda of the discipline charged with the job. WID-like classes in English departments, on the other hand, have been dogged by the problem of student expertise not shared by teachers and by a certain theatricality that attends the creation of these versions of academic discourse for an audience not engaged in producing them. Neither the community of (Writing in) Discipline X, on the one hand, nor the community represented by the English department, on the other, seems adequate to the task. Yet as far back as 1989, Joseph D. Harris suggested expanding the notion of community beyond idealizations of academic practice:

> While I don't mean to discount the effects of belonging to a discipline, I think that we dangerously abstract and idealize the workings of "academic discourse" by taking the kinds of rarified talk and writing that go on at conferences and in journals as the norm, and viewing many of the other sorts of talk and writing that occur at the university as deviations from or approximations of that standard. It may prove more useful to center our study, instead, on the everyday struggles and mishaps of the talk in our classrooms and departments, with their mixings of sometimes conflicting and sometimes conjoining beliefs and purposes.[50]

Harris's revision of community was offered in another context, of course, but I think his basic suggestion to make *the classroom itself* a primary object of inquiry can help resolve some of these problems in WID pedagogy.

Consider the genre of the memo. In many business and technical writing classes, the memo is taught as a genre practiced by members of a specific discipline or field. When I say that WID classes involve a certain theatricality, I mean an assignment like this: *You are a mid-level employee in a chemical products company. You have found a problem with the inventory control software recently purchased to handle the influx of raw materials. Write a memo to JS, the company's Chief Technology Officer, advising the CTO of the problem and suggesting a solution.* Such assignments are not uncommon in WID textbooks. But the knock-on effect of an assignment like this is that the teacher (or the student reader) must stand in for JS, pretending to read the memo in JS's terms, while not generally in possession of the kind of perspective JS would bring to the situation. The student knows that, although the memo is written for JS, the audience of consequence is the teacher. And so the student is caught between two audiences, and neither the student nor, I would suggest, the teacher is fully capable of assigning priority to either one until the moment of evaluation.

In the AWD course outlined above, the memo is not (or not only) taught as a category in use by a particular academic discipline. The audience for the context memo is *the classroom*: the point of the memo is to explain and justify the rhetorical decisions that have been made in other documents. This approach differs from one dismissing the imagined audience as "fake."[51] The imagined audience is, rather, all too real—writer, peer students, and instructor acknowledge that reality in the dynamics of composition and evaluation. But the local reality of the classroom is also acknowledged through such documents as the context memo, the peer review, the response letter, and the reflective note. In fact, these documents provide key mediating spaces between the imagined audience of the unit paper and the material audience of the classroom and teacher.

Reflection in a successful AWD course must be regular and integrated. Not only in the unit reflection, but throughout the semester, students are asked to reflect on their goals, purposes, and decisions. This is a deliberate strategy designed to incorporate reflection into the warp and woof of the class rather than make it simply an end-of-term exercise. Recall that the LG statement includes written reflection on writing processes and their role in critical reasoning as a goal (Goal 7). It would be difficult to imagine a student demonstrating such reflection if the portfolio reflection essay itself were the only significant instance of written reflection in the course. In considering this goal, the final reflective essay becomes a reflection on previous reflective activity. We might say that AWD seeks to maximize the opportunities for reflection in the hope that some of them might result in reflexivity.

III

> Please, please, kids, stop fighting. Maybe Lisa's right about America being the land of opportunity, and maybe Adil's got a point about the machinery of capitalism being oiled with the blood of the workers.[52]

Is Homer Simpson's capsule summary of American economic contradiction a moment of critical effectivity? Not quite. In "The Crepes of Wrath" (from the first season of *The Simpsons*), Simpson son Bart has been sent to France for three months as an exchange student, replaced in the Simpson household by Albanian student Adil Hoxha (who secretly spies on the nuclear power plant where Homer works). Lisa Simpson and her temporary brother Adil view the United States through opposing Cold War ideologies, and Homer "resolves" their argument by means of a classic parental gambit: you've both got a point.

The history of writing instruction in America is marked by a series of such resolutions. Does first-year composition initiate students into the university or serve as another moment of exclusion? You've both got a point. Should writing instruction be reformed or abolished?[53] You've both got a point. Are we preparing workers or citizens? You've both got a point. Should composition be the responsibility of English faculty or of faculty in all disciplines? You've both got a point.

David S. Kaufer and Patricia L. Dunmire capture the conundrum of WAC/WID instruction when they observe that "Although . . . actuaries, accountants, and insurance adjusters write on the job, no one seriously designs writing programs with the tasks that cross their desks each day" in mind.[54] Their response to this observation—that much of the writing that will be professionally important for students is largely unacknowledged in writing program design—anticipates some of the ideas of the present paper. In particular, Kaufer and Dunmire insist on the need to foster "reflection on the conventions of academic writing" as "an integral part of students' productive practices."[55] Their concept of "knowledge design" leads toward "a curriculum that would provide students with the tools they need for understanding how historical context both enables and constrains positions that can be argued and actions that can be taken within that context."[56] Knowledge design is of a piece, I think, with other concepts explored here—Durst's reflective instrumentalism, McComisky's social process, the brake of reflection—all of which seek to create spaces for critical effectivity while acknowledging, even exploiting, the subject-forming activity of higher education.

But where should that resistance take place? One approach to program design is to pair a first-year composition requirement (to be taught in English or rhetoric departments) with upper-level WID courses distributed throughout the university. This replicates at the level of writing program administration the increasing specialization generally found in the higher education calendar. But it also puts first-year composition at odds with advanced writing and tends to dichotomize the critical and pragmatic dimensions of writing instruction.

Locating advanced writing in a centralized program rather than following the popular distributed WID model has the following advantage: the development of critical effectivity is not, in this scheme, left entirely to first-year composition. Whatever pragmatic losses might be entailed by having non-experts work with advanced students in the disciplines may be made up for by the hope that reflexivity will be cultivated when students come face-to-face with the demands of their profession.

It is worth recalling that, in "The Crepes of Wrath," the real moment of critical effectivity belongs to Bart, who is mistreated by his French hosts and who discovers that they put antifreeze in the wine. Bart, however, lacks the ability to speak French and is therefore unable to communicate his plight to the authorities. The crucial breakthrough comes while he is reflecting on his inability to learn:

> I'm so stupid. Anybody could've learned this dumb language by now. Here, I've listened to nothing but French for the past *deux mois, et je ne sais pas un mot. Mais, je parle Français maintenant! Incroyable!*[57]

Once armed with this new literacy, Bart then *hails a police officer* in a manner that precisely inverts the Althusserian roles. Whereas Althusser has the police officer hailing the subject, here the officer is the object of Bart's hailing cry: *"Hey, Monsieur, aidez-moi!"*

What I find interesting about Bart's transformation is that his experience has not been designed to help him master French and that the knowledge he does gain leads to the exercise of another kind of power entirely. It is the alienating character of his experience that defines it; it is this reflection on failure that precipitates his momentary intervention.

WID pedagogy and critical writing pedagogy have different dreams. The WID classroom's common dream is the sudden onset of disciplinary mastery. One of the central hopes of critical writing pedagogy, on the other hand, is to get "students to theorize their own experiences rather than articulate the meaning of other people's experiences."[58] A truly critical WID program must be designed with the knowledge that, while WID programs align well (too well?) with the pragmatic goals of higher education institutions, critical writing pedagogy is (on the whole) on its own. If critical reflection in the writing class is truly to provide a brake on the processes of interpellation, the critical dimension of the writing program must be given adequate institutional support. One way to do this—I do not say the only way—is to keep WID programs in an English or rhetoric program where such perspectives have a chance to be acknowledged.

Notes

1. Michael Carter, "Ways of Knowing, Doing, and Writing in the Disciplines," *CCC* 58, no. 3 (2007): 386.
2. Carter, "Ways of Knowing, Doing, and Writing," 388 (emphasis added).
3. Carter, "Ways of Knowing, Doing, and Writing," 387 (emphasis added).
4. Judith Goleman, *Working Theory: Critical Composition Studies for Students and Teachers* (New York: Bergin & Garvey, 1995), 69.
5. Goleman, *Working Theory*, 70.
6. Goleman, *Working Theory*, 70.
7. Goleman, *Working Theory*, 71.
8. Goleman, *Working Theory*, 93.
9. Frederic Jameson, *Marxism and Form: Twentieth-Century Dialectical Theories of Literature*, New ed. (Princeton: Princeton University Press, 1974).
10. Goleman, *Working Theory*, 46.
11. Goleman, *Working Theory*, 46-47.
12. Goleman, *Working Theory*, 18.
13. Goleman, *Working Theory*, 18.
14. Goleman, *Working Theory*, 107.
15. Louis Althusser, "Ideology and Ideological State Apparatuses: Notes Toward an Investigation," in *Lenin and Philosophy* (London: Monthly Review Press, 1978).
16. Althusser, "Ideology and Ideological State Apparatuses," 145.
17. Goleman, *Working Theory*, 19.
18. Goleman, *Working Theory*, 47.
19. Althusser, "Ideology and Ideological State Apparatuses," 174.
20. Althusser, "Ideology and Ideological State Apparatuses," 155.
21. David Bartholomae, "Inventing the University," in *When a Writer Can't Write: Studies in Writer's Block and Other Composing-Process Problems*, ed. Mike Rose (New York: Guilford, 1985), 134.
22. Peter Elbow, "Being a Writer vs. Being an Academic: A Conflict in Goals," *CCC* 46, no. 1 (1995); Patricia Bizzell, *Academic Discourse and Critical Consciousness* (Pittsburgh: University of Pittsburgh Press, 1992). As Bizzell notes in her introduction, the essay that gave this work its title was eventually abandoned for journal publication "because I developed serious doubts about the argument while writing it" (20).
23. For an important recent discussion of labor market intermediaries and their role in constructing contemporary literacy, see Michael Pennell, "'If Knowledge is Power, You're About to Become Very Powerful': Literacy and Labor Market Intermediaries in Postindustrial America," *CCC* 58, no. 3 (2007).
24. National Commission on Writing, "Writing: A Ticket to Work . . . or a Ticket Out: A Survey of Business Leaders," (College Board, 2004).

25. Russel K. Durst, *Collision Course: Conflict, Negotiation, and Learning in the Composition Classroom* (Urbana: National Council of Teachers of English, 1999).

26. Durst, *Collision Course*, 37.

27. Durst, *Collision Course*, 50.

28. Durst, *Collision Course*, 174.

29. Durst, *Collision Course*, 178, 179.

30. Durst, *Collision Course*, 179.

31. William H. Thelin, "Understanding Problems in Critical Classrooms," *CCC* 57, no. 1 (2005): 117. See also Russel K. Durst, "Can We be Critical of Critical Pedagogy?," *CCC* 58, no. 1 (2006); William H. Thelin, "William H. Thelin's Response to Russel Durst," *CCC* 58, no. 1 (2006).

32. Bruce McComiskey, *Teaching Composition as a Social Process* (Logan, UT: Utah State University Press, 2000), 20.

33. McComiskey, *Teaching Composition as a Social Process*, 1.

34. Donna Qualley, *Turns of Thought: Teaching Composition as Reflexive Inquiry* (Hanover, NH: Boynton/Cook, 1997), 11.

35. See, for example, Karen Kurzman, "Reflection," *The English Journal* 87, no. 3 (1998), Margaret K. Willard-Traub, "Reflection in Academe: Scholarly Writing and the Shifting Subject," *College English* 68, no. 4 (2006), Kimberly Emmons, "Rethinking Genres of Reflection: Student Portfolio Cover Letters and the Narrative of Progress," *Composition Studies* 31, no. 1 (2003), Barbara Gleason, "Self-Reflection as a Way of Knowing: Phenomenological Investigations in Composition," in *Into the Field: Sites of Composition Studies*, ed. Anne Ruggles Gere (New York, NY: Modern Language Association of America, 1993).

36. Kathleen Blake Yancey, "Making Learning Visible: What You Can't See Can Change Response," in *The WAC Casebook: Scenes for Faculty Reflection and Program Development*, ed. Chris M. Anson (New York: Oxford University Press, 2002), 70.

37. Yancey, "Making Learning Visible," 70.

38. Yancey, "Making Learning Visible," 70.

39. Yancey, "Making Learning Visible," 70-71.

40. Yancey, "Making Learning Visible," 71.

41. Yancey, "Making Learning Visible," 70.

42. As Durst points out, the University of Cincinnati "was the first college in the [United States] to develop a program of cooperative education almost a hundred years ago, and it still has the nation's largest." Durst, *Collision Course*, 12.

43. Mary Balestraci et al., *Writing for Academic and Professional Situations: Exploring Experience Through Research* (Boston, MA: Pearson Custom Publishing, 2002; reprint, 2003).

44. Journalism and history majors satisfy the AWD requirement within their programs; these exceptions were negotiated some years before I came to Northeastern. The description of AWD provided here of the program here does not apply to those courses.

45. Edward M. White, "The Scoring of Writing Portfolios: Phase 2," *CCC* 56, no. 4 (2005).

46. White, "Scoring Phase 2," 583.

47. White, "Scoring Phase 2," 586.

48. David Kellogg and Susan Soroka, eds., *The AWD Toolkit*, Second ed. (Kendall/Hunt: Dubuque, IA, 2007). This short text supplements the major, discipline-specific texts for individual AWD courses.

49. In my AWD classes, only the final unit papers and the final portfolio receive letter grades. Drafts, context memos, peer reviews, response letters, unit reflections, and other writing receive other grades which adjust their final grade at the margins.

50. Joseph Harris, "The Idea of Community in the Study of Writing," *CCC* 40, no. 1 (1989): 20.

51. See George D. Gopen, "Why So Many Bright Students and So Many Dull Papers?: Peer-Responded Journals as a Partial Solution to the Problem of the Fake Audience," *The WAC Journal* 16 (2005).

52. Wesley Archer and Milton Gray, "The Crepes of Wrath," in *The Simpsons* (Fox Network, 1990). All dialogue from this episode is taken from The Simpsons Archive, <http://www.snpp.com/episodes/7G13.html>, accessed August 7, 2007.

53. Robert Connors, "The New Abolitionism: Toward a Historical Background," in *Reconceiving Writing, Rethinking Writing Instruction*, ed. Joseph Petraglia (Mahwah, NJ: Lawrence Erlbaum Associates, 1995).

54. David S. Kaufer and Patricia L. Dunmire, "Integrating Cultural Reflection and Production in College Writing Curricula," in *Reconceiving Writing, Rethinking Writing Instruction*, ed. Joseph Petraglia (Mahwah, NJ: Lawrence Erlbaum Associates, 1995), 217.

55. Kaufer and Dunmire, "Integrating Cultural Reflection and Production in College Writing Curricula," 227.

56. Kaufer and Dunmire, "Integrating Cultural Reflection and Production in College Writing Curricula," 230.

57. Archer and Gray, "The Crepes of Wrath."

58. Henry A. Giroux, "Who Writes in a Cultural Studies Class? or, Where is the Pedagogy?" in *Left Margins: Cultural Studies and Composition Pedagogy*, ed. Karen Fitts and Alan W. France (Albany: State University of New York Press, 1995), 11.

Chapter Seven

Location, Location, Location: The Radical Potential of Web-Intensive Writing Programs to Challenge Disciplinary Boundaries

Catherine Gouge

Disciplines are defined by groups of objects, methods, their corpus of proposi-tions considered to be true, the interplay of rules and definitions, of techniques and tools: all constitute a sort of anonymous system, freely available to who-ever wishes, or whoever is able to make use of them.
—Michel Foucault (1972)

Michel Foucault's 1972 definition of academic disciplines ought to draw our attention, as David Bartholomae reminds us, to the constructed, "artificial nature of divisions."[1] This is not to say that the artificiality of disciplinary distinctions makes them any less real, nor does it preclude our being deeply affected by them. Indeed, such divisions are lived. As faculty members, we bump up against them when we apply or are asked to apply for grant money to fund research, when we attempt to get a new course approved, or when our promotion and ten-ure committee decides whether and how to count something we publish that might be considered "outside" the specialized area for which we were hired. These kinds of academic events make us all too aware of the ways in which we are deeply affected by disciplinary assumptions, assumptions which instill and reinforce presuppositions that define our professional identities and successes. Foucault's somber qualification that disciplinary discourses are not simply "freely available to whoever wishes" but only to "whoever is able to make use of them" acknowledges this. And we relearn that crucial disciplinary lesson every day: there are ways of participating in disciplinary conversations that count, and there are ways that do not count. Those practices that count—those that "correctly" observe the artificial boundaries of disciplinarity—are also constitutive. They are iterations of what Foucault termed an "anonymous system." In our experience of it, this system is a lot like the "consensual hallucination" that William Gibson named "cyberspace" in *Neuromancer* (1984): those who have the access and specialized knowledge that counts can participate in making the hallucination "consensual" by "jacking in" and defining the system through their activity in it. While in that privileged and exclusive imaginary space, the concurrent consensuality and anonymity of the hallucination can combine to make it seem terrifyingly powerful.

As a faculty member in the English Department at West Virginia University (WVU) who was hired to teach professional writing and to design and adminis-ter a set of web-based writing courses, I have had an interesting, if intense and challenging, experiential education in the consensual, anonymous system of disciplinarity over the past five years. When I started the position, I became si-multaneously a first-time tenure track faculty member and a first-time adminis-trator. I approached both these new positions from the perspective Henry Giroux describes (via Foucault) as common to educators coming from a Cultural Stud-ies background: I was not only aware of, but deeply invested in, thinking criti-cally about the ways in which I and my colleagues "always work and speak within historically and socially determined relations of power."[2] I considered it vital to the integrity of my new positions that I reflect critically on my newly authorized roles in the academy. Because of this critical perspective from which I approached my new position and, much to my relief, with the full support of the Director of our also newly-formed Center for Writing Excellence, I was par-ticularly concerned with ensuring that our web-based writing program prioritize its value and service to the public good by helping students become better criti-cal thinkers, and not exacerbate "the turn to downsizing and deskilling faculty" that many[3] have written may be the most lamentable intervention of distance education in the future of academia. While I agree that this intervention would be, and maybe already is, lamentable, I want to argue that we ought to work now for a different legacy for web-based writing programs. Indeed, with a critical administrative approach, I believe that it is possible for distance writing pro-grams to be the site of disciplinary intervention of a much more desirable kind: one that challenges disciplinary boundaries by contesting their consensuality and anonymity.[4] In order for this to happen, the administrators of such programs must compel their institutions to participate in conversations about and critical reflection on what Giroux assesses is lacking in the "corporate discourse on schooling":

> any analysis of how power works in shaping knowledge, how the teaching of
> broader social values provides safeguards against turning citizen skills into
> simply training skills for the work place, or how schooling can help students
> reconcile the seemingly opposing needs of freedom and solidarity in order to
> forge a new conception of civic courage and democratic public life.[5]

Currently, there is no clear structure in place that can accommodate the challenges posed by the new uses, and institutionalization, of a growing array of instructional technologies. Web-intensive programs are, therefore, having a destabilizing effect for existing institutional operations, forcing many institutions to revisit, revise, and create new policy[6] and reconfigure administrative structures of power. Now is the time to intervene in the conversations required to respond to the institutional instability that newness creates.

I. Location, Space, and Situatedness

Like the distance writing program I coordinate at WVU, most web-intensive writing programs are institutionally located in English Departments. That is, courses offered are listed through the English Department; and the coordination and decision-making about courses, instructors, and students are often the primary responsibility of one or more English Department faculty members. Sometimes such a program is even further embedded in the institution's disciplinary structure, as ours is at WVU, in a composition and rhetoric program which is a sub-division of the English Department. In spite of this apparently specific disciplinary location, however, and unlike on-site writing programs, my experience suggests that the location of a web-intensive program ought not to be defined in the ways that on-site programs are: in terms of the physical and departmental orientation/affiliation of its primary program administrator. Indeed, because such programs rely on the staffing, support and, consequently, decision-making and problem-solving of so many different programs, centers, and offices on campus—most of which are both physically and disciplinarily outside of the English Department—web-intensive writing programs often have deeply interdepartmental systems of support. Power is distributed and flattened in this way and is distinctly inter-disciplinary, drawing on the financial, labor, and intellectual resources of people from a wide range of disciplines. In fact, while the corporatization of higher education is often cited as the most depressing trend for those of us who believe in protecting academic freedom from the demands of the marketplace, one of the characteristics of the administrative structure of web-intensive programs that enables its radical potential is a characteristic that is similar to turn-of-the-twentieth-century corporate management structures: the increasingly horizontal distribution of power.[7]

Often the only criteria for participation in this cross-campus interaction are involvement in a program that is significantly web-dependent and a willingness to devote the time required to join the conversations taking place on the seemingly endlessly proliferating number of the committees that form to coordinate relevant university resources and make policy decisions. These committees at many institutions are currently engaged in making critical decisions that will in large part determine the ways that distance education will influence institutions of higher education, for better or worse. For example, this past year the WVU eCampus[8] Advisory Council was responsible for developing an electronic "Student Evaluation of Instruction" (called "eSEI" at WVU). In addition to making some technical decisions about submission format and processes, this committee—which consists of a dean, staff from our Instructional Technology Resources Center and Office of Information Technology, and faculty from various colleges on campus—determined which questions students would answer to evaluate their web-intensive courses and instructors. The content of these questions and how they are worded have the potential to affect 1) how the teaching of involved faculty will be evaluated by their promotion and tenure committees and 2) the perceived success of the programs in which those faculty teach.

Because program functioning takes place administratively in conversations and various support activities across campus, the institutional location of web-enhanced programs is functionally inter-disciplinary. This inter-disciplinarity is not, however, necessarily progressive, radical, or anti-disciplinary. As Ryan Claycomb and Rachel Riedner note in this volume, such an institutional infrastructure often works in the service of conventional disciplinarity and is valued by the institution primarily for the ways that it distributes the financial burden and labor required to keep the programs viable; this kind of inter-disciplinary distribution of resources does not necessarily translate into intellectual progressivism, challenging artificial, neo-liberal disciplinary boundaries. However, rather than assuming that inter-disciplinary groups formed because of economic imperatives preclude anti-disciplinary interventions, we ought to take advantage of the fact that such inter-disciplinary structures of power can be leveraged to challenge the boundaries of disciplinarity and enact a progressive anti-disciplinary approach to program administration. Because these programs are functionally inter-disciplinary to a greater extent than their on-site counterparts, the administrators who coordinate web-intensive writing programs are uniquely situated, not just to interact with and benefit from many different disciplines, but to regularly and frequently participate in institutional conversations with faculty, staff, students, and other administrators from many different institutional locations. Moreover, because these conversations influence and sometimes define policy at the college and often at the university levels, each of these conversations has the greater potential to challenge disciplinary boundaries. If their radical potential is realized, these conversations can, in other words, be the site of disciplinary resistance and the administrators who participate in them can be activists for anti-disciplinary transformation.

To understand better the context for such conversations, we need to consider the ways in which web-intensive writing programs constitute an unstable and thus more flexible kind of disciplinary space, a "practiced place," as Michel de Certeau has defined postmodern conceptions of space: "composed of intersections of mobile elements."[9] Like space in de Certeau's formulation, the institutional location of web-intensive writing programs at this historical moment is not a static, fixed place; rather, it "occurs" and is "the effect produced by the operations that orient it, situate it, temporalize it."[10] The flexible disciplinary location of web-intensive programs is, even without the deliberate, critical force of any explicitly anti-disciplinary intervention, a location that is deeply unstable as it constitutes and reconstitutes, and is constituted and re-constituted by, the interaction of the members of every program, center, and office required to support its daily functioning. This inherent instability can be extremely challenging for program administrators since it requires an almost constant revision of where resources are and how to accomplish what are usually the most routine tasks: student registration, content delivery, course evaluation, and classroom access. However, the same aspects of the instability that can make web-intensive programs such administrative challenges are also those aspects which contain its radical anti-, or perhaps even post-, disciplinary potential.

II. Space, Efficiency, and the Logic of Sameness

What theories of disciplinarity and administration can emerge when disciplinary location is considered to be a flexible, unstable space?

Recognizing that "the anxiety of our era has fundamentally to do with space,"[11] Foucault writes that traditionally "space was treated as the dead, the fixed, the immobile."[12] However, "to trace the forms of implantation, delimitation and demarcation of objects . . . the organization of domains mean[s] the throwing into relief of processes."[13] For many administrators, these processes are about money. The efficient use of space determines "value" to the institution for these budget-conscious administrators. These budget-driven definitions of space and value are deployed by these administrators to argue for starting web-intensive programs as a way of responding to the budget crises so common at many institutions. This argument has been made successfully at state institutions like the University of Central Florida, which became a forerunner in substantially web-enhanced, or "mixed-mode," courses and programs when it became so desperate for seat space in 1999 that it had to rent out a local movie theater during the day to conduct "on-site" classes. "We didn't serve popcorn," recalls Steven Sorg, assistant vice president for distributed learning at the university, "but we used the seats and they served as lecture halls."[14] At night, they rented space from a nearby high school. On their website, UCF currently lists six undergraduate "degree completion" programs, ten graduate programs, and ten graduate certificate programs which can be completed primarily through what it calls "mixed-mode" and 100% online instruction. They report offerings of more than 180 mixed and online courses. Their "mixed-mode" courses, the site says, "combine Web delivery and synchronous or live class delivery where the Web-based instruction substitutes for face-to-face class time . . . a 3-hour [mixed-mode] course will now have one or two live class meetings rather than the usual three."[15]

In 2002, Texas Tech piloted a mixed-mode writing program, Interactive Composition Online (ICON), and has since received a good deal of attention from those interested in composition studies and writing program administration. Their in-house course management system, called TOPIC (Texas Tech Online-Print Integrated Curriculum) supports the "distributed grading" of ICON, allowing document instructors to more efficiently respond to the writing of first-year composition students.[16] ICON assigns multiple document instructors to review, comment on, and grade student submissions. These comments are viewable by all document instructors, but grades are not viewable among document instructors, so that new graders are not influenced by prior evaluations. While no outside assessment results have been published,[17] Texas Tech's in-house assessment of their hybrid first-year composition program is quite positive. In their overview of the program, they emphasize repeatedly that ICON "support[s] the fairer grading of essays and the ability to assign more frequent student writing."[18]

The economic benefits of ICON are not explicitly emphasized on the program's web-site; rather, the site highlights the relationship between their separation of documents from classroom instructors and "consistency," "fairer grading," "coherent instruction," and "objective evaluation."[19] Perhaps most notably, the ICON website sidesteps or attempts to mediate the subjectivity of its document instructors by arguing that the "fact that student writing is anonymously evaluated by instructors who may or may not be other than those teaching particular students means that the criteria for effective writing must be shared among all instructors and ensures far more consistent and coherent instruction program-wide than ever before."[20] This emphasis on shared criteria and consensus among different subjective graders—which will ensure consistency, equity and, therefore, objectivity in grading—is a faulty logic at best. Any busy program administrator can certainly understand the temptation to work toward consistency among courses since consistency is easier to monitor, especially if the consistency derives from criteria we design ourselves. Indeed, when the priority is efficiency, giving the power to develop criteria for what counts as effective writing to less-experienced instructors, who may not have composition as their primary focus of graduate study, across many sections, can seem to be a very risky and dangerous proposition.

However, as the example of Texas Tech's ICON program illustrates, program administrators ought to be more concerned about the ways in which time and labor efficiency are being used to determine program policy and to discipline student writing under the guise of disciplinary integrity. In exhorting the value and desirability of objectivity in evaluation, ICON reinvests in a consumerist academic culture which is honored for its efficiency and anonymity. Such a culture is invested in—and thus values—the reproducibility of "things" like, most disturbingly, student writing and the evaluation of student writing. These values are driven by a logic of sameness like that which makes McDonald's and Starbucks so appealing—you know what to expect going in and, for the most part, you will find food and drink at these places which is almost identical in every location. At Texas Tech, this presumption of the desirability of consistency has resulted in a program founded on a myth of objectivity, a myth that is ultimately a fantasy of control predicated on a logic of sameness which sees difference as threatening.

Left unchecked, such a logic will further define academic culture according to the values and priorities of corporate culture. It will, in other words, participate in the reproduction of capitalist spatiality. As Cary Nelson and Stephen Watt argue, "No longer a space for political struggle, culture in the corporate model becomes an all-encompassing horizon for producing market identities, values, and practices."[21] However, intervention in the culture is possible if we take advantage of the instability of that process of becoming that Nelson and Watt describe. "The production of capitalist spatiality," as Edward Soja writes, "is no once-and-for-all event. The spatial matrix must constantly be reinforced and, when necessary, restructured—that is, spatiality must be socially reproduced, and this reproduction process is a continuing source of conflict and crisis."[22] Due to budget crises and the temptation to respond to them with instructional technology (IT), as I explain the University of Central Florida and Texas Tech have, many universities are experiencing an intensification of the rate at which these moments of "conflict and crisis" are cropping up around IT-rich programs. In my estimation, though, all administrators ought to use their positions to intervene. The trend toward looking to IT to solve budget crises further places the responsibility for intervention onto administrators of IT-rich, web-intensive programs, rather than their on-site counterparts.

In order to maximize the radical potential of the flexible disciplinary space opened up by the conflicts and crises that are a part of "becoming" processes, web-enhanced program administrators need to resist the institutional trend to define space at the university as student seat space. We can do this by emphasizing the priorities of such programs to promote critical thinking so that students are better able to be more thoughtful about epistemological processes like those Foucault addresses in *Discipline and Punish*: What knowledge can be made? Under what conditions? How is that knowledge authorized?

III. The Distance Writing Program at West Virginia University

WVU's Distance Writing Program provides a case study with which to illustrate more specifically the ways that such programs are structured and to explore other ways in which this conflict and crisis can become opportunities for intervention in disciplinary conventions. Like many distance programs, the Distance Writing Program at WVU originated in disciplinary thinking and economic efficiency, but I hope to show how the web-intensive delivery of the program has enabled a critical administrative approach that has the potential to leverage a new, more flexible disciplinary space. Indeed, I hope to clarify how a critical administrative approach can be adopted by other web-intensive writing program administrators to leverage the radical anti-disciplinary potential of the programs for which they are responsible. If institutions of higher education continue to develop their web-intensive course offerings, as the data over the past years suggests they will,[23] the implications of this administrative and disciplinary transformation might be far-reaching and significant for the future of disciplinarity in every area of these institutions, not just those that are web-intensive.

At WVU, it is true, as Cary Nelson and Stephen Watt predicted in 1999, that "profit-making departments [have] become the first priority for institutional resources, and the profit-making function within those departments begins to dominate their other activities, from student recruitment to faculty hiring to curriculum design."[24] And I do not see this being undone or reversed at any state institution like WVU, where deans are scrambling to find ways to balance their budgets without any hope of significantly increased state funding. Indeed, I think that what is more likely is that internal grant funding and funding for new hires will continue to go to a) departments that the institution sees as most important to the college of which they are a part because of numbers of majors graduated and "service courses" offered and b) the programs that use technology to increase the efficiency of the institution by increasing the rate at which students matriculate. This is not news. And it is not particularly uplifting to think about. But it does point to the places where the institution is most likely to be open to intervention: departments that "own" introductory courses required of all students—the greater the number of students served, the more open the field for intervention. Changing the structure from within is an admittedly risky strategy. My point, however, is that even though upper-level administrators of institutions of higher learning may be using the rhetoric of corporate culture in their communication with parents and students and faculty and community members, individual faculty members like myself are participating in conversations that define for the university what all of that rhetoric means and, perhaps more importantly, determining for upper-level administrators what is possible and what is not.

For example, anticipating the seat space challenges we now face at WVU, our Distance Writing Program was initiated in response to a call from the Office of the Provost to develop web-based versions of high-enrollment courses in the name of efficiency and to help students who were unable, due to time and/or distance issues, to attend traditional on-site courses. In October of 2000, when the Office of the Provost established the "West Virginia University Entrepreneurial Learning Innovation (ELI) Grant Opportunity," the focus of the grant was, as the language of the grant detailed, "two-fold":

> One goal is to stimulate colleges to develop learning innovations for large en-rollment courses that increase retention, student interaction with the content and individual mastery of objectives through instructional technologies. The second goal is to increase educational opportunities for students located at a geographical distance from the Morgantown campus or who have time con-straints that restrict access to courses on campus.[25]

In spite of the fact that she was explicitly asked to find a way to move online—in whole or in part—one of the two introductory writing courses required of all WVU students, the director of our Center for Writing Excellence, Dr. Laura Brady, instead submitted a proposal that the English Department hire someone full-time to design and pilot English 101 and English 102 only for an adult learner population, as the "Division of Extended Learning" defined them (at least twenty-five years old, part-time, and out of school for at least four years), who were physically distant from WVU's main campus in Morgantown, WV. Rather than increase course size in the name of efficiency, the proposed student enrollment for each course was set at sixteen students (a much lower cap than our on-site sections of twenty-two). After an initial pilot year, Dr. Brady pro-posed that the courses' effectiveness be assessed by the course designer and the director of our Center for Writing Excellence—those she believed would keep the course goals as the priority in assessment. The proposal explained that only if the online versions of English 101 and 102 were determined to provide a valu-able learning experience to that adult-learner population would the dedicated course designer continue to design the other four writing courses.

By the time I was hired to begin the design of courses, then, the intent of the new courses was defined very specifically as a way to "help adult learners, who are constrained by time and/or distance, meet the requirements of a degree pro-gram at WVU."[26] To this end, over a period of two years, I designed and piloted a series of six different 100 percent web-based writing courses, in the following order: the two introductory writing courses required of all students at the univer-sity (English 101 and 102), an advanced composition and rhetoric course (Eng-lish 201), a technical editing course (English 302), a professional writing course (English 304), and a technical writing course (English 305). Adult learners can now choose to complete only the introductory writing courses required of all degree-seeking students at WVU, or they can choose to take the full sequence of online writing courses and earn what we call a "Professional Writing and Edit-ing" minor, certificate, or concentration. Whether a student earns a minor, con-centration, or certificate depends on that student's major and degree status.[27]

What is noteworthy here is, I think, the cautious and careful way in which our proposal was constructed to serve a specific population in the state of West Virginia who might not otherwise be able to earn a college degree. Furthermore, the power of assessment was localized; therefore, the power to determine the future delivery of web-based writing courses was retained by members of the English Department who would guard against any use of the courses that might compromise their academic integrity or value to students. The money acquired through the ELI grant would not support the matriculation of high numbers of students as some of our upper-level administrators had hoped it might. In my interview process, I was clear that, while I did not believe in moving introductory writing classes online for traditional students, the research at the time suggested that retention rates were higher for adult learners and that, in the state of West Virginia, such courses would be particularly welcome to adults outside of Morgantown, since winter travel in the mountains can be extremely difficult, if not impossible, at times, and the state does not have a community college system that might allow this student population to return to school and complete the requirements of a degree program. It has certainly not been easy because of both pressure from upper-level administrators and pressure from traditional on-site students who want the scheduling flexibility the online courses would allow; however, for the past six years, we have managed to keep the cap size to sixteen students and to restrict the courses to the adult-learner population the courses were designed to serve.

Radical Potential Inside of the Program

Many students who take the online professional writing courses are currently employed as technical and professional writers and report that they are taking the coursework so that they can get a promotion or a better job. We are offering a certificate we believe will be desirable to an adult-learner population because doing so will help them get a job or a promotion. In a historically economically depressed state, this helps adults—more than 80 percent of whom are women—meet their basic needs and those of their dependents. In light of that reality, I must resist the impulse to raise the course caps to make more money for the institution and, at the same time, negotiate student needs for economic viability. Giving students access to coursework that might help them be more financially secure has got to be a priority. I have tried, therefore, to design a program with courses that give students both economic viability and the power to read and think critically about the "anonymous system" within which they must participate to secure their basic needs. Using the wide range of communication tools (chat room, white board, message board, internal email) that are a part of our course management system, the courses call for substantial individual, as well as small and large group, reflection as part of the process of taking the course. These opportunities for reflection are important to a program that seeks to facilitate critical pedagogy because they encourage students to practice critical engagement with the course and course content.

One course begins, for example, with a small group activity for which students meet in a chat room to discuss the course goals and report back to the message board the results of the conversation they have about what those goals mean. This small activity is meant to help them become familiar with an important course technology but, more importantly it is intended to invite their participation in formulating goals for the term. Asking them to discuss the meaning of the course goals before they have completed any other work for the course is intended to signal to them that all meaning is negotiated, including that which is commonly used as the foundation for the courses they take. I hope that including them in the process of determining what the class will look like helps students see their participation in the course as constitutive of the course itself, rather than as a response to an already established set of requirements. Through such approaches to course design and instruction, I hope to create and make transparent for students the kind of flexible institutional space I imagine myself to be a part of as an administrator of a web-intensive program. In this way, I negotiate what can otherwise seem like contradictory administrative roles: helping students who are a part of the program become more economically viable and arguing against prioritizing economic efficiency outside of the program. Inside of the program, I have designed courses which offer students a professional certificate that is authorized by a state university in exchange for becoming more critical and aware students and citizens; outside of the program, I use my role on university and college committees as an opportunity to challenge the disciplinary boundaries which seek to reproduce uncritical laborers and consumers.

Radical Potential beyond the Program

There is a great deal that could be done to pursue radical opportunities intellectually and institutionally outside of an online Professional Writing and Editing Program like the one I coordinate—a program that was conceived of as 1) a way to offer training so that students can get or keep jobs and 2) institutionally located and authorized by an English department. Such a program could expand its course offerings to include a "Writing for Activism" course, for example. In the context of what usually constitutes professional writing and editing coursework, this would indeed be a radical move. Along these lines, our program at WVU is currently in the process of getting official approval from the faculty senate for a course that would create an opportunity for instructors to, in effect, teach activist writing. If approved, the course will be required of all PWE minors, concentrators, and certificate seekers, and will be listed as "Writing Theory and Practice." The course is meant to be an advanced rhetorical theory course that helps students prepare arguments for public discourse. Of course, the extent to which the public discourse produced by students might be considered radical or activist depends in large part on the students and the instructors in any given term. As the program coordinator, however, I will support and encourage instructors to keep the boundaries of public discourse open, and I am optimistic about the contribution this theory and practice course will make to our PWE sequence.

To push even farther outside of the conventional disciplinary boundaries of a professional writing program, we could also consider the possibility of creating alliances with activist groups outside of the university. This might, in fact, be a natural extension of the work students do in the program, since our program does currently encourage students to pursue writing projects with non-profit organizations during the required capstone course/internship. In fact, all of the students taking the capstone course I am currently teaching are working with non-profit agencies. Many are writing pieces that have the potential to be important activist interventions: speeches for politicians who make appearances at fundraising events for their non-profit organizations; articles for local and national publications that make pleas for public involvement; and pieces that contribute to grassroots efforts to improve the social and economic independence and health, in some cases, of people who are struggling at the local and state level. Because WVU is a state institution located in Appalachia, our program might partner capstone students with an activist organization such as Myles Horton's Highlander Center in Tennessee. The Highlander Center is an Appalachian adult education center for community workers involved in social and economic justice movements. Among its many outreach programs, the center has a "Grassroots Think Tank" which defines its mission as "giv[ing] people an opportunity to discuss some of the most critical problems facing us and develop[ing] new ideas and new approaches to the difficult but vital task of social and economic change."[28] Such a partnership might help challenge the imagined boundaries and disciplinary location of a Professional Writing and Editing program. A program that would create and support such activist opportunities for students would, indeed, be one that would help students and upper-level administrators rethink what can and should "count" as "professional training." Coursework that might have been thought by many to support the uncritical reproduction of workers could, accordingly, be reconceived as coursework that teaches students about the potential value of all forms of public discourse to social and economic justice.

Also, beyond the disciplinary boundaries of the small program I coordinate are great opportunities for disciplinary intervention within the college and university administrative coordinates. Part of my existing critical administrative approach is, thus, to recognize and seize the many opportunities for intervention that are all around me every day. These opportunities are many and varied, but most of them are opportunities that I have to define institutional goals and policies—and it is these goals and policies, of course, that motivate the way resources are allocated and "official" priorities are set. As the coordinator of WVU's online Professional Writing and Editing program, which we call the "Distance Writing Program," I find such opportunities when I participate in even the most seemingly ordinary administrative tasks: maintaining and revising the courses, training and supporting the graduate students and faculty members who teach the courses, and teaching one online course a year. Furthermore, I am asked to serve on nearly every task force and committee at the department, college, and university levels that has to do with instructional technology. I write reports for the Dean of the College of Arts and Sciences and our Provost that describe how the department uses instructional technology, what instructional technologies faculty would like to use in the next five years, and what kinds of support we need in order to incorporate those instructional technologies into our courses in meaningful ways. To do this, I must define what "meaningful instructional technology implementation" means to the English Department for our chair, dean, and provost. I serve on committees that name technology platforms for the university, determine what questions all university students will be asked to evaluate their technology-enhanced classes and the instructors who teach them, and decide what research needs to be done by the university about IT (what counts as "faculty incentives" for IT use for faculty and what technology should be available to faculty and students that currently are not). We work on problems such as student evaluation of instruction, student privacy and password issues, and library access for off-campus students. On one of these committees, I am called a "Point of Contact" and am expected to give voice to—essentially, authorize—the concerns and interests of all of the English Department faculty and to communicate important information to the faculty from the IT folks. To do this, I must determine what counts as "important" and what language to use to communicate that information to other faculty and graduate students.

IV. Conclusion

In order to challenge disciplinarity in meaningful ways both "inside" and "outside" the presumed ideological and institutional locations of the programs we coordinate, administrators need to write critical reflection and activism into our core curriculum. We need to seek out opportunities to partner with and learn from non-academic institutions that are models of social and economic justice. But perhaps as important is that we not forget to be activists in our most mundane administrative interactions and tasks, to act locally and find ways to encourage our administrative colleagues to develop critical administrative practices that can redirect the momentum of the "corporatization of the university" toward more radical ends. To do this, we need not only to participate in, but to initiate and influence, conversations in a way that will create opportunities for university administrators at all levels to think critically about our priorities and their implications for the future of higher education. To help us prepare for this challenging and important work, we might consider versions of the questions Claycomb and Riedner[29] advocate that instructors help their students address.

Namely, how can administrators—even deans and provosts who are responsible for balancing budgets and allocating resources—recognize the disciplines as contested sites? How can we work with other program administrators to illuminate for upper-level administrators and instructors the ways in which the disciplines are used to justify and demystify the circuit of capital? Can we advocate administratively for the critical reading of disciplinary structures as a strategy for entering into social and political struggle? How can we encourage upper-level administrators to recognize academic counter-disciplines that encourage students to vocalize "oppositional ideas about voice, authority, identity, writing, and even democracy"?

A critical administrative approach that takes seriously the opportunities for intervention, such as those I discuss, can help us demystify the processes by which institutional spaces are constituted and help us interrogate the individual roles we play in allowing those processes to continue. Accountability has got to be seen as the responsibility of all members of the academic community and, in particular, of those who have the most access to critical conversations, such as those to which web-intensive program administrators often do. If web-intensive programs are indeed creating the kind of institutional crisis and conflict I discuss, and if in this historical moment web-based program administrators have an opportunity to leverage the radical potential that such crisis and conflict creates, then we need to consider that an education in critical thinking need not move in only one direction: from deans to faculty or instructors to students, for example. We ought to consider and take seriously that, as program administrators, we have an opportunity and a responsibility to speak "up" in every sense of the word.

Notes

1. David Bartholomae, *Writing on the Margins: Essays on Composition and Teaching* (Boston: Bedford/St. Martin's, 2005), 132.
2. Henry Giroux, "Doing Cultural Studies: Youth and the Challenge of Pedagogy," *Harvard Educational Review* 64, no. 3 (Fall 1994): 278.
3. In particular, authors that take this on most directly include Henry Giroux, Cary Nelson, and David Noble. Henry Giroux's 2007 article "Academic Repression in the First Person: The Attack on Higher Education and the Necessity of Critical Pedagogy" in *The Advocate* (February 2007) http://gcadvocate.org/index.php?action=view&id=124; Cary Nelson and Stephen Watt's 1999 text *Academic Keywords: A Devil's Dictionary for Higher Education. Routledge, 1999*; and David Noble's 2001 article "The Future of the Digital Diploma Mill" *Academe* 87, no. 5 (September-October 2001): 29.
4. I am taking as a given that program administrators ought to work to create courses that allow instructors and students the flexibility to work in anti-disciplinary ways. The focus of this article assumes that should be done and makes an argument for what else can be done—to effect institutional and, one hopes, more lasting change.

5. Henry Giroux, "The Corporate War Against Higher Education," *Workplace* 5, no. 1 (October 2002). http://www.cust.educ.ubc.ca/workplace/issue5p1/5p1.html (accessed September 5, 2008).

6. Copyright issues, student evaluations of instructors, student and instructor privacy, and access issues, to name only a few of the many issues being reconsidered. I will discuss this in more detail later in the essay.

7. There are some interesting and important implications of using the language of corporate culture to describe academic administrative infrastructure. I will discuss these a bit later in this article. For now, I intend to describe the de-centralized, horizontal distribution of power that characterizes the administration of web-intensive programs and courses and to invoke the rhetoric of corporate culture. Terrence Deal and Allan Kennedy discuss this trend in *Corporate Culture* (New York: Addison Wesley [1982] 2000) and *The New Corporate Cultures: Revitalizing the Workplace After Downsizing, Mergers, and Reengineering* (New York: Basic Books, 1999).

8. "WVU eCampus" is the name we use at WVU for the course management system we license from Blackboard. The product is called "Vista" (version 4), but one of the tasks of this advisory committee this past year was to rename that product for the institution so that we could "brand" it and come up with an institution-specific banner and graphic.

9. Michel de Certeau, *The Practice of Everyday Life* (Berkeley: University of California Press, 1984), 117.

10. de Certeau, *The Practice of Everyday Life*, 117.

11. Michel Foucault, *Discipline and Punish: The Birth of the Prison*, trans. Alan Sheridan (New York: Vintage Books, 1995), 23.

12. Foucault, *Discipline and Punish*, 21.

13. Foucault, *Discipline and Punish*, 21.

14. Jeffrey Young, "'Hybrid' Teaching Seeks to End the Divide between Traditional and Online Instruction: By blending approaches, colleges hope to save money and meet students' needs," *The Chronicle of Higher Education*. Information Technology. March 22, 2002.

15. "UCF Distributed Learning: Scope and Policies." http://online.ucf.edu /cdl/dlp_plain.htm (accessed June 1, 2006).

16. The ICON website indicates that the program hopes to transition fall 2006 – summer 2007 into using commercial software to support the distributed grading process. Currently, the most commonly used CMS on university campuses is Blackboard, which bought WebCT in spring 2006.

17. An April 2006 article in the *Chronicle of Higher Education* reported that a formal WPA assessment was conducted in March 2006, though to my knowledge it has not been made public.

18. "Overview of the Changes" Texas Tech TOPIC webpage: http://ttopic.english.ttu.edu/manual/manualread.esp.

19. "Overview of the Changes" Texas Tech TOPIC webpage: http://ttopic.english.ttu.edu/manual/manualread.esp.

20. "Overview of the Changes" Texas Tech TOPIC webpage: http://ttopic.english.ttu.edu/manual/manualread.esp.

21. Cary Nelson and Stephen Watt, *Academic Keywords: A Devil's Dictionary for Higher Education* (New York: Routledge, 1999), 86.

22. Edward Soja, *Postmodern Geographies: The Reassertion of Space in Critical Social Theory* (New York: Verso, 1989), 129.

23. Between 1999 and 2004, the number of students participating in web-based courses has risen from 60,000 learners to almost 2.5 million. The 1999 number comes from Sir John Daniel's "Lessons from the Open University: Low-Tech Learning Often Works Best," *The Chronicle of Higher Education*. September 2001, 24. The 2004 number comes from the 2005 Sloan Consortium study, *Growing by Degrees: Online Education in the United States, 2005*. The reason I choose to compare numbers from two different sources is that the Sloan Consortium, which produces the most comprehensive and current of such studies, has only been conducting these studies since 2002.

24. Nelson and Watt, *Academic Keywords*, 86.

25. Unpublished. "ELI Grant Opportunity" offered by the Office of Extended Learning at West Virginia University.

26. In-House "ELI Report" produced for WVU's Office of Extended Learning at the conclusion of internal grant funding.

27. This available focus—because it supports the production of workers—is admittedly market-oriented and, thus, could be argued to reproduce the very capitalist logic I critique above.

28. Highlander Research and Education Center Grassroots Think Tank Web Page: http://www.highlandercenter.org/p-grassroots.asp (accessed September 10, 2007).

29. Material quoted in the following list of questions comes from Ryan Claycomb and Rachel Riedner, "Cultural Studies, Rhetoric Studies, and Composition: Towards an Anti-Disciplinary Nexus," *Enculturation* 5, no. 2 (2004): http//enculturation.gmu.edu /5_2/Claycomb-Riedner.html.

Chapter Eight
Discipline and Indulgence

Cathy Eisenhower and Dolsy Smith

An Introduction and a Disclaimer

After a stint teaching college writing, I became a librarian, and now I am attached to the first-year writing course at my university, where my job is to help students cultivate a critical practice of research. Pedagogy—a concept undercultivated in the discourse of librarianship—is my intellectual link to the work I used to do, and to the teaching faculty with whom I currently work. By *pedagogy*, I think I mean the promise of an occasion where teacher and student attend to the demands of reason and the imagination's needs, wrangling side by side with the doubts, uncertainties, chimeras, and differences that come flocking when we reflect on our place in the world. This promise is the ideal to which I want to stay faithful, however inadequate is my practice day by day. But if a lot of my fellow librarians abstain from such fuzziness, that is not surprising. For while teaching has become central to academic librarianship, the general model remains the "one-shot" session, in which the librarian, ensconced behind a keyboard or in the aura of an LCD projector, expounds to bored students about web pages and databases—an exercise that often fails to make an impression, for good or bad, on the research habits of the students. And considering the way many students (and faculty) treat librarians—as service providers of last resort—one has a hard time imagining what pedagogy *could* apply to this model, unless it were a pedagogy of the drive-in. Inside the aura of the projector, which describes the complete circle of your skill, your aims at least are clear (if their utility is not). Point, click, expound, repeat. Any questions? No? All right, then; goodbye.

As librarians, we have a certain, let us *say*, intimacy with discipline at its most insidious. I mean the discipline of information and technology, which is a kind of transcendental discipline, in which the content of specific discourses—their histories and politics, their ethical constellations, their crises and failures and outcries, and what in them remains difficult to bespeak or define—fades out before the presumption of a generalized utility. This utility, in turn, falls prey to an efficiency that wants to streamline all transfers in order to maximize profit and minimize time and personal contact. Information is the pure form of discipline; as Michel de Certeau suggests, it is one with the technocratic desire to *inform* the masses, whose crazy and recalcitrant materiality cracks up every project undertaken for the sake of profit or an ideal social order (ends that tend to conspire). The technocrat's problem, according to de Certeau, is how to get live bodies to conform to their representation as abstract units stacked against a norm (labor-hours, numbers of commuters, dollars of market demand, years alive, and so forth).[1] In the public sphere (cue up Habermas), the informing proceeds apace thanks to seductive technologies: in the barrage of images, reports, and statistics; through moralistic fictions that mimic a journalistic determinateness; and through news broadcasts and talk shows that turn lived moments into moral narratives. Not to mention the advertising that underwrites it all, dangling before our eyes the reward for good behavior (a body *sans* dirt, *sans* debility, and beyond the embarrassment of time and gravity and the grave).

School is supposed to be the place where one stands at "critical distance" and puts off the passions and paranoia of the marketplace. In many academic disciplines, it happens that this distance only imparts a certain finesse—one learns how, under set conditions, to manipulate predetermined *topoi* (as in marketing, the rhetoric of the technocrat). In the purer disciplines, a model of reflection holds court, the constituents of which are reading, writing, experiment, discussion, and peer critique, in a space of abstraction designed to free the heart from its ordinary determinants. The discourse of these disciplines is *exceptional*; but how often does the liberty they confer come at the price of indifference, in a language purged of the very stuff to which they seek to inspire commitment, i.e., creativity, sympathy, desire? And in place of these purged what-have-you's, or superimposed on their etiolated images, there arises a standard of consensus which can be taken for universal, but only to the extent that it patrols its borders, establishes shibboleths, and repels all claims of an immanent necessity, which are bound to be local, excessive, and contradictory.[2] When discourse circulates with the chief aim of meeting this standard (underwritten by the institutional conditions of its reproduction, such as publication and tenure), the practice of reflection becomes *self-reflexive*, a serpent swallowing its tail.

If reflection, as George Santayana suggested, always begins *en medias res*, we do our students, and ourselves, a disservice to keep it pure—it is less a baptism than a flailing about, a dogged attempt to stay afloat. But we do an even greater disservice by merely anticipating the demands of labor and capital: turning students into "critical consumers of information," or better workers in the "knowledge economy." These dicta, at the heart of the librarian's official pedagogy, suggest that the discipline of information exceeds itself: there is just too much of it! But how could it not exceed itself? After all, the undisciplined materiality of the masses is, on another view, their spirit, their desire for forms.

What follows began as an exchange between two academic librarians, carried out over the course of a few months via a private blog. Originally, we had intended to turn these desultory expostulations with our professional selves into a proper academic argument, but each question we posed seemed only to lead further afield, away from that unity and clarity of focus and purpose on which scholarship depends. Unable to answer anything resolutely, we indulged in the evidence of our impressions, personal histories, sensibilities, and (for my part, at least) a kind of wavering play of speculative conviction, half belief, half the desire for belief. If this indulgence proves excusable, I would like to believe that it is because reflection itself involves a kind of indulgence—and that if a discipline is constituted at the expense of forgetting that indulgence, pedagogy might be what recalls it to itself. (DS)

Q: What are you trying to teach your students?

The point of reading, writing, and research is, for me, one and the same: to wrestle possibility, to pin it down a little while on the actual earth. Not in order to defeat possibility, but to ennoble, maybe, the ground. As a librarian teaching research in a writing class, I get to work with students during their first attempts to grapple with their topics, when the imagination should be at its most limber. I don't have to worry about the crunch, the inevitable tense pounding of a sensibility against an idiolect that can't quite get it right, or that totally misses the point and eats dirt. I don't (so much) have to wince at the gaps in logic, the missed opportunities, the flagging attention, the ludicrous stamina of a poor analogy. I don't have to bring my students back to the arbitrary reality of a grade.

I find myself interested in *sensibility*—does that term have a place in our pedagogy? Or is it a fugitive from the idealism of *critical thinking*? If I say I am inclined to imagine teaching as the cultivation of sensibility—and this is pure idealism, dreaming along a languid inclination—I don't exactly mean habits of thought, or not at least with reference to the Herculean efforts of a reason that would cast out the appeals of pathos, clean the heart's stables, and overthrow all mutiny of inarticulate desire. Nor do I mean "learning styles": an approach that tackles personal differences as the varieties of a capacity to *learn*, assuming that the thing to be learned remains the same for each person, as does the aim, i.e., to make us all more productive, to "enrich" the human capital in our lives. Critical reason respects differences; nevertheless, its discourse treats difference, from time to time, as an object, as something to be discerned and rendered objective within a disciplined, that is, a normative, order of words. The ethical form of this critical practice—emphasizing the ideals of tolerance, skepticism, and the freedom of informed choice as the products of non-coercive discipline—this ethical form does, indeed, seem to fulfill the unique destiny of reason itself, which I might, in a haphazard moment, call the refinement of satisfaction and motive. But if the action of reason is a perpetual refinement, where does the impetus to it lie?

The differences of sensibility are the figures of individual necessity. Neither personal history nor self-interest, sensibility is, I think, a matter of how the understanding realizes itself and feels itself happen in the grappling of experience with desire. It is not desire as an inert body to be understood, discerned inside self-knowledge, re-formed with the aid of restraints freely chosen or else imposed; it is, rather, the wage of that knowledge, and the curvature of what buckles under that restraint. If there are forces converging within ourselves that we cannot possibly understand, the question becomes, how can they be withstood?

I fall short, I mis-step, I miss the point. What brings me back from the arbitrary reality of words?

My own sensibility leads me to believe that certain forms of thought count as action: when I teach, I reach for the fulfillment of that belief, asking questions and devising exercises to "get them to think," hunting among sour looks and furrowed brows for that elusive animal, enthusiasm, and betting on the glimmer of a response to what is, in the final analysis, the needs of my sensibility. Is this just? Do I mis-take for the freedom of thinking what my students regard as an obligation—or perhaps as the satisfaction of an arbitrary ritual in the name of deferred rewards? Are we both being fleeced? A fellow in the front row stretches out his long, hirsute limbs, aware that the fact of an idle body is the best defense against my impertinent questioning. What do I do with his resistance?

One might seek to understand the classroom, like the history of Western reason itself, in terms of the *agon* that satisfies a special competitive sensibility. There, under ideal conditions, the resistance to being in-formed refines the appetite for it, even as the resistance to discipline escapes into whatever, in the images of an intellectual tradition, flatters sensibility: the dandy quotes Proust, the punk-rocker dog ears her Che Guevara. If learning can lead to praxis, surely it must begin with the development of a rhetoric persuasive to oneself. Isn't that, after all, where teaching begins? Yet this is not the position from which I teach, when I am teaching people how to use a database, how to find information, *how to be competent.* Often I feel helpful. Seldom do I feel like a steward to the imagination, or anything that matches the rhetoric with which I am accustomed to exalt myself.

Today, on the side of reason, we have models of competence. And on the side of sensibility, keeping company with the abstraction of our productive capacities, we have a rhetorical marketplace of selfhood—the self becoming a commodity traded on Facebook and mySpace, which gamely let everyone make up in the expression of personality and desire what he lacks in the determination of his own capacity to make something of individual value. Vast resources of sensibility are marshaled for the soft politics of consuming collectively.

What am I trying to teach my students? I don't know. Writing about it, I find myself trying to dodge the topic, to escape: from information, research, and pedagogy; from the discipline of others; from the intimate boredom of the classroom, with its pent shapes napping or anxious or distracted; from the performance of concern. If one day we dropped the enchanted thread of decorum that holds us here, we might all throw up our hands.

And writing? Again and again I come back to the folds of cadence and idea, as to the place where a sensibility consumes itself. (DS)

Q: If the ACRL Information Literacy Competency Standards were an animal, what kind of animal would they be?

Competence, it strikes me, is a fantasy of the human animal, dreaming of a state past the necessity of subjective experience, beyond the pricking flux of sublunary life. By studying their behavior and picking them apart, we objectify animals, and at work, in school, in the declining light of our social institutions, we try, without end, to objectify each other—but wouldn't the ultimate comfort come if we could objectify ourselves—judge ourselves without feeling—correct our faults in the absence of hope or remorse? Which one of us stands competent in the things that really matter? In the light of these things, which don't dare cross professional lips, competence is at once an impossible goal and an inconsequential consolation.

Tautology is the symptom of a discourse that fears being rendered illegible. "Information Literacy Competency": what do each of these words add to our understanding of the term?[3] I'd like to pick on *information* now. Which one of us is not, at every minute, being informed? We are bombarded. Saturated. Unwitting antennae, one and all. In *The Structural Transformation of the Public Sphere*, Jürgen Habermas says that modern capitalist society, riven by antinomies of interest and class struggle, feeds on a dream of the public sphere, empty as a soap-bubble; the mass media inspires us to think that we are participating in the democratic project, yet the flow of public information tends only one way, and that is downward and inward.[4] We are supposed to be competent to *evaluate* this information: but how, when the presumption of its value is, in large degree, ingrained in us from the beginning? From the first difficult blink of our newborn eyes we are *informed* by structures whose preservation demands our acquiescence, even as they stimulate deep-seated needs—the assorted ideologies of family, social class, religious and ethnic affiliation, school and nation, all increasingly mediated by the streaming twenty-four-hour corporate hortatory, the bright dithyramb of Times Square: *BUY, BUY, BUY!* It's like studying the cards a card-shark plies you with, with one important difference: by some trick of mirrors, the closer you look, the more the shark resembles yourself.

At the 2007 conference of the Association of College and Research Libraries, held in Baltimore, you couldn't escape the seafaring metaphors, deployed everywhere in a paroxysm of packaging ("Sailing into the Future!" "Uncharted Waters!"), or the word *marketing*—as if there lay a discovery wrested from the vast mouth of Capital. Competence and marketing are two sides of the coin of the realm. The utility of librarians, which in "the marketing piece" lures students in, consists in making them competent—that is, in rendering them fluent human capital, objects of utility. Standards say, *teach students to evaluate information.* Does this differ from putting a price on it—whether in terms of time, grades, or desired socioeconomic status? How do we evaluate our own standards? What values do we advance—what values do we ourselves, as people, infuse into our professional capacities? I don't believe in standards as a refuge from judgment, nor in critical thinking as a free and value-neutral zone. There are only values spoken aloud, values hushed or soft-spoken (marketing), and values that lie mute and intricate with practice (competence). Does the effort to pronounce value count as resistance? Is it enough?

In the Baltimore aquarium, the sharks swam passively underneath the trampling of hundreds of feet. We were not part of their element. (DS)

Q: Where do you get your values?

My values come directly from my experiences, like those of most people. Having grown up in a steel town that shut down in the late 70s, I went through a lot of angst about class as my father lost his job, and we lost our house, while classmates of mine whose parents were doctors and lawyers didn't seem to feel the blow. Even at that age I was feeling the pain of globalization and understood it as such—steel and cars being made abroad made my father's job obsolete.

This did not fill me with rage or indignation. It just filled me with shame. As a child I wanted to grow up and have more money than my parents had so I could take care of them and live in relative luxury. Until then, I would pass—by not inviting friends to my house, by getting a part-time job so I could pay for designer labels, or at least the counterfeit ones. The shame and pretense lasted through my higher education, at a small liberal arts college where families with money sent their children. How did I end up there, at a southern Baptist university, I, an agnostic who had never even visited the South until I stepped onto campus for orientation? I ended up there because my parents had never attended college, so had no idea how to advise me, and my seventeen-year-old brain chose no doubt based on frivolous yearnings toward a leafy quadrangle and publicity photos of happy undergrads sharing books under brick archways.

As a math/econ major I enrolled in an intro to women's studies course to fulfill an elective. That class changed my life—we read Derrida, Freud, Irigaray—and I was suddenly very angry at the way my vision shifted. I started writing bad, angry poems, the first step at turning shame into a critical consciousness that could work on the world. The nascent values of justice, equality, freedom, and a sense of moral responsibility for local and global communities surfaced, all values counter to the profit-motive logic of hypercapitalism. That's why I went to graduate school and ended up teaching writing—because I had faith in higher education as a place where people develop their moral faculties along with critical abilities that create responsible citizens involved in their own governance and fate.

Adjuncting at a school where students had already come to treat their education as a business transaction, themselves as consumers, and me as a service provider, forced me out of higher education and into the nonprofit world. (CE)

Q: Do you bring these values to work? How so?

Sometimes I do, sometimes I don't. Sometimes I'm not sure how to integrate my own values into the work that I do. As a writing instructor I had a lot of autonomy in creating courses that performed the "critical social imperative of educating citizens who can sustain and develop inclusive democratic public spheres," or at least that I hoped performed this imperative.[5] In the library, my autonomy is limited and the mission articulated through policy and procedure and administrative decisions that constrain my own work and what is possible. I'm thinking now about what I do that reflects my values. Some examples: Being the librarian for women's studies, romance languages, and English allows me to support scholarship that makes a difference. As a poet, I place a lot of importance on poetry as a cultural form through which I can play and build on the oppositional poetics of the past and present. As a librarian, I can build, and educate students about, collections that put dissident poetries alongside mainstream work that has absorbed a disturbing logic: one that puts words together in ways received and manipulated by media that strip issues of their complexity. Charles Bernstein said this about that:

> Dissent is a form of saying no, to echo Dickinson's remark in a letter, "Don't you know that 'no' is the wildest word we consign to language." Too much of the "popular" poetry of the time is affirmative but I want an "unpopular" poetry of "anaffirmation" that expresses confusion, anger, ambiguity, distress, fumbling, awkwardness. Oddly, it is a form of dissent these days to hold out that art that doesn't get the market share can actually be as valuable as the art that does, that ideas that are hard to understand may have something to say that ideas you can understand can't begin to get at. I'm for the ketchup that loses the race.[6]

My work with women's studies also feels really valuable to me—right now I'm working with two faculty members on "Women in and Beyond the Global," which we're still conceptualizing, but will involve international scholars on prisons, households, and cities coming together virtually and physically to consider these problems—of domestic workers, of gentrification, etc.

In other parts of my work, I'm not so sure. Right now the library is hosting a consultant who is streamlining our technical processing of books and electronic resources. Her proposal to us, and the administration's push to accept her changes, makes clear that the corporate value of efficiency trumps all other considerations, and that increasing journal inflation in the sciences will gnaw away at the monograph budgets for the humanities. And the university is not raising our budget commensurate with inflation, which has happened for the three years I've been at GW. I find myself (along with one or two other librarians) constantly in the position to defend the humanities to people who fail to see the vocational use of, say, literary studies, for our students. The humanities shrink, the sciences swell, and many librarians around the country view this shift as either appropriate, because the university determines on which disciplines to focus and it's none of our business, or as inappropriate because of a feeling of territoriality and self-preservation rather than a concern for higher education and our faux democracy.

This disturbs me—when I went to library school, I thought that this profession busted at the seams with people who think higher education must fulfill that critical social imperative Giroux talks about. Instead, I find a profession that calls students "customers" and that doesn't see it as a civic or moral responsibility to engage in campus discourse, or national discourse, about higher education. Of course, I'm exaggerating, but not too much.

Recently I read an interesting article by a librarian, "Information Criticism: Where Is It?" in which Jack Andersen suggests that librarians use the term "information" rampantly because it keeps them at a distance from the values implicit in disciplinary discourses and other kinds of rhetorical communities.[7] Though organizations like the American Library Association advocate against the USA Patriot Act, censorship, intellectual property, and other related issues, they never, as far as I'm aware, participate in public critiques of how corporatization is destroying higher education. Librarians seem to limit their concerns to the library. Even in discussions about corporate funding of university research, the question that generally arises is, "Are we getting any of that money for library materials?" rather than, "Why do corporate interests have so much say in what scholars do at this and other universities?"

This is not the case with all librarians, but our library school educations, which feed us techno-managerial speak and quash questions beyond practitioner level, raise broods of liberal faux social-scientists with strident opinions about what users need and how we should serve them, but few thoughts on larger cultural trends that are dismantling our educational systems, such as they are.

To be honest, I'm not sure what to do about this. I'm not a Cultural Studies scholar and, even if I were, I'm not sure how I would write to an audience of librarians and get them to listen. I'm doing this writing project with Dolsy for just that reason—to figure out how my day-to-day work relates to social justice, how I can make it relate, and how to do some public thinking in the library community and beyond with others who have similar concerns. (CE)

Q: What value do you assign to the act of reading?

Some people behave as though this trait had become vestigial, ceding to the expediency of newer pastimes. And perhaps it has. *Information processing* subsumes reading, which becomes just one of its modes, preliminary to, and less important than, the modes that produce new packets of information or discourse.[8] But these terms—discourse, information—too easily become neutered creatures, mascots of an imaginary that wants the operations of capital to be clean and smooth. The life of information, on this view, is a chaste fecundity.

That's why I turn to a text like Robert Burton's *Anatomy of Melancholy,* which puts this fecundity in another light:

> To be counted writers . . . to be thought and held polymaths and polyhistors . . . to get a paper kingdom . . . in this precipitate, ambitious age . . . and they that are scarce auditors, *vix auditores,* must be masters and teachers, before they be capable and fit hearers. They will rush into all learning . . . divine, human authors, rake over all indexes and pamphlets for notes, as our merchants do strange havens for traffic, write great tomes, *cum non stint re vera doctiores, sed loquaciores,* whenas they are not thereby better scholars, but great praters . . . A fault that every writer finds, as I do now, and yet faulty themselves . . . all thieves; they pilfer out of old writers to stuff up their new comments, scrape Ennius' dung-hills, and out of Democritus' pit, as I have done. By which means it comes to pass, "that not only libraries and shops are full of our putrid papers, but every close-stool and jakes" . . . they serve to put under pies, to lap spice in, and keep roast-meat from burning.[9]

Among other things, discourse partakes of the body's prolific appetites and the productivity of its fundament (and if Burton's Baroque horror at this productivity seems quaint, we would do well to pay it more attention in our own world). Beyond the scatological, Burton reminds us that the substance of information is material and social—the abundant papers, the writers' desires—and that its nature is to run to excess, to overwhelm, to accumulate, to be in flux. Think of the junk mail stuffing the trashcan, the rumors and gossip, the news on twenty channels, some of it *meant* to be false—not to mention, in the interstices of the rest, and hovering above our highways and cityscapes, the constant retinal onslaught of the Great Ad Age. Inside the library's disciplined geography, we forget these facts; as in Borges' fable, the library belabors the dream of a universal order, with the content of the volumes expressing nothing more than the permutations of a singular, original, and inflexible discipline—"the fundamental law of the Library," as expounded by "a librarian of genius":

> all the books, no matter how diverse they might be, are made up of the same elements: the space, the period, the comma, the twenty-two letters of the alphabet. He also alleged a fact which travelers have confirmed: *In the vast Library there are no two identical books.* From these two incontrovertible premises he deduced that the Library is total and that its shelves register all the possible combinations of the twenty-odd orthographical symbols (a number which, though extremely vast, is not infinite): in other words, all that it is given to express, in all languages.[10]

As Borges' narrator concludes, there is thus "not a single example of absolute nonsense" in the whole universe.[11] Here is the function of *information,* of its concept: to exorcise from communication the specter of the absurd.[12]

Consider, for instance, the database JSTOR: "a high-quality, interdisciplinary archive . . . of over one thousand leading academic journals across the humanities, social sciences, and sciences," whose contents are fully searchable and

readable online (to anyone with access privileges, that is).[13] The technology of
JSTOR promises to condense discourse (but isn't discourse meant to meander?)
into a stream that can be tapped with precision and efficiency—no more haunt-
ing the library stacks late into the night, no more allergens, cramped hands, and
sloppy photocopies. But more subtly, the technology promises a fullness (every
possibly important article! available in full text!) that verges on the ecstatic. The
ideology of JSTOR: *find what you need.* I said *ideology* because the user is led
to expect a satisfaction that cannot be had: by matching texts from its archive
against the keywords she enters, JSTOR offers her "relevant" results—never
mind that relevance is a creative act, and that what the database provides, thanks
to its algorithms, are merely materials for a possible relation, on the basis of
language stripped of its referential dimension, reduced in the guts of the computer to a glorified alphabet soup. Before the articles can be judged relevant, one
has to read them and, in doing so, to invent their relevance. Of course, the scholar knows better. But why are we bemused by the desire of students to get that
one hit that will close the case and complete the circuit? It's not unlike what
drives us when we visit the grocery store, or the department store, nomads in a
storm of things supposedly designed to suit us, but in fact demanding that we fit
our lives to them, except that the demand is made worse, in the student's
case, by the estrangement of academic discourse and the threat of reproof.

I can't forget David Bartholomae's point that student writers must learn the
conventions of this discourse by imitation, which is a process fundamentally
uneven, unpredictable, and uncomfortable, with disparate results that can embar-
rass both student and teacher.[14] How does reading bear on this obscure toil?
Surely, in the light of mimesis, the habits and "tactics" (to poach a term from
Michel de Certeau) that I absorb unconsciously while reading are at least as important as the explicit sense that I can make of what I have read—even assuming
that my sense of a text can be made explicit at all. But is what I have said ever
more than the moiety of what I wanted to say? I am wandering into a thicket
here, but I find some help in an idea from George Santayana, that discourse
forms part of the experience of "animal life": an orientation to obscure objects
of belief whose force draws us along.[15] In the philosopher's example, we take
bread to be a substance in the world, and we talk about it as such, not because
we can measure it and describe it and decompose it into its ingredients, but because we can seize it and eat it up. As social animals, it is through discourse that
we obtain what we need to subsist. Given our discursive orientation to action
and belief (and survival!), punctuated as it is by "shocks" from threatening or
unfamiliar sources, what we call thinking is less like a computer, in which information is "stored" and "retrieved," than a theater, where sensations and emotions and desires play out their play. The virtual nature of consciousness has
profound implications for our understanding of the discourse of others: "it is not
the words, any more than the action and attitude which accompany them, that
are his *understanding* of the words, or his *sense* of his attitude and action. These
can evidently be apprehended only dramatically, by imitative sympathy."[16] Contemporary psychological research seems to confirm this notion, viz., that in in-

terpreting another's experience, or even the representation of her experience—e.g., watching someone hit a baseball, or seeing a character on TV get hit in the face—the spectator virtually plays out the physical actions in his own mind, together with the emotions associated with them.[17] How far this "dramatic sympathy" pertains to abstract concepts remains obscure, but why would it not? According to Edmund Burke, the meaning of a word like *patriot* or *liberty* is a palimpsest comprising the emotional history of our encounters with the word—and, by implication, variable from person to person.[18] In any event, thoughts ghost corporeal forces. In Santayana's words, "in order to communicate thought, it is necessary to impose it."[19]

The imagination is our capacity to be flexibly determined. This is the idea I want to impose on you, Dear Reader. I take my cue here from Michel de Certeau, who would have us heed the ways in which every reading, for every reader, is a creative act: a process of selecting, combining, filling in gaps, or perforating and inverting what is supposed to be a smooth and lawful surface. In de Certeau's marvelous phrase, the reader reading is "oscillating in a nowhere between what he invents and what changes him."[20] So how does a text change and determine us? Off the top of my head, I propose a schema:

- as information (that is, facts that we can cite or recall to our own purposes)
- as representation (of a coherent intention that we can impute to the author of the text, which, in the case of works with an express rhetorical purpose, we call the *argument* or *logos*, but which may also depend on moral judgments of the writer)
- as rhetorical cornucopia (that is, an array of lexical, syntactical, figurative, and prosodic tactics—the schemes and tropes—that we can "store," mimetically, for our future use)
- as an occasion of sympathy (or what rhetoricians called *pathos*, which has a more or less dramatic structure, in Santayana's sense of the virtual imitation of an attitude or a feeling)
- as a field of imagery (the stuff that fantasies and dreams are made of)
- as musical forces (rhythm and cadence, with their strong connection to bodily ways of being, such as balance, muscular tension, and breath)
- ?

The list is not meant to decompose the dimensions of "sense"—there may be others I have missed—nor is it intended to capture a succession of phases, for surely, if the process could be described in serial terms, the "representational" would come last (as the supposed plenitude that would gather up the parts and make them whole). I offer the list merely as a gesture toward the obscure, moving from those kinds of meaning that we make our regular business—and the objects of our discipline—to those that must be experienced rather than explained.

I am reminded of how Emily Dickinson describes the experience of reading good poetry—as though the top of your head had been taken off. In that nebulous territory where sense gels because of suggestion and echo, and persuasion crosses over into motivation, inspiration, even ecstasy—in this territory, the text becomes illegible, rising from itself like a mist, or shooting off like a rocket capsule. Dickinson's poetry is itself a great example: having had to re-invent for herself a literary language that was not meant to accommodate a woman of genius, much less one capable of such profound spiritual doubt, she wrote, from the perspective of her contemporaries, *illegibly*. In large measure, her work remains illegible—and in this lurks its remarkable power. If we seldom have the patience these days to take pleasure in such work, we nevertheless seek, in our more immediate literacies, memoranda from the forbidden territory she evokes (like a bullet-point to the head). In what we choose to read, to see, to hear, our imaginations demand to be strongly determined, even violently so. In the face of this aptness to be in-formed, the challenge of pedagogy is to cultivate the flexibility of the imagination.

To do so means to slow down the pace of information-processing, and to balk the ferocious onward grasping of discourse.[21] When I help first-year students do research, I try to induce them to stop and read; just to skim a scholarly monograph, chosen almost at random, while trying to winkle out the keywords of its argument, is good practice for the student primed to mine texts for their facts alone. But to induce people to imagine, and to connect their academic encounters with other modes of reading and memory and judgment—I don't know where to begin. My own encounters with academic texts are often anything but vitally imagined. And who knows why some things lodge in the head, while the rest passes through us, eluding an expectation so foolishly refreshed? Recently, reading a justly famous tome, I came away with three or four ideas, among which this quote from Marx stands out, like a momentary tattoo on the brain: the "open book of the human faculties."[22] Part of the special pathos of this phrase is the hope it reposes in reading and writing as instruments of self-determination. That set me wondering: what would it look like, a pedagogy addressed to whatever is illegible in our labor? (DS)

Q: What value do you assign the act of reading?

These values shift at each page turn or eye movement, don't they? Reading acts are often invisible, often cannot be disentangled one from another. Now that it's all text all the time, we never get a break, and I'm tired of trees. My reading has grown rhizomatic after many years of "academic reading," loosely defined for me as reading to produce eventually a reasoned argument within a set of disciplinary constraints that sap the pleasure out of the text altogether. The act of reading in an academic context transformed my choices of reading objects into a series of requisite texts that would develop in me enough expertise that I could construct a relevant, disciplined argument. Seminal is a dirty word. I want a mass of biographies, chick flicks, poems, buildings, jelly labels, and physics equations that bear only metaphorical relations to each other constructed by the reader in a moment of love. How do you teach that? Do we even want to? Does this sentence have to connect to the previous one? I should hope not.

That said, there is power in reading beyond aesthetic pleasure, in experiencing potential worlds, both narrative and of mere idea. We can see the literal worlds we inhabit as we read them, both in their reconstruction on the page, screen, platform, and in their appearance and re-appearance around us. Then we have tools to tear those down and build them up again. We may also feel helpless at painful insights that clarify our overwhelming situations, but I hope we do this communally and pool our capacities. Reading is essential to struggling for social justice—reading defined variously through myriad literacies, whether Freirean critical literacy that teaches us to "rewrit[e] . . . what is read" and become conscious of our subject positions historically, politically, socially, or literacies focused on particular cultural forms or through particular ideological lenses (not that these are mutually exclusive).[23]

As a woman, oh boy. We have to read to know the language we've inherited, in some ways all we have—if you agree with Richard Rorty that we can really only take an inherited language and reconstruct it into new metaphors, paradigms, etc., notwithstanding Audre Lorde's "The master's tools will never dismantle the master's house." Especially in the case of identities, we need to construct ourselves through oppositional narratives and images that explore our potential as women and, to do that, we first have to read the narratives and images already there. As Barthes says, we write to read what we want to read, but also to write who we want to be.[24]

This is not news, nor is it pedagogically new, so I'm wondering what it means in the context of libraries. Part of my responsibility as a librarian (and all of this ultimately connects to responsibility, social and otherwise) is to read the library and its classification and information systems, just to take two examples. Some librarians are doing this work—Marvin Taylor at NYU has written about collecting the Downtown arts scene from Manhattan in the 1970s. One writer, David Wojnarowicz, created *Memories That Smell Like Gasoline*, an illustrated text delving into not only his experience as a man with AIDS but also his life in the culture of downtown Manhattan as a gay man. The library processed the book and classified it as RC607—in the section on medicine and AIDS. Taylor points out, using Foucault, that the classification system does a kind of violence to this text by denying Wojnarowicz the identity of an artist and writer, instead regarding him as an AIDS patient with a story to tell. Wojnarowicz, ironically, had repeatedly visited book stores and moved his books from the AIDS section to the arts section in protest of his relegation to the role of AIDS artist at best.[25] The way Taylor reads the library reveals it as a system of discourse not functioning "objectively," as some would like to believe (a goal of libraries that Dolsy explains rather well), but rather labeling and placing texts in indexical and proximate relations to other texts, which transforms them in ways that do violence to identity. There are many stories like this one, but there are many more systems in libraries that we need to critique, and maybe students can help us do that. (CE)

In Lieu of Conclusion

What is the critique to which this builds, from the perspective of teachers and librarians who view classrooms and libraries as collaborative spaces in which we put ourselves in relation to texts and to each other, where we venture to examine together how texts have been classified in libraries and why, how scholars often classify themselves through disciplinary conventions and markers, and how and why writers who intentionally or accidentally resist classification force us to sharpen our critical faculties—thus reading against and toward the text and its physical and virtual (thus virtually infinite) context, without the signposts that encourage glossing over disciplinary landscapes? Attempts to teach research with goals of efficiency and prescribed competencies for the student, a model made possible by the cataloging and classification of knowledge, are rewarded by institutions that prize assessable outcomes and cost-benefit analyses of educational programs. Big surprise. Though overstated to the point of hilarity, the below conclusion to an article articulates assumptions that undergird much of library instruction in the U.S.—even when instruction programs, and the ACRL information literacy competency standards, pay faint lip service to "critical thinking" as a learning "outcome" (thus measurable):

> This essay has been an argument for an obvious way to evaluate student search strategies. It should not be assumed that students (and faculty) automatically control the system merely by the fact that they are using it. Control is especially important in a database the size of MEDLINE in which a search of a single word or phrase could retrieve thousands of citations in many languages. Control increases relevancy. In addition, I believe that when a student demonstrates control over a search interface (OVID or PubMed), the very act of control assumes that the student was using critical thinking (consciously or subconsciously). Because of today's online environment, control replaces critical thinking as the preferred evaluative technique. We want our students to be skilled researchers, not lucky ones.[26]

The language of libraries—bibliographic control, controlled vocabulary, and mastery or control over systems of control, control over evaluating student control of controlled systems (ahhh!)—reveal that the key to research is, yes, "control." It increases efficiency of finding "relevant" "information"—relevant being code for appropriate to the researcher's discipline and topic within that discipline. The library as a system facilitates "research" by organizing information and teaches "research" through designing standards by which student achievement *can be measured*. And here I thought we created relevancy by thinking and writing, not by controlling bibliographic systems of control. Where's the messiness? Research as a sanitized, controlled *strategy*, tantamount to Herman Hesse's "bourgeois cleanliness"—" a paradise of cleanliness and spotless mediocrity, of ordered ways"[27]—rejects the serendipitous, the accidental, the irreconcilable, the absurd extra-academic, extra-disciplinary juxtapositions that gnaw at us until we link vehicle to tenor in a new metaphor (i.e. we *think*).

Are we creating Foucault's "docile bodies" by exercising control over student research techniques rather than developing environments that encourage play and court the absurd, that is, imaginative connections that form new knowledge that calls us to imaginative action? We have to question as Foucault does what he calls "unities"—books, disciplines, libraries.[28] The similarities, overlaps, insinuations are more obvious to students, most likely, than to ourselves; institutions have trained us to sort texts and their forms into pre-conceived taxonomies, but students often have no clear idea what "scholarship" is, let alone its disciplinary genres. And, as Martha Stewart would say, "That's a *good* thing." What is obvious to us is not obvious at all, and we would probably do well to remember that.

The questions of praxis and how we act in "constrained circumstances" acknowledge that constraint often courts control and efficiency—absent the luxury of time, librarians lapse into (were born into?) meticulous environments that mask the chaos that is thought—and I suppose disciplinary conventions do the same, so does grammar, for that matter. Maybe that's why I'm a poet, why Dolsy and I are writing this as a private blog instead of an article to publish in the void. I don't know what I'm doing when I teach. I never have. And I'm both comfortable and uncomfortable with that—which may drive more of my pedagogy than anything. If I knew how to avoid praxis, I would, but I have to do *something*—"Gotta bring home the bacon," as Warhol used to say. I go into the classroom and try to make it appear to observers that whatever is happening is not too chaotic, while encouraging students to ask questions and think about "*dispositions* toward emergent occasions" [author's italics], as Van Hillard puts it.[29] Far from revolutionary. Does it work? I have no idea—I can hardly have goals for students whom I barely know. That would be completely presumptuous. Wouldn't it?

As Schrödinger's equation has suggested, matter is in all states of potential conditions at all times—not following prescribed paths, but all potentialities at once. When we observe matter, whether to measure or to see it, we experience *state vector collapse*—all of those potentialities collapse into a single image or measurement to make it actual, which may tell us more about the observer or the measurement method than about matter itself. Research is like this—all potential, and the frustrations of it for me often stem from the collapsing of that potential into the actual. Writing is the same, for that matter. I observe this with students as well—their excitement at the possibilities and their disillusionment with the systematic research methods taught and expected in many cases in order to measure their performance. Stepping in to evaluate, or even guide, for non-arbitrary purposes at arbitrary moments, the institution, the professor, the librarian, serve a limiting function in actualizing and directing what could form the chaotic birth of an intellectually rich citizenry [cue violins]. (CE)

Notes

1. Michel de Certeau, *The Practice of Everyday Life*, trans. Steven Rendall (Berkeley: University of California Press, 1988), 34-39, 166-67, etc.
2. Another way to say this is to enumerate what would *not* be present in "good writing" under a given disciplinary rubric. Take literary criticism, for instance (as it is practiced by scholars in English Departments): excessive sympathy with and/or erotic longings for the characters in a text, similes and metaphors (one or two, fine—but four or five?), outright value judgments, polemical disrespect for one's contemporaries in the field, silence with respect to one's contemporaries, statements whose force aims elsewhere than the demonstrable, allegiances to different forms of cultural authority at the same time (highbrow and popular, historical and contemporary, etc.), a style that imitates the kind of writing under consideration, displays of melancholy or outrage . . . . I'm not claiming that examples of these things do not exist in the canons of the discipline, but I maintain that the *disciplinary model*, as practitioners are compelled to imagine it, excludes these elements, which the critic introduces into her work at her own risk. The model, however, introduces a contradiction of its own, because it coexists with a demand that new work be "innovative," "imaginative," and "necessary." There is a double boundary, dividing, first, the ordinary from the exceptional and, second, the acceptable from the excessive. In competition with one's colleagues and oneself, one is always trying to cross the first boundary, which moves ever further away; the second, meanwhile, floats just ahead of one's steps—one false move, and lo, we have work to do here, we can't accept *that*, it's just the way things are, etc.
3. Association for College and Research Libraries, *Information Literacy Competency Standards for Higher Education*, American Library Association, http://www.ala.org/ala/acrl/acrlstandards/informationliteracycompetency.cfm (accessed July 2, 2008).
4. Jürgen Habermas, *The Structural Transformation of the Public Sphere: An Inquiry into a Category of Bourgeois Society*, trans. Thomas Burger (Cambridge: MIT University Press, 1989).
5. Henry Giroux, "Vocationalizing Higher Education: Schooling and the Politics of Corporate Culture," in *Beyond the Corporate University: Culture and Pedagogy in the New Millennium,* ed. Henry Giroux and Kostas Myrsiades (Lanham: Rowman and Littlefield, 1999), 29-44.
6. Charles Bernstein, "Charles Bernstein: Interview," *readme* no. 1 (1999), http://home.jps.net/~nada/issueone.htm (accessed November 15, 2007).
7. Jack Andersen, "Information Criticism: Where Is It?" *Progressive Librarian* 25 (Summer 2005): 12-22.
8. I have noticed that some of my colleagues and friends who teach writing feel similar pressures—pressures which are both bureaucratic and disciplinary—to de-privilege or even neglect their students' needs as *readers*.
9. Robert Burton, *The Anatomy of Melancholy*, ed. Holbrook Jackson (New York: New York Review of Books, 2001), 23.
10. Jorge Luis Borges, *Ficciones*, trans. Anthony Kerrigan (New York: Grove, 1963), 54.
11. Borges, *Ficciones*, 57.
12. The term *allegory* originally meant "to speak otherwise than in the marketplace." If the market has no more fixed place, being at once nowhere and everywhere, we might

suppose that all communication becomes allegorical, yet without a key to unlock its meanings. Or rather, there are countless, competing keys.

13. JSTOR, "The Archives," 2008, <http://www.jstor.org/page/info/about/archives /index.jsp> (accessed July 3, 2008).

14. David Bartholomae, "Inventing the University," in *When a Writer Can't Write: Research on Writer's Block and Other Writing Problems*, ed. Mike Rose (New York: Guilford, 1986), 134-66.

15. George Santayana, *Skepticism and Animal Faith* (New York: Dover, 1955), 193-244.

16. Santayana, *Skepticism*, 252.

17. Giacomo Rizzolatti, Leonardo Fogassi, and Vittorio Gallese, "Mirrors in the Mind," *Scientific American* (November 2006): 54-61.

18. Edmund Burke, *A Philosophical Enquiry into the Origins of Our Ideas of the Sublime and the Beautiful*, ed. Adam Phillips (Oxford UP, 1990), 149-62.

19. Santayana, *Skepticism*, 251.

20. De Certeau, *The Practice of Everyday Life*, 173.

21. It is common to say that language is a game; do we assume thereby that its rules can be illuminated? This assumption might be part of a game that *we* play, as those already in the know, who stake our livelihoods on our performance. It almost says, there's not so much at stake—i.e., it's *just* a game—in order to drive from our conscience the specters of those who, despite our coaching, *just don't get it*. After all, why do we find the ludic metaphor more suitable than others: Discourse as a hunger? As contagion? Isn't there something embarrassing about these ideas—to be frank, something high-school-creative-writing-teacherish? We picture the poet manqué in rubbed corduroy, or with frizzy hair and a tacky skirt. But if language is a game, it often ends badly, the dropped ball lost in the deepening shades. . . .

22. Raymond Williams, *Marxism and Literature* (New York: Oxford University Press, 1977), 60.

23. Paolo Freire and Donaldo Macedo *Literacy: Reading the Word and the World* (London: Bergin & Garvey, 1987), 36.

24. Roland Barthes, *The Pleasure of the Text*, trans. Richard Miller (New York: Hill and Wang, 1992).

25. Marvin Taylor, "'I'll be your mirror, reflect what you are': Postmodern Documentation and the Downtown New York Scene from 1975 to the Present," *RBM* 3, no. 1 (2002): 32-51.

26. Dean E. Cody, "Critical Thoughts on Critical Thinking," *Journal of Academic Librarianship* 32, no. 4 (July 2006): 403-7.

27. Herman Hesse, *Steppenwolf*, trans. Basil Creighton. (New York: Picador, 2002), 14-15.

28. Michel Foucault, *The Archaeology of Knowledge*, trans. A.M. Sheridan Smith (New York: Pantheon, 1972).

29. Van Hillard, "Navigating the Social Turn: Information Literacy as Situated Literacy," in *Teaching Literary Research: Challenges in a Changing Environment*, ed. Steven Harris and Kathleen Johnson (Chicago: American Library Association, forthcoming).

Part III

Writing Across the (Anti) Disciplines

There are, of course, many institutional obstacles to such collaboration. Among them is institutional fear on both sides. Disciplinary fear. The social sciences fear the radical impulse in literary studies, and over the decades, we in the humanities have trivialized the social sciences into their rational expectation straitjackets, not recognizing that, whatever the state of the social sciences in our own institution, strong tendencies toward acknowledging the silent but central role of the humanities in the area studies paradigm are now around. Sustained and focused discussion is all the more necessary as the boundaries of disciplinary knowledge are being redrawn.

—Gayatri Chakravorty Spivak, *Death of a Discipline*, 19.

Chapter Nine
"Only Connect":
Doing Dickens, Cultural Studies, and Anti-Disciplinarity in the University Literature Classroom

Eric G. Lorentzen

Only connect! That was the whole of her sermon. Only connect the prose and the passion, and both will be exalted, and human love will be seen at its height. Live in fragments no longer. Only connect, and the beast and the monk, robbed of the isolation that is life to either, will die.

—E. M. Forster, *Howards End*[1]

Any professor or instructor committed to a student-centered critical pedagogy in the university literature classroom practices the kind of connection between the subjects they teach and their students' actual lives that Forster's quote above embodies. One of the predominant strategies of progressive critical educators relies on the premise that "one secret to good teaching is the ability to discover fresh dimensions in celebrated material,"[2] and thus to make schooling relevant to students as a vital force in their own contemporary worlds. However, the recent intensification of the disciplinary climate in America's universities, replete with numerous and varied forms of challenge to academic freedom, threatens to make an authentic pedagogy of connection more difficult. These limitations on public intellectuals are more significant in the humanities, and are fraught with remarkably dangerous implications, in particular for professors of literature. In an academic era in which we find increasingly frequent hostile workplace restrictions that discipline what may and may not be taught in various university disciplines, the practice of reading literature alongside inter-disciplinary texts and popular texts becomes crucial in maintaining the democratic mission of truly liberating education. In this essay, I argue for the efficacy and exigency of adopt-

ing a Cultural Studies pedagogy in the university classroom that engages in inter-
disciplinary, multi-disciplinary, and anti-disciplinary methodologies that result
in, and reveal the necessity for, precisely the kind of "only connect" moments
between literature and lives that recent policies attempt to contain.[3] In particular,
I will illustrate the specific benefits of this critical pedagogy by detailing the
ways in which I transformed a senior seminar on Charles Dickens from a
"straight" literature course into a course in which students "did" Dickens through
multi-disciplinary Cultural Studies lenses.[4]

I

Since the beginning of the culture wars in the late 1980s, led by Allan Bloom, E.
D. Hirsch, Jr., and William Bennett, attempts have escalated to limit the discursive ground that professors at American universities may cover. Since the terror-
ist attacks on September 11, 2001, debates over, and warnings about, the radical
professoriate, on the one hand, and potential limitations to academic freedom, on
the other, have seemed to take up more and more space both in the public air-
waves and print, and in professional journals and scholarly conferences. Even
though the "back to the basics" arguments about the parallel declines of Western
civilization and university standards had already resulted in legislative attempts
to teach to the test, standardize curricula, corporatize democratic public space,
and suppress free speech on university campuses for years, the tragic events of
the early twenty-first century have led to even more profound assaults on academic freedom in higher education.

In my own experience as an assistant professor of nineteenth-century British
literature at a liberal arts university in Virginia, my own understanding of the
threats to academic freedom on campus crystallized during a department meeting
during the 2005-2006 school year. Although, as a scholar and teacher who had
long researched and practiced critical pedagogy in the university classroom, I
had been rather conscious of these threats before, I was about to experience their
limitations in a way that was all too first-hand. Our faculty were informed of new
"hostile workplace" regulations that were to take effect in institutions of higher
education in Virginia, which seemed at first merely to contain common sense
legislation relating to sexual harassment and workplace violence on campus.
However, a few of my fellow faculty members also noticed some of the less obvious directives contained in the hostile workplace material, which included new
guidelines about the kinds of things we should (and should not) be talking about
in our courses. For one, these edicts sought to discursively limit what we professors addressed in the classroom to our putative areas of specialization (in my
case, nineteenth-century British literature), rather than casting wider scholarly
nets to include lines of inquiry associated with today's politics, institutions, social constructs, identity formations, media representations, market economies, or

systems of government. Additionally, the implication was that professors who did not abide by these guidelines could be threatened with disciplinary action, litigation, and so forth. Although most of my colleagues reacted to these directives by responding that such mandates for disciplinary isolation were both foolish and counter-productive, if not practically impossible, most of us also seemed to recognize the writing on the wall: the imminent danger to the protection of free democratic exchange that makes a university education genuinely critical and transformative for its students. This epiphany was not merely a theoretical one, either; these issues were being raised for us right here, right now.

What we experienced as a faculty here in Virginia is symptomatic of a larger national trend aimed at silencing public intellectuals and disciplining both professors and students alike. In the wake of the "war on terror," we have seen a shift in the ways terms like "patriotism" and "freedom" have been deployed in limiting teachers at all levels of American schooling. In *The Abandoned Generation: Democracy beyond the Culture of Fear*, Henry Giroux describes one of the more insidious national attempts to police political ideas and pedagogical praxes in the name of patriotism. Situating this particular movement amidst a number of similar reactionary backlash movements, Giroux describes a recent high-profile attack on academic freedom:

> [Lynne Cheney] and Senator Joseph Lieberman founded an organization called the American Council of Trustees and Alumni, which published the recent report, "Defending Civilization: How Our Universities Are Failing America, and What Can Be Done about It." This report includes a list of 117 statements made by faculty and students in the wake of September 11 and points to such comments to argue that American campuses are "short on patriotism and long on self-flagellation." The report not only suggests that dissent is unpatriotic but it also reveals the names of those academics who are allegedly guilty of such crimes. The report was sent to 3,000 trustees, donors, and alumni across the country, urging them to wage a campaign on college campuses to require the teaching of American history and Western civilization and to protest and take actions against those intellectuals who are not loyal to this group's version of patriotism.[5]

Like the hostile workplace guidelines, this organization seeks to silence educators who do not conform to the conventional master-narratives that supposedly offer objective knowledge about the everlasting truths upon which our history and culture are based.

But what they do not acknowledge in these attacks is the multiplicity and subjectivity inherent in all historical accounts, literary traditions, and in the very notion of truth itself. Master-narratives create truth rather than merely excavating an authentic cultural, historical, political, and social past. Therefore, whenever figures such as Cheney and Lieberman and their ilk suggest that subjects like literature and history should be taught within narrowly defined disciplines that reflect an absolute truth, we recognize that self-interest plays a large motivational part in singling out *their* particular versions of these subjects; master-narratives traditionally have been used to consolidate power for those who have it, and to continue to marginalize those who have suffered oppression and domination within (and because of) those ostensible eternal truths. In addition, suggesting that such subjects should be separated from the realm of the political is, in itself, one of the more aggressively political maneuvers in which one can engage.[6] From this standpoint, the essentially disciplinary and punitive elements of such policies seem all too conspicuous, as professors continue to feel and fear "the limits prescribed by the institutional setting itself. As individuals, teachers dare not lead their students into political struggles without incurring risks that might result in loss of employment."[7] The loss of freedom on campus thus accords with and reinforces the dominant images in media and other societal networks of representation that construct the reality of our daily lives. Although these sites of power can also afford paradigms for resistance to dominant ideology, the current crisis has led to a refusal to "only connect."

While those of us who study education in nineteenth-century literature and culture may find it easy to recognize that pedagogical institutions today are still too often much more about disciplining, marginalizing, and containing students than liberating them, the consensus in general society is that the classroom is a place of empowerment where diligent students will unquestionably improve their lives. Many of us believe this premise, of course, because it is one of the primary messages about schooling with which we are incessantly bombarded while at schools ourselves. However, as a society, we need to identify the ways in which education often seeks to reproduce citizens that uncritically accept their worlds in terms of the dominant ideology of the status quo. As George Lipsitz urgently argues:

> Educators, students, and parents rarely recognize the role of the classroom as a place where labor is socialized, where people learn the requisite values, attitudes, and behaviors needed to make them docile, compliant, and productive workers and citizens. Instead, the classroom in our culture is seen as a site for upward mobility, a place where workers might gain the resources needed to make themselves supervisors, where entrepreneurs might become professionals, where professionals might join the ranks of upper management. This creates a "hidden curriculum" that influences every aspect of learning and teaching.[8]

Indeed, this hidden curriculum actively excludes connection between academic disciplines, with their standardized subject matter "knowledge," and the ways in which students might use their learning to negotiate their own identities, social roles, and the strategic possibilities to fight domination and exploitation in their daily lives.

When schools adopt a disciplinary regimen that features any standard curriculum, which reifies a core body of knowledge, and which then must be transmitted from teacher to student for the sake of mastering the compartmentalized subject matter, the objectives of the hidden curriculum become clear: discipline and mastery. What Paulo Freire has called the banking concept of education, this pedagogical methodology strives for the normalization of its students, rewarding obedience and stifling free thinking, and creating good students rather than critical ones.[9] In "A Good School Revisited," an article in which she attempts to diagnose why her previous schooling seemed so unsatisfactory, Mary Evans recognizes these forces at work in her own pedagogical experience of women writers of the nineteenth century like Jane Austen and Charlotte Brontë. By excluding any connection to her own life, she and her fellow students:

> were taught to see these texts as confirmations of the rewards of good behavior and generally abiding by the rules.
>   The rules were not, of course, just the written school rules which we were told about in our first year. The rules which mattered were rules about conformity and obedience and learning the limits of creativity and originality.[10]

This disciplinarity of the hidden curriculum results in a pedagogy of disconnection rather than an educational dynamic that is student-centered and engaged.

Of course, the recent movements to curtail academic freedom by concretizing this form of disciplinarity on our nation's campuses similarly divorce subject matter from relevance. Instead of advocating a student-centered pedagogy that authorizes possibilities for agency in their day-to-day schooling, "students are silenced by being denied the opportunity to engage texts within a context that affirms the histories, experiences, and meanings that constitute the conditions through which students exercise their own voices."[11] Students must be able to apprehend the connection between the works they study in the university and the ways those works speak to their own lives in the twenty-first-century United States, if we hope to preserve pedagogy as an essentially indispensable element in affirming vigorous individual and collective democratic identities. If we as professors succumb to policies that disconnect, how can we expect our students to do otherwise when they enter our classrooms? Yet the legislative forces that increasingly exert themselves on schools demand just that, by corporatizing higher education, silencing dissent from progressive intellectuals, devaluing contemporary connection with students' lives in the classroom as anti-intellectual, and instituting pedagogical praxes that emphasize rote memorization of "facts," embrace "teaching to the text" philosophies, and champion more standardized curricula and means of evaluation. A university education must be seen as a passport to becoming a critical citizen, not just a credential that certifies a student's ability to memorize and regurgitate certain canons of disciplinary information, or perform a set of specialized skills at the end of four years of training. As public intellectuals we must resist these pedagogies of negation and "only connect," realizing "no university that wants to hold up its head in the face of the twenty-first century can afford to turn dispassionate eyes away from the problems . . . that beset our world."[12]

One of the more significant obstacles that twenty-first-century professors face in trying to connect is the increasingly corporate environment found on many of the United States' university campuses. This corporate ideology does more than merely put the bottom line first in administrative decisions about university resources; it also indicates a shift in ideology, from prioritizing students and their access to counter-hegemonic dialogue in their courses to hierarchizing the value of university resources, departments, courses, and professors directly in terms of the training they can provide for students' future entry into positions in the labor force. As in the majority of institutions in the corporate United States that these universities now primarily serve, access to voices that might challenge dominant power networks and ideologies virtually disappear. Some of the tactics that the corporate university deploys to discipline academic life include the hostile workplace normalization about which I have been writing, corporate notions of accountability such as raising test scores, and constant attacks that rewrite progressive critical pedagogy as the unpatriotic dissent of tenured radicals.[13] The corporate university thrives on the fallacious postulate that an objective transmission of universal verities is possible, and demonizes intellectuals who attempt to "flip the script," while masking that their own eternal truths are just as subjective as the narratives they attempt to discipline.

This normalization of higher education has led to the increasing number of appointments of corporate CEOs to positions of leadership within education, such as roles as university presidents and members of educational boards and committees, a development that offers perhaps the most profound threat yet to higher education.[14] One of the ways in which corporatized education actively discourages involvement in decision-making processes is through standardized testing, since an inherent element in the "hidden curriculum is that testing is used as a ploy to ensure that teachers are de-skilled as they are reduced to mere technicians, that students be treated as customers in the marketplace rather than as engaged, critical learners, and that public schools fail so that they can be eventually privatized."[15] An anti-disciplinary Cultural Studies methodology, especially in the university literature classroom, is precisely the kind of critical pedagogy of connection that can resist and talk back to these disturbing trends in higher education today.

II

Perhaps in more than any other area of academic endeavor, the necessity for embracing an "only connect" pedagogical philosophy in the literature classroom is of utmost importance. As Michael Bérubé argues:

> Literature is after all one of the fine arts, and not an explicitly social discipline . . . and it is on these grounds that cultural conservatives have criticized teachers like myself, who stress the social ramifications of literary works, for under-

emphasizing aesthetic considerations at the expense of political considerations. But literature cannot avoid being a *representational* art, which is why the ancients, in their wisdom, spoke not merely of its capacity to delight but of its potential to instruct as well. Literature . . . tends to be propositional, and on occasion it even contains specific propositions about the disposition of human social organization. I find it impossible, in ordinary classroom practice, to discuss literature in ways that do not involve worldviews, even when I am trying to make the simplest case about authorial intentionality.[16]

Indeed, the study of literature in the university demands a number of connections—between literary texts and students' lives, between popular culture and putatively canonical texts, between theory and experience, between English and a vast variety of texts and experiences from other disciplines, between the past and present, between academic realms and actual societal realms desperately in need of social justice reform—all of which lead to a critical reading of the world coalescing with a critical reading of the word.[17] Cultural Studies theorists and practitioners have long sought to achieve these vital conjunctions, and their insistence on trans-disciplinary work proves crucial to progressive professors and students of literature, by insisting that "some forms of advocacy are not merely *permitted* but positively *mandated* by certain fields of study."[18]

Although scholars have different degrees of anti-disciplinarity in mind when they invoke Cultural Studies, all are in agreement when it comes to the mandate to get beyond the reductive practice of working in hermetic areas of specialization.[19] Perhaps the most fundamental characteristics of Cultural Studies pedagogical praxes are a determination to be both inclusive and critical in analytical examination. These criteria often mean that professors must strategically move beyond the authorized texts traditionally available in their disciplines, and actively seek out alternative texts, literacies, epistemologies, and intellectual communities, since the "safe, superficial themes often foregrounded in anthologies and school textbooks do not usually lead us into authentic forms of Cultural Studies unless ways are found to engage the realities of the historical and cultural contexts in which we live."[20] The challenge is to move from canonical disciplinary notions of textuality to inclusive approaches to critical "alternative literacies" education that seeks what a number of critics call "useful knowledge," wherever it is to be found—in canonical or popular texts, in primary works or theoretical approaches, across disciplines and beyond university walls.[21] As Freire has suggested, we must read the world critically as well as reading the word critically, and our hermeneutic paradigms should incessantly strive for connection among these seemingly disparate readings; as Lisa Langstraat asserts, "we must theorize experience, but we must also experience theory."[22]

Hence, a Cultural Studies pedagogy may (or may not) begin with literature, but it subsequently moves across genres and forms, and away from traditional aesthetic expectations. In "doing" Cultural Studies, both students and professors should experience liberation, not only from conventional disciplines and pedagogical methodologies, but also from the "typical" lines of inquiry that usually over-determine and restrict where the analysis of intellectual communities in and out of the classroom can (and should) travel. Allen Cary-Webb offers a terrific model of a potential Cultural Studies methodological journey:

> In exploring a particular issue or theme, a cultural studies approach might involve doing a close and careful reading of one or more literary works, along with studying a television program, doing library research, and reading prose essays. Research papers can be combined with literary analysis, personal reflection, and argumentation. A cultural studies approach might lead us to compare traditional canonical authors with contemporary popular materials, including the mass media. Cultural studies invites a wide variety of new and potentially invigorating writing into teaching, such as interviews, ethnography, testimonials, surveys, film, and media analysis. It urges us to be self-reflective but not cavalier about the disciplines we work in. While mixing genres and crossing disciplinary boundaries, cultural studies spurs us also to consider how the establishment of genres and disciplines has functioned historically.[23]

This widely heteroglossic approach authorizes a truly student-centered environment for all learners in an intellectual community, allowing students to offer their own subjective areas of expertise to the collective scholarly conversation and validating their own life experiences as both important and worthy of academic inclusion. Furthermore, the final turn to self-reflexivity here establishes another crucial connection in a Cultural Studies methodology, the imperative commitment to be meta-critical in our own classrooms, to make our schooling itself visible to critique even while we are engaged in it.

Another crucial connection in an anti-disciplinary Cultural Studies pedagogy is between the past and present, which involves both the theoretical tactics of what Ann Cvetkovich and others call "presentism"—"understanding historical inquiry to be motivated by contemporary concerns that demand considerable attention to current conditions"[24]—and what James Clifford and others refer to as "Counter-Historicism."[25] The project with regard to each of these terms is to read history, past culture, and public memory not in a way that simply excavates an unassailable universal past, but to critique what historical narratives can reveal about the social and political conditions in which they were written. What might they tell us about the power dynamics and conditions of representation and production at that particular moment, and how do these concerns have continuing ideological consequences for the ways in which we are situated socially today? In other words, whose history and culture has been recorded? Whose history and culture has been marginalized or elided? What individuals and groups benefit from these *master*-narratives and which ones suffer because of the ways in which public memory gets co-opted and used as a tool of domination? What can we learn from seeing similar hegemonic patterns of oppression in historical, literary, and cultural narratives that speak to means of resistance and social justice in the present and future?[26] In an authentic Cultural Studies pedagogy of

connection we must certainly historicize, but also re-historicize; we must transcend passive reading practices that merely absorb a totalizing brand of history,
and become writers of alternative histories who critically produce culture as
well.

Hence, an anti-disciplinary Cultural Studies methodology must not only
practice counter-historicism, but also "what Antonio Gramsci calls 'counter-
hegemony.'"[27] Put simply, this kind of pedagogy insists on connecting all academic endeavor to democratic questions of social justice, the resistance to domination and oppression, and the actual transformation of conditions of suffering in
daily lives. Although this approach eschews becoming hegemonic itself, Cultural
Studies must remain political in the face of supposedly objective detractors, and
it must strive to achieve increased freedom and empowerment for all populations.[28] A genuinely liberatory pedagogy must *use* its resources as more than just
aesthetic or formal representations of a venerated discipline; in the case of literature, with all due respect to W. H. Auden, poetry must make something happen.
As Simon During reminds us: "Most individuals aspire and struggle the greater
part of their lives and it is easier to forget this if one is just interpreting texts
rather than thinking about reading as a life-practice."[29] Without this commitment
to actual social transformation, even reading various texts from a range of disciplines does not qualify as an authentic Cultural Studies pedagogy. As Peter Murphy insightfully maintains:

> Cultural Studies needs to unite its criticism of contemporary culture with a
> practice of cultural change. Rather than establishing a newer and shinier inter-
> disciplinary studies program, cultural studies can work to create a progressive,
> insurgent culture. The reason to bring together a communications department
> with a sociology department is not just to allow sociologists to examine popular
> culture but to teach them to make subversive videos. The reason to unite liter-
> ary theorists with drama professors is not to make better theater critics but to
> make better (that is, politically progressive) theater.[30]

The ultimate goal of an "only connect" Cultural Studies pedagogy is nothing
short of changing the world as we know it.

III

Although an anti-disciplinary Cultural Studies approach works well across literary genres and time periods, the nineteenth century proves an ideal moment to
scrutinize, since it is, as I have often told my students, the age in which the past
becomes the present. This quality is most tangible when studying the Victorian
novel in particular because of the tendencies of Victorian novels to be volumi-
nously dialogic and markedly didactic works.[31] Unfortunately, these texts are
rarely taught or written about in an "only connect" sense, since the predominant

materials available to professors of nineteenth-century British literature perpetu-
ate conventions that embrace disciplinarity in many forms. As Jay Clayton writes
about the "disconnect" between the Victorian age and our own worlds:

> the various schemes of periodization familiar to most literary scholars and his-
> torians of science actually serve to conceal the existence of any relationship be-
> tween these two times. Hence it is necessary to work toward a new understand-
> ing of cultural parallels in history, one that is as sensitive to disjunction as to
> recurrence, as careful in delineating gaps, discontinuities, and altered meanings
> as in making the comparisons that urgently need to be made.[32]

However, these comparisons generally are infrequent, as most students I first
encounter in nineteenth-century literature courses are accustomed to reading
these novels in isolation and from a present position of privilege and impunity.
They may find the gender oppression in Austen, Brontë, or Dickens lamentable,
or even shocking, but they do so in a way that belies their relief that things have
changed so much since these antiquated cultures existed, and that they, happily,
do not have to worry about such concerns anymore.

This disconnect is precisely why an anti-disciplinary Cultural Studies approach is so important; by only connecting, we offer an interventionist pedagogy
that allows students to apply what they read to their own lives, and examine the
continuity of forces in Victorian literature and culture with similar powers today.
Christine L. Krueger argues: "Rather than . . . reaching across a postmodern historical rupture when we construct a functional Victorian past, we may instead
begin to suspect how far we haven't come in one hundred years, that we appeal
to Victorian culture in order to think about problems and needs that are not
wholly unprecedented."[33]

Using this methodology in teaching the Victorian novel thereby disabuses
students of the previous hostile-workplace insularity that they have experienced
throughout their educational careers. In my experience, once students begin to
see this correlation with their own lives, they start engaging these texts in far
more meaningful ways, often finding them less intimidating and elitist, and certainly warming up to the challenge to share their own connections with our intellectual community.

However, professors as well as students often exhibit such an entrenchment
in disciplinarity that embracing an authentic form of anti-disciplinary Cultural
Studies seems problematic for them as well. As I personally have experienced on
the job market, at conferences, in the processes of publication, and elsewhere,
many intellectuals seem afraid of mixing up the traditional disciplines with regard to Victorian literature. Many undergraduate classrooms and English departments are resistant to opening up the curriculum in these ways.[34]

There have been some recent scholarly texts that embrace an inter-
disciplinary approach to Victorian literature in new and exciting ways, by connecting nineteenth-century cultural texts with postmodern forms, in an emergent

field tentatively labeled "Post-Victorianism." However, most of the criticism still refuses to take the final step toward political and pedagogical transformation.[35] Despite the exigency for these connections in terms of a Cultural Studies philosophy, some of these practicing scholars are unabashedly dismissive of such a methodological link.[36] I will suggest instead that a political Cultural Studies pedagogy that takes up Victorian studies can result in an enormous gain.

Although I employ an anti-disciplinary Cultural Studies methodology in all of the courses I teach, a single-author senior seminar in Charles Dickens might at first seem to pose more of a challenge than other subjects. First of all, on top of all the contextual historical material about the nineteenth century, and the pertinent background and narrative theory about the novel genre that one must cover, there is the daunting task of getting undergraduates to read multiple texts that approach one thousand pages in length in a single course. Second, very few scholars are publishing on Dickens from a Cultural Studies perspective, so there is a conspicuous lack of models for this pedagogy.[37] Hence, if a Cultural Studies approach can yield significant benefits despite these obstacles, it can work well in any literature classroom.

When I had my first opportunity to teach the senior seminar in Dickens after years of teaching the novels, I approached it in exactly these terms; I was determined to address Dickens with an inter-disciplinary or anti-disciplinary "only connect" mentality. We began the course with general discussions about why we read literature in the first place, exploring what we might hope to learn about our own twenty-first-century lives from imaginative texts written 150 years ago. Slowly but surely, my students began to identify the aspects of our worlds that literature helps us to negotiate: social constructs like race, gender, class, nationality, and sexuality; institutional forces exerted by schools, churches, workplaces, government agencies, law enforcement, military spheres, and mass media; and emotional resonances in their own lives like love, friendship, family, death, grief and loss, hope and fear, and individual identity. As a few students noticed at this point, these elements were all "connected" and all had to do with power, in different but related forms. Although they were somewhat puzzled at first that we had not yet uttered the word "Dickens" in a seminar supposedly devoted to him, they were clearly intrigued about the common denominator of empowerment our broad discussions about literature seemed to suggest.

After these general discussions, we read deeply about nineteenth-century (not just Victorian) historical, social, and cultural contexts, covering the French Revolution, the rise of mass literacy, charity and Sunday schools, increasing government control and social unrest, the age of reform, evolution, the Industrial Revolution, the "Woman Question," empire and colonialism, the rise of the novel, poverty, filth and disease, and the daily conditions and occupations of men and women across social hierarchies (such as the uneasy position of the governess). We then discussed the effects of periodization itself, and what it really means when we call something or someone "Victorian." Finally, we read the Romantic poet William Wordsworth, who exerted more influence over Victorian novelists than perhaps any of the previous era's writers, to prepare us for Dickens's treatment of such themes as memory and forgetting, the continuity of the self, and the disparities between the country and the city.

At this point, a couple of weeks into the course, my students were clearly thinking that it had to be time to read some Dickens. Nonetheless, we then turned to various inter-disciplinary and theoretical texts with which we could connect both the contextual material we had just read, and the Dickens texts we would soon (I promised) be reading. Some of the texts we read firsthand, other concepts I delineated in group discussion; we studied some central texts right away before beginning Dickens, but I also integrated others as they became primarily applicable. Over the semester, in addition to Dickens, we covered theoretical texts which included Nietzsche on truth, lies, language, and power; Foucault on panopticism and normalizing judgment, and other critics who invoke Foucault, such as D. A. Miller and Judith Butler; Althusser on ideological state apparatuses; Freud and others like Peter Brooks who take up Freud; Armstrong and Spivak on the link between gender, domestic space, nationality, and colonialism in the English novel; Gilbert and Gubar on gender and women's writing; Showalter on sexuality; a number of Cultural Studies texts by scholars like Giroux, Raymond Williams, and others about whom I have written in previous sections of this essay. We also introduced, as an intellectual community, a number of texts from popular culture, including films, television, advertising, animated works, popular fiction, mythology, fairy tales, amusement parks, network news, and other media. When we turned to the novels themselves, we were ultimately prepared to "only connect" Dickens with an abundance of other disciplines and with real lives outside of the university, a process to which I referred as our final "exigency move." As my students were now well aware, I would insist on this exigency component of the course in both class discussion of the novels and outside papers.[38] With the remaining space I have in this essay, I will briefly reproduce some of these valuable connections we made as an intellectual community, during our reading of (and correspondent writing about) three Dickens novels: *Bleak House, Hard Times,* and *Great Expectations.*

In reading *Bleak House,* we covered many of the topical themes one might expect: education and literacy, colonialism and empire, poverty and horrible living (and dying) conditions of the Victorian era, social class, and Dickens's scathing contempt for institutions such as the court of Chancery. However, with our anti-disciplinary approach, my students were far more prepared to make transcendent connections with our Dickensian texts, to both historicize and re-historicize, to make "Boz" meaningfully relevant to the here and now. We began by discussing the dangerous varieties of education and literacy in the novel, a subject for which we were well prepared by our lessons in historical context. My students immediately recognized such nineteenth-century issues as the trivial "accomplishments" education for girls, and the equally trivial classical education for young gentlemen, which significantly reduces Richard's acumen for living and working in a real-life setting. They easily identified those marginalized by their education, such as Caddy's inky bouts with literacy, the Smallweeds' Utilitarian education, and Krook's suspicious auto-didacticism, as well as the dangerous sites of education in the novel, like Turveydrop's school of deportment, Chadband's oppressive catechisms of Jo, and the school at Chesney Wold that indoctrinates its students in ruling-class dominant ideology. We also scrutinized Dickens's treatment of the disciplinary tactics deployed in nineteenth-century education to marginalize and compartmentalize at-risk learners such as women, the working classes and poor, and colonial populations—rote memorization, the catechistic method, and primers that taught literacy with scripts that reinforced subordination and exploitation.

As compelling as these discussions were, my students became even more engaged when we made those final "exigency" connections. In the case of education, we were able to apply *Bleak House* to many of the Cultural Studies writings we had read earlier and, hence, to our own encounters with schooling. My students, rather than deploring such unfortunate conditions in Dickens's era, began to notice similarities with our own times. One student argued that schools even today, with their reading groups in early grades and correspondent systems of tracking throughout, are much more about social control and hierarchizing social classes and job opportunities than they are about liberation or empowerment. Another student pointed to the disparities among academic resources and their connection to capital via such economic forces as property taxes. Another noted the differences in the quality of education based on one's race or gender, and how contemporary pedagogy, both in schools and popular media, still enforces limitations on individuals (boys do analytical math and science; girls pursue the more emotional humanities). Their readings in Althusser allowed them to identify the school as the primary "civilizing" state ideological apparatus, their study of Foucault prepared them to recognize the ways in which schools make docile bodies visible (attendance, pop quizzes, seating in rows) and how that contributed to the conformity of normalizing judgment. These theoretical lines of inquiry coalesced when they realized that education was merely one of these sites of power and control in their lives.

Indeed, they "only connected" education with the forces of colonialism in the novel, when a few students had the epiphany that Dickens might be attacking a number of social institutions in similar ways. Hence, we discussed colonialism and empire in the novel not just in terms of the nineteenth-century texts we read, or the theoretical positions we had explored, but again in terms of our own twenty-first-century lives. My students were able to chart the similarities between England's presence in India, Africa, and the Caribbean, and the United States' occupation of many locations around the world, most prevalently, of course, the Middle East. We critically addressed Dickens's concerns about neglecting "obligations of home" in favor of imperial expansion with the United States' Gulf Wars abroad, in spite of the tremendous social problems we still suffer at home, such as homelessness, poverty, and the constant neglect and demonization of our youth. My students ably made comparisons between Dickens's Telescopic Philanthropy and the "war on terror" tactics of distraction, and also connected spurious philanthropy overseas with a religious hegemony and thirst for global power. They also diagnosed how charity was tied to class warfare, both in *Bleak House* and today. Jo's homelessness and the Victorian attitude that poverty was the fault of the poor, a symptom of moral failing on their part rather than an indication of systemic oppression, triggered discussions about welfare reform and Rudolph Giuliani's "solution" for the poor in New York City, who, like Jo, were told to "move on." Skimpole's suggestion that Jo would be better off in prison than on the streets, since he cannot find sufficient food or medical care, and his subsequent smallpox contamination of Esther, led students to note with great excitement Dickens's continuing relevance on such issues as universal healthcare, socialized medicine, and crime and punishment. In more ways than perhaps ever before, Dickens really mattered to my students and their lives.

In reading *Hard Times*, the class quite naturally turned to education first in this novel as well, since much of Dickens's text deals directly with the perils of a Utilitarian educational system that adjures students to "never wonder." Having examined a number of themes about the dangers of education today during our inter-disciplinary Cultural Studies work, my students were able to "only connect" Dickens's critique of Utilitarianism with the increasing corporatizing of schools today and the very hostile workplace directives about which I have been writing throughout this essay. One student noticed how destructive this "just the facts" education was for Louisa, who throws herself away on Bounderby; Tom, who becomes both whelp and criminal; and Sissy, who has her vital individuality and free thinking both disciplined and punished by the catechistic method. Another recognized how this pedagogy of "disconnection" provides Louisa precise scientific knowledge of insects without any practical knowledge of the men and women in societal forces, while it also creates corporate monsters like the servile Bitzer. Others connected *Hard Times* to our current losses of arts, music, and humanities programs, in favor of business, computers, and skills courses, and the subsequent lack of preparation for social challenge and transformation that such a curriculum promotes. A few particularly perceptive students suggested that Dickens's alternative literacies in the text, such as the circus, fairy tales and adventure narratives, and the industrial landscapes and fires that Louisa reads, actually anticipate a Cultural Studies mentality that looks for epistemologies beyond books—reading the world as well as the word.

My students again discerned how the different ideological state apparatuses worked together, identifying the ways in which the school prepared one for future exploitation in the factory in Dickens, or in the corporate United States today. *Hard Times* spoke to them directly about such concerns as favoring industry and technology over individual quality of life, losing democratic free speech, stopping the ravages of pollution and the decimation of the environment, and leveling the great inequities dividing the two nations of rich and poor, both in Victorian England and twenty-first-century America. They connected Coketown and Victorian writings by Engels and Mayhew, on the poverty of the "great towns" and the segregation of rich and poor, to a similar strategy of invisibility that obtains in our own great towns like Baltimore, with its tourist-driven "Inner Harbor" and hidden tenements only blocks away. They analyzed the division of labor in both eras, as well as the infantilizing of the poor and the correspondent, seemingly paradoxical paternalism that constantly invades workers' privacy and extends work space and time,[39] yet cuts benefits, health care, pensions, and other programs that might make their lives more humane. We also explored the representations of the country and city in Dickens with similar media representations of inner city populations in network news, sit-coms, and film, theorizing such images as performative interpretations. As my students realized, schools paved the way ideologically for all of these various social conditions.

In reading *Great Expectations*, we again dealt briefly with education (with Miss Havisham's damaging tutelage of Estella) and social class, and the corrupting influence of business life in the city, touching on Jaggers, who washes the filth of commerce away with his scented soap, and Wemmick, whose home is literally his castle, replete with a moat for protection against the sordid influences of public life. But we moved quickly beyond these issues to address normalizing judgment in the novel, especially in terms of gender and class, embodied in Dickens's layered use of the word "gentleman." My students aptly noticed the chasm between society's definition of the term and the challenges and complications that Dickens seemed to have in mind. Pip's conventional understanding of the category led us to explore how our own gender and class identities are constructed for us in everyday life. We discussed reigning conceptions of gender that saturate the media, and the cultural pedagogy that associates hypermasculinity, violence, and cold stoicism with being a man, and the objectification of physical beauty and submissiveness that inscribe popular conceptions of femininity for women. We scrutinized texts from both periods during this study, reading Robert Browning's poems "Porphyria's Lover" and "My Last Duchess" to reveal possessive, controlling, and violent masculinity, and submissive and abused women in the Victorian age, alongside Disney animated films such as *The Little Mermaid* and *Beauty and the Beast*, which normalized for very young viewers male dominance, female sacrifice, domestic abuse, and terrifying messages about physical beauty. We then screened documentaries about gender by the Media Education Foundation, *Killing Us Softly 3* and *Tough Guise*, which amplified gender connections and added elements of class and race to constructions of desire.

When we returned to *Great Expectations*, a number of students recognized how strictly Dickens's characters adhered to contemporary definitions of identity. They especially noticed how normative gender roles for women were—all of Dickens's good women, like Biddy and Clara, conformed to the domestic ideal of sacrificing women in the Victorian age; *all* of the women who stepped beyond such narrow constructs, such as Estella, Mrs. Joe (a telling name), Miss Havisham, Molly, and Joe's mother, were disciplined and punished, all physically and psychologically abused, wild beasts tamed. My students connected this

domestic abuse with other Dickens moments, such as the abusive brickmakers in
Bleak House, but also to their encounters with domestic abuse in their own lives,
which provided some of the most profound moments of class discussion of the
entire semester. Eventually, most students concluded that the predominant objective of Dickens's novel is to offer more liberatory alternative definitions of both
gender and class, using Joe to rewrite both categories as an authentic "gentleman."

When it came time to approach our writing assignments in our anti-
disciplinary study of Dickens, I again insisted that my students transcend the
typical university literature papers that frequently investigate particular themes,
characters, or historical and literary connections, but almost always succumb to a
disciplinary paradigm that allows them to remain exclusively in the realm of the
text. Although they began to write papers within this more expected literary
style, I reminded them that their papers should be adding to the collective voice
of the intellectual community that we created together. Hence, only connecting
their literary analysis with multiple and various discursive epistemologies and
methodologies would be required, as would making the leap from the mid-
Victorian age of Dickens to our own times. Most importantly, their writing
equally must connect the scholarly interests that they desired to explore in Dickens with crucially important forces that they faced in their daily lives, preferably
in such a way as would prove potentially transformative in negotiating specific
social ills. Although they would begin with Dickens' text, and deploy many of
the critical writing strategies upon which English students often rely, they would
also go beyond that limited arena. They did not, as many critics of Cultural Studies often fear, ignore Dickens' texts in favor of more polemical "victim studies"
narratives; a Cultural Studies pedagogy never raises a binary "either/or" di-
lemma, but rather embraces a "this *and* that" dynamic. In other words, if my students historicized Dickens's novels, they also re-historicized them in the context
of their own lives. To some degree, they wrote in ways that were already very
familiar to them; in other ways, they were integrating and transcending academic
disciplines in a manner that they had never imagined possible.

The papers I received were as profound and exigent as the class discussions.
One young woman wrote about mental illness in *Bleak House*, diagnosing the
ways in which institutional forces wear away at the mind and soul, for characters
like Miss Flite, Gridley, Richard, and Skimpole, and connecting this analysis to
her own father's struggles with life in the military and, subsequently, the business world. Another student wrote about the alternative conceptions of family
that the circus community authorized and validated in *Hard Times*, and how
Dickens helped him to negotiate his own alternative family dynamic. Yet another
examined Pip and Esther Summerson in terms of trauma theory, primal scenes,
and Freud's notion of the compulsion to repeat, with regard to the continuity of
her own personal trauma. In each case, this student-centered, anti-disciplinary
Cultural Studies approach led to both a better knowledge of the primary works
and historical context, and a transcendent engagement with literature that spoke

directly to real lives. Instead of learning in strict disciplinary ways that hostile workplace directives dictate, my students were able to "only connect," and that made all the difference.

Notes

1. E. M. Forster, *Howards End* (New York: Signet Books, 1992), 148.
2. David Sadker, "Foreword," in *Women in Literature: Reading Through the Lens of Gender* (Westport, CT: Greenwood Press, 2003), xxi.
3. I have argued elsewhere for the benefits of adopting a Cultural Studies approach in the university literature classroom. See, for example, Eric G. Lorentzen, "Why the Novel (Still) Matters: Doing Student-Centered Cultural Studies in the Literature Classroom." *The Review of Education/Pedagogy/Cultural Studies* 26, no. 4 (October-December 2004): 289-311. This article serves as a more general introduction to the subject, and deals predominantly with teaching lower-level general education courses in literature, using George Orwell's *Animal Farm* as its primary example. My general premise, that a Cultural Studies methodology in the university literature classroom is a necessity, serves as the foundation to the more detailed and specific argument I am making here. Furthermore, I do not deal with the issues of hostile workplace legislation nor with the specific applications of this methodology for upper-level capstone courses, such as a senior seminar in Dickens, in my previous article.
4. In terms of my own ostensible "discipline," I was hired as an assistant professor of nineteenth-century British literature and, although I am fortunate that the liberal arts university at which I teach largely supports and often practices the kinds of inter-disciplinary approaches about which I am writing, my putative professional area of expertise is in the Victorian novel—hence the senior seminar in Dickens. Some of the methodological classroom examples I use in this article have originated in a variety of my upper-level courses in Victorian literature and the Victorian novel, in which I taught Dickens.
5. See Henry A. Giroux, *The Abandoned Generation: Democracy Beyond the Culture of Fear* (New York: Palgrave Macmillan, 2003), 23. Giroux goes on to argue about this particular case that: "Patriotism in this view becomes a euphemism for shutting down dissent, eliminating critical dialogue, and condemning critical citizenship in the interest of conformity and a dangerous departure from what it means to uphold a viable democracy. Needless to say, teachers in both K-12 and higher education are particularly vulnerable to these forms of censorship, particularly if they attempt to engage their students in discussions that critically explore the historical, ideological, and political contexts of the attacks and the underlying causes of terrorism, not to mention any controversial subject that calls into question the authority and role of the United States in domestic and foreign affairs. Such censorship shuts down critical inquiry in the schools and prevents students from learning how to distinguish an explanation from a justification" (24).
6. See Peter F. Murphy, "Cultural Studies as Praxis: A Working Paper," *College Literature* 19, no. 2 (1992): 39, who argues: "Professors as intellectuals can no longer deceive themselves into believing they serve some neutral, objective truth 'when in fact they are deeply involved in battles 'about the status of truth and the economic and political role it plays.'"

7. Carol Stabile, "Pedagogues, Pedagogy, and Political Struggle," in *Class Issues: Pedagogy, Cultural Studies, and the Public Sphere* (New York and London: New York University Press, 1997), 217.

8. George Lipsitz, "Class and Consciousness: Teaching about Social Class in Public Universities," in *Class Issues: Pedagogy, Cultural Studies, and the Public Sphere* (New York and London: New York University Press, 1997), 10. See also Henry A. Giroux and Susan Searls Giroux, *Take Back Higher Education: Race, Youth, and the Crisis of Democracy in the Post-Civil Rights Era* (New York: Palgrave Macmillan, 2004), who, citing Walter Lippman, argue similarly about the project of schooling for "the masses, whose education would train them to be obedient workers and passive spectators rather than participants in shaping democratic public life" (6).

9. For the banking concept of education, see Paulo Freire, *Pedagogy of the Oppressed* (New York: Continuum International Publishing Group Inc., 2000), 71-86. See also Ronald Strickland, "Pedagogy and Public Accountability," in *Class Issues: Pedagogy, Cultural Studies, and the Public Sphere* (New York and London: New York University Press, 1997), 166, who argues against both disciplinarity and the banking concept of education for postmodern pedagogies.

10. Mary Evans, "A Good School Revisited," in *Women's Lives into Print: The Theory, Practice and Writing of Feminist Auto/Biography* (New York: St. Martin's Press, 1999), 174. She continues: "Central to that experience of school was, I now think, a feeling of emotional and political impotence. How was I ever to claim a place, indeed make a place, in the public world, if we were taught in ways that seemed set on its eternal evasion? . . . Even if we were (very fully) encouraged to do well in education, there seemed to be a sense of unwritten boundaries, of how far we could go without destroying the whole edifice of learning and education."

11. Henry A. Giroux, "Reading Texts, Literacy, and Textual Authority," in *Falling into Theory: Conflicting Views on Reading Literature* (Boston: Bedford Books, 1994), 69. Giroux also addresses the dangerous implications of pedagogical domination more particularly in terms of literacy education and the English classroom, arguing that "students are silenced in the interest of dominant culture that wants to produce citizens who are passive rather than critical and actively engaged in the reconstruction of society."

12. The phrase is Stuart Hall's, quoted in Lawrence Grossberg, *Bringing It All Back Home: Essays on Cultural Studies* (Durham & London: Duke University Press, 1997), 380.

13. See Giroux, *The Abandoned Generation*, 27, who argues that we must recognize and expose that "consumerism and the squelching of dissent are mutually reinforcing aspects of a patriotism in which citizenship is more about the freedom to buy than the ability of individuals to engage in 'critical public dialogue and broadened civic participation leading (so it is hoped) to far-reaching change.'" See also, Henry A. Giroux, *Impure Acts: The Practical Politics of Cultural Studies* (New York: Routledge, 2000), 11, for his related commentary on recognizing the dangerous effects of corporate schooling.

14. A representative example would be James Carlin's appointment to the Massachusetts Board of Education in 1998. As a multi-millionaire former insurance executive, his prescriptions for higher education indicate just how dangerous corporatizing the university can be. See Giroux, *The Abandoned Generation*, 175: "First, he argued that higher education had to model itself after successful corporations, and this means that colleges and universities have to be downsized. Second, he echoed the now familiar call on the part of corporate culture to abolish tenure. Third, he made it clear that democratic governance was not in keeping with the corporate model of the university and that faculty

have too much power in shaping decisions in the university. Finally, he explicitly condemned those forms of knowledge whose value lie outside of their practical application in the marketplace."

15. Giroux, *The Abandoned Generation*, 73.

16. Bérubé, *The Employment of English: Theory, Jobs, and the Future of Literary Studies* (New York and London: New York University Press, 1998), 174, original emphasis.

17. Paulo Freire, *Teachers as Cultural Workers: Letters to Those Who Dare Teach* (Boulder, CO: Westview Press, 2005), 40, original emphasis. See also, Paulo Freire and Donaldo Macedo, *Literacy: Reading the Word and the World* (Massachusetts: Bergin & Garvey Publishers, Inc., 1987), 122.

18. Bérubé, 178, original emphasis. A number of scholars have commented on the ways in which a rigid professional disciplinarity endangers the efficacy of teaching literature in the university English classroom. See also Ronald Strickland, "Pedagogy and Public Accountability," in *Class Issues: Pedagogy, Cultural Studies, and the Public Sphere* (New York and London: New York University Press, 1997), 168-69; Stabile, 216; and Giroux, *The Abandoned Generation*, 189-90.

19. For example, see Peter Brooker, "Why Brecht, Or, Is There English After Cultural Studies?" *Essays and Studies* 40 (1987): 27, who argues: "From its elected position on the margins of the academic establishment, cultural studies offers neither a discipline, nor multi-discipline base for a reconstructed English, nor a new set of courses and texts. Instead, it presents a radicalizing mentality, both intellectual and political, which is applicable to all texts." See also Rory Ryan, "The Social Life of Literature: Cultural Studies, Cultural Ethnography and the Future of Literary Studies," *Journal of Literary Studies* 12 no. 1-2 (1996): 4, who suggests that "the practice of cultural studies has never made claim to being a discipline. Rather, it has been a response, an intervention, and an intellectual politics." See Peter F. Murphy, "Cultural Studies as Praxis: A Working Paper," *College Literature* 19, no. 2 (1992): 31 who maintains: "Cultural Studies, embodies not just an inter-disciplinary approach but at times an anti-disciplinary perspective." See also Carolyn Williams, "Introduction: Victorian Studies and Cultural Studies," *Victorian Literature and Culture* 27, no. 2 (1999): 356, who, echoing Ed Cohen, insists that as "a disciplinary formation, cultural studies is marked by its resistance—its interdisciplinarity, transdisciplinarity, or even its saliently 'undisciplined' character." Williams also stipulates for cultural studies' "attempt to reconceive inter-disciplinary studies with an eye toward a greater historical, social, and methodological self-consciousness" (356) and "its central concerns with issues of identity, power, and representation, its aim to analyze forms of social determination and to identify individual and group agency in specifically cultural terms" (356). Similarly, Henry A. Giroux, in "Is There a Place for Cultural Studies in Colleges of Education?" in *Education and Cultural Studies: Toward a Performative Practice* (Routledge: New York and London, 1997), 233, emphasizes that the "slavish adherence to structuring the curriculum around disciplines is at odds with the field of cultural studies, whose theoretical energies are largely focused on issues regarding gender, class, sexuality, national identity, colonialism, race, ethnicity, cultural popularism, textuality, and critical pedagogy." He adds that "cultural studies is premised on the belief that the traditional distinctions that separate and frame established academic disciplines cannot account for the great diversity of cultural and social phenomena that has come to characterize an increasingly hybridized, postindustrial world" (235). See also Grossberg, who propounds that "cultural studies renounces the power of the institutional boundaries

of disciplines in favor of doing the work necessary, wherever it is, to begin to provide better answers" (14).

20. Allen Carey-Webb, *Literature and Lives: A Response-Based Cultural Studies Approach to Teaching English* (Urbana: National Council of Teachers of English, 2001), 25.

21. See Richard Johnson, quoted in Brooker, 27, who distinguishes this kind of a Cultural Studies pedagogy of useful knowledge "by its openness and theoretical versatility, its reflexive, even self-conscious, mood and, especially, the importance of critique. I mean critique . . . in the fullest sense: not criticism merely, nor even polemic, but procedures by which other traditions are approached both for what they may yield and for what they inhibit. Critique involves stealing away the more useful elements and rejecting the rest. It involves appropriation, not just rejection. From this point of view cultural studies is a process, a kind of alchemy for producing useful knowledge." See also Simon Frith, "Literary Studies as Cultural Studies—Whose Literature? Whose Culture?" *Critical Quarterly* 34, no. 2 (1992): 19, who combines these elements of connection and critique in slightly different terms: "cultural studies should be an exploration of how the 'commercial' and the 'literary' between them articulate the 'popular.'"

22. See Freire, *Teachers as Cultural Workers*, 34 and Freire and Macedo, 35; and Lisa Langstraat, "Gender Literacy in the Cultural Studies Composition Classroom: 'Fashioning' the 'Self' Through an Analysis of Popular Magazines," *Works and Days* 14 (1996): 170.

23. Carey-Webb, *Literature and Lives*, 8. See also Mary Poovey, "Cultural Criticism: Past and Present," in *Understanding Others: Cultural and Cross-Cultural Studies and the Teaching of Literature* (Urbana: National Council of Teachers of English, 1992), 4-5.

24. Ann Cvetkovich, "Histories of Mass Culture: From Literary to Visual Culture," *Victorian Literature and Culture* 27, no. 2 (1999): 498.

25. Quoted in Kate Flint, "Counter-Historicism, Contact Zones, and Cultural History," *Victorian Literature and Culture* 27, no. 2 (1999): 507-11. See also Carey-Webb, *Literature and Lives*, who argues: "Meaningful cultural studies themes emerge out of social and historical realities and they challenge us to identify and forge authentic connections between the present and other time periods, and between our cultures and those of other people" (25). For a more specific example of this practice, see chapter 4 (79-105), entitled "Shakespeare and the New Multicultural British and World Literatures," in which his pedagogical objectives include "putting Shakespeare in context, examining the relevance of his work to the controversies of his day, and developing conceptions of history that connect Shakespeare's time and our own, offer to rescue Shakespeare from an abstract 'greatness' and make his works meaningful to students and their lives in today's world" (80).

26. See Giroux, *The Abandoned Generation*, 29, who expostulates: "Public schools should play a decisive role in helping students think about the relationship between history and the present, incorporating a critical understanding of events that are often left out of contemporary interpretations that define the roles students might play as critical citizens. American history should not be presented to students free of the many conflicts and struggles waged by women, workers, people of color, and others who have tried to erase the gap between the reality and the promise of democracy." Giroux writes frequently and compellingly about our need to connect the past, in terms of history and public memory, to the present. For example, see *Impure Acts*, 36-37, and Giroux and Searls Giroux, 105.

27. Freire and Macedo, *Literacy*, 36.

28. Indeed, as Giroux writes in, "Disturbing the Peace: Writing in the Cultural Studies Classroom," *College Literature* 20:2 (1993): 14, "Cultural Studies must be grounded, in part, in a project that deepens and expands the possibilities for radical democracy both in the United States and abroad. Democracy in this sense is the discursive face and lived experiences of struggling to expand the conditions for social justice, freedom, and equality across all the major political and economic spheres that shape, position, and locate people in everyday life." See also Giroux and Searls Giroux, 111, who argue: "While no pedagogical intervention should fall to the level of propaganda, a pedagogy that attempts to empower critical citizens can't and shouldn't avoid politics. Pedagogy must address the relationship between politics and agency, knowledge and power, subject positions and values, and learning and social change, while always being open to debate, resistance, and a culture of questioning"; and Brooker, 22-23, who similarly suggests that cultural studies is not about proselytizing: "These emergent, and of course often marginalized forms, in writing, music, publishing, theatre and in community politics have no single academic discipline at their centre, and no single political party either, but exert a political influence and have points of real contact all the same, both inside and outside the educational establishment."

29. During, 2. Brooker argues in a related vein: "'specific' intellectuals, in different areas and institutions, are also answerable to the criterion of 'useful knowledge.' Marx spoke of philosophers as only interpreting the world when the point is to change it. But this is a thesis we need now to revise as we recall it. For interpretations, or what we might prefer to call ideological constructions or representations, do have power in the world. They help define and control our place in it. A critique of dominant 'interpretations' can therefore *help* redefine and so change the world. *If* this critique and the new meanings it puts into circulation are useful, and gain consent. This is a limited, oblique, and uncertain power for change, but if modern 'philosophers,' including writers, teachers, and critics, and students of literary discourse, do not exercise it, they will assist in maintaining the world as it is" (28, original emphasis). See also Stuart Hall: "The work that cultural studies has to do is to mobilize everything that it can find in terms of intellectual resources in order to understand what keeps making the lives we live, and the societies we live in, profoundly and deeply anti-humane" (quoted in Grossberg, 380).

30. Murphy, 38.

31. For my discussion of the efficacy of Cultural Studies for other genres beyond the Victorian novel, such as poetry and the short story, see Lorentzen, 305-6.

32. Jay Clayton, *Charles Dickens in Cyberspace: The Afterlife of the Nineteenth Century in Postmodern Culture* (Oxford: Oxford University Press, 2003), 9. Clayton's connections between the time periods are often fascinating, although his analysis belongs more firmly to the emergent practice of "Post-Victorianism" than it does to cultural studies: "There are odd parallels between the two times, conjunctions that share a weird, long-hidden logic. Some of the most notable of these parallels include: the telegraph and the Internet; Babbage's Analytical Engine and the digital computer; nineteenth-century sound technology and virtual reality; Frankenstein's monster and genetic clones; automata and artificial life research" (8). His methodology also includes looking consciously at Victorian culture for what it might reveal about getting beyond disciplinarity today.

33. Christine L. Krueger, "Introduction," in *Functions of Victorian Culture at the Present Time* (Athens, OH: Ohio University Press, 2002), xii. She stipulates: "Even in our most anxious, ambivalent, or hostile responses to Victorian culture, we often find ourselves contributing to a critique—of capitalism, nationalism, gender roles, for exam-

ple—that had its counterpart, if not origins, in Victorian cultural criticism." Williams argues similarly: "Global Anglophone culture has been in the making for hundreds of years, and it must be studied across the entire trajectory of its lengthy history, from the perspective of our present moment (of transnational capital) and from the perspective of the Victorian period as well, for the perhaps altogether obvious reason that it was the crucial period of imperial expansion. Both cultural studies and Victorian studies, in other words, have their national dimensions, and their transnational or global dimensions. Exploring the conjunctions and disjunctions of these various perspectives—'Victorian,' 'transatlantic,' and 'global'—should be one of our primary goals" (362). Cvetkovich expands on her idea of presentism thus: "So much of what we take for granted as the present has its origins in the nineteenth century, including most of the disciplinary categories through which we produce knowledge. Thus the Victorian period is not simply the past as other. At the same time, it is not simply the same; part of its fascination is the possibility of doing what Nancy Armstrong has called an ethnography of our own culture, seeing familiar cultural trends estranged enough to be able to see them anew" (498-499). See also Michael Steig, *"David Copperfield* and Shared Reader Response," in *Approaches to Teaching Dickens's David Copperfield* (New York: The Modern Language Association of America, 1984), 147.

34. See Lorentzen, 291, where I argue: "To talk about gender roles and the patriarchal gaze with respect to Robert Browning's poetry is to neglect the form of the dramatic monologue; to examine Brontë's treatment of classist education in *Jane Eyre* in light of today's politics of education is somehow to do a disservice to 'real' or 'actual' history; to enlarge the range of texts we read in an English course to include films, television, museums, shopping malls, comic books, fashion magazines, and other works of popular culture is to ignore the essential 'serious' texts we putatively share as a civilized culture." I am arguing against such prevalent attitudes here. See, for example, John Kucich, "Cultural Studies, Victorian Studies, and Graduate Education," *Victorian Literature and Culture* 27, no. 2 (1999): 478, who writes about the invasion of what he characterizes as a Cultural Studies mentality in his graduate courses: "These days, when we discuss a text in my graduate seminar, my students have only two general questions they want to answer. First: how racist, sexist, or classist is this text? And, second, what generalized forces of subversion, discursive or otherwise, might it mobilize anyway? I don't quite understand how we've gone from discovering that these are good questions to ask, to assuming that they're the only questions worth asking."

35. I am thinking primarily of Clayton's interesting work, the collection edited by Krueger, and another text, *Victorian Afterlife: Postmodern Culture Rewrites the Nineteenth Century*, ed. John Kucich and Dianne F. Sadoff (Minneapolis: University of Minnesota Press, 2000). Many of the studies found herein make remarkably cogent connections between our time and the Victorian era, and constitute a body of criticism that is one of the more fresh and exciting approaches to Victorian studies today. However, few of them take the final steps toward exigency, resistance, empowerment, and transformative pedagogy upon which a Cultural Studies philosophy insists.

36. John Kucich, for example, writes of Cultural Studies as a blight on Victorian studies rather than as an opportunity for fostering students' agency: "It seems to me that the unilateral political imperatives of cultural studies impoverish not just literary knowledge, but general cultural knowledge as well. Victorian studies, which has been and ought to remain such a fertile area for cultural studies research, given the explosion of printed popular materials—as well as the development of other popular media like photography—in the nineteenth century, has suffered, I think, an enormous loss as a result"

(478). His words of caution about "the unilateral political imperatives of cultural studies," a premise with which I disagree, to me co-exist uneasily with the collection he co-edited on Victorian literature's relevance for postmodern culture (see note 34), and seem to indicate a nostalgia for certain facets of disciplinarity. He writes of his students: "They all need to find a hot new topic, and to politicize it fast. Before we can reform the intellectual structures of our discipline, we had better come to terms with the marketplace forces that are deforming our intellectual landscape so terribly" (480). I would add that we must take cautions about institutionally devaluing Cultural Studies, such as Grossberg has made, to heart: "In too many places, cultural studies is being institutionalized in ways that merely reproduce the structure of area studies, or of the English or communication departments in which so many of us were educated and are located. One result is that 'interdisciplinarity' is often used as a rhetorical weapon against the disciplines instead of as a productive challenge to build new relations and to change our own research practices. The fact is that what passes for interdisciplinarity is too often little more than cross-disciplinary theoretical dabbling" (2).

37. Jay Clayton, however, does insist on the necessity for connecting Dickens and postmodernism, albeit more from a critical and scholarly perspective than a pedagogical one. See Jay Clayton, "Dickens and the Genealogy of Postmodernism," *Nineteenth-Century Literature* 46, no. 2 (1991): 184.

38. In terms of the writing I have asked my students to do in a number of courses, one that "only connects" their own lives with the texts we read, I have been influenced, in part, by Giroux's concept of "border writing." See Giroux, "Disturbing the Peace," 18-24.

39. In Dickens's text, through Bounderby's treatment of Stephen; in twenty-first-century life, via computer monitoring, cell phones, and PDAs.

Chapter Ten
From *Things Fall Apart*
to *Freedom Dreams*:
Black Studies and Cultural Studies in the
Composition Classroom

Randi Gray Kristensen

Michael Omi and Howard Winant, in *Racial Formation in the United States*, cite the Phipps case of the early 1980s, where the plaintiff lost her suit against the state of Louisiana to change her racial classification from black to white. Their analysis pursues the question of what the meaning of "race" is in America.[1] The question that interests me is why Phipps wanted to change her classification. What was wrong with being black? If Phipps had a traditional U.S. education, she probably had every insight into blackness as lack and pathology, and little to no awareness of black intellectuality and agency. These absences reflect the unfinished business of race in America.

Some of our students grow up in multicultural America, and are more sophisticated than many of their instructors; many more still grow up in what I call apartheid America, racially and often class-segregated enclaves where they are taught selective notions about themselves and their "Others." As Audre Lorde notes:

> Institutionalized rejection of difference is an absolute necessity in a profit economy which needs outsiders as surplus people. As members of such an economy, we have all been programmed to respond to the human differences between us with fear and loathing and to handle that difference in one of three ways: ignore it, and if that is not possible, copy it if we think it is dominant, or destroy it if we think it is subordinate. But we have no patterns for relating across our human differences as equals. As a result, those differences have been misnamed and misused in the service of separation and confusion.[2]

The course I'm about to describe draws on Black Studies and Cultural Studies to begin an intervention; I make no pretense that at the end of it we have formed new patterns for relating across our human differences as equals. But at least we have called into question whether "fear and loathing" are worthy responses to difference.

The George Washington University's new literacy requirements require students to take "University Writing," a four-credit class in their first year, and one Writing in the Disciplines class in each of their sophomore and junior years. The first year courses share a template, but each course takes its own theme. We hope students will choose classes that develop their writing skills through engagement with material that both interests and challenges them. For several years, I taught a version of University Writing with the theme of "Writing Cultures in Africa and the African Diaspora," where writing is a verb—to write about cultures—and an adjective—cultures that use writing.

African and African Diaspora texts are often openly self-reflexive in their consideration of questions of language and argument. They deliberately foreground issues of audience, purpose, evidence, and rhetorical strategy in ways that draw the attention of students back to fundamental assumptions about critical thinking, reading, and writing, thus renewing student engagement with writing and its possibilities. Using these texts has proved very useful for moving students, who may well be competent writers within the template of their high school writing instruction, into a more careful, thoughtful, and academically rigorous stance toward their own writing. In addition, because of the cultural specificity of the texts, the reading and writing assignments draw student attention to the significant role of context—cultural, disciplinary, and generic—in affecting rhetorical choices.

Most accounts of using African and African Diaspora texts in composition focus first on their significance for students of African descent, and second on the ways they demonstrate specific African American tropes. I focus on how such texts are also significant in multicultural classrooms. I argue that they deconstruct disciplinarity and Eurocentricity, as well as draw fresh attention to the power of language, and language as power. The first part of this chapter discusses the theoretical basis for this approach, and the second part demonstrates the application of these theories with examples from the texts and assignments used in the course.

The incorporation of Cultural Studies into the U.S. academic paradigm has prompted a crisis for Black Studies programs and advocates by threatening to reproduce the history of American amnesia toward Black intellectual productivity. In effect, Cultural Studies offers to absorb the critical perspectives of traditionally under-represented groups in the academy by offering a protective umbrella in politically beleaguered times. The notion of an academic Rainbow Coalition has its attractions and strategic usefulness, but many practitioners of Black Studies are compelled to remind their enthusiastic colleagues that, from the point of view of Black Studies, Cultural Studies is "old wine in new bottles." That is, if Black Studies imagines a historical origin in W.E.B. Du Bois' *The Souls of Black Folk* (1903),[3] Cultural Studies' identifiable practices of interdisciplinarity, historical contextualization, and critical attention to popular culture and academic practice have been mainstays of the Black intellectual tradition, which has been (and arguably continues to be) much less enthusiastically wel-comed. Negotiated responses have ranged from articulating the specificity of Black Studies as an emerging discipline without reifying its borders, which Ma-rio Azevedo calls for in "African-American Studies and the State of the Art," to connecting Black Studies with British Cultural Studies of the London and Bir-mingham Schools as a global field, as do Manthia Diawara and Stuart Hall, to Wahneema Lubiano's call for the visibility of the Cultural Studies project within Afro-American studies. Mae G. Henderson and Barbara Christian argue for Black Cultural Studies as a historical and contemporary project of multi-disciplinary, cross-cultural, attention to Black culture and experience that simul-taneously "challenges received and conventional disciplinary paradigms in the construction of knowledge."[4] Manning Marable responds to that call in the 21st century, noting that the Black intellectual tradition is not only descriptive and prescriptive, it is also corrective because it has made a "concerted attempt to challenge and to critique the racism and stereotypes that have been ever present in the main discourse of white academic institutions."[5]

In class, I draw attention to the struggles of Black people to construct a Self in language, usually that of their oppressive Others, that incorporates the quali-ties of the Other without reproducing the hierarchical epistemological violence of the initial model. Since most critical, feminist, literary, economic, psycho-logical, anthropological, social and cultural theory has been developed either in the absence of or in contrast to the devalued qualities of Black people, this work relies on the corrective re-visioning of scholars who have either posited the cen-trality of Black experiences in the modern era, or examined closely the signifi-cance of peripheral, marginal, or oppressed locations. This approach is less cen-trifugal than perspectival. I am not arguing to replace Eurocentric models with Afrocentric ones, but rather am asking what we are able to perceive if we locate Black people's experience as fundamental human experience. In other words, the ongoing project of decolonizing higher education can be furthered by (a) not presuming the universality of prior theory based on a limited, and exclusive, range of human experience and (b) illuminating particular contributions by Black writers that offer useful lenses for renegotiating the historically oppressive and repressive relationship between Self and Other which has produced the ne-cessity for such decolonizing work. Thus, the class aims to bring to the surface a counter-narrative of resistance to the dehumanization that has resulted from his-torical mutual antagonism, a counter-narrative that suggests the possibility of mutual recognition.[6]

In the writing class, I draw on the theory of the "rite of passage" as a peda-gogical framework and an aspect of course content. Anthropologist Victor Turn-er describes three stages to the rite: separation, the threshold or liminal period, and reaggregation. First-year students entering the composition classroom have clearly achieved the first stage: separation, or "leaving home." I do not promise "reaggregation" in fourteen weeks; rather, we discuss the writing process in terms of their four-year progress through the university, and draw their attention to the possibilities of the liminal, where they have room to work with ambiguity, and where they are passing through what Turner calls "a cultural realm that has few or no attributes of the past or coming state."[7]

The liminal period of the college years offers a valuable opportunity to enable students to think critically about the world and their place in it. Russian formalist Mikhail Bakhtin's comparison of authoritative discourse and internally persuasive discourses enables students to consider the discursive challenges they face in a college writing class. Bakhtin describes authoritative discourse as "indissolubly fused with its authority—with political power, an institution, a person."[8] Most students arrive well-versed in authoritative discourses, including anonymous textbook certainties and prior pronouncements on their writing abilities. By contrast, Bakhtin describes the internally persuasive discourse as that which makes the word, or language, one's own. Intention replaces allegiance and the reproduction of meaning changes to "newer ways to mean."[9] The internally persuasive discourse is in "interanimating relationships with new contexts" and remains "open"[10]; it provides an arena in which students can become participants in meaning-making through language.

Thus, Turner's articulation of the liminal zone suggests openings in discourse; Bakhtin's discourse distinctions offer what might be negotiated in that opening. Mary Louise Pratt's theory of the "arts of the contact zone"[11] offers some ways of thinking about how those negotiations take place. So we have the where, the what, and now the how. Pratt's "arts of the contact zone" can be read as elaborating on Bakhtin's assertion of "interanimating relationships," and introduces students to the negotiability of language and the impingement of power relations on discourses. Using examples as local as her son's development of literacy through his engagement with baseball card trading, and as distant as the Inca Guaman Poma's 1613 letter to King Philip II of Spain, she argues for a formation she calls "contact zones," which she defines as "social spaces where cultures meet, clash, and grapple with each other, often in contexts of highly asymmetrical relations of power."[12] In these contact zones, "members of subordinated or marginal groups select and invent from materials transmitted by a dominant or metropolitan culture."[13] It is this process of selection and invention (and revision) that I find present in African and African Diaspora texts, and that I draw attention to for first-year college writers. Thus, in a first year college writing class, there can be multiple contact zones: within texts, which seek to convey historically excluded knowledges in dominant languages; between students and texts; between teacher and students; between students as peers; and within students, between multiple authoritative and internally-persuasive discourses, and between the known and the unknown, the space of learning. Thus each contact zone is also a zone of liminality, filled with possibilities and choices. The opportunities in each contact zone are not identical, but they are analogous. Reading and writing assignments echo this process of shifting from authorized certainties to internally-persuasive possibilities in ongoing negotiation with ever-changing contexts.

The title of this chapter not only reflects the texts we use to frame the class, Chinua Achebe's novel *Things Fall Apart* and Robin Kelley's history *Freedom*

Dreams, but it also echoes the process that many students experience. Things *do* fall apart when the five-paragraph theme, the list paper, or the report is no longer the adequate, or exclusive, template for communicating their ideas. Ideally, breaking that mold and essaying different forms of writing will lead to a sense of, if not freedom, then choices as a writer.

Within the semester, students write in a variety of ways that offer smaller versions of the larger trajectory of the class. After reading and critiquing Pratt's essay, all students write an autoethnography. Pratt defines an autoethnography as "a text in which people undertake to describe themselves in ways that engage with representations others have made of them."[14] The specific assignment is to write an autoethnography that reflects the place and use of language in each student's family/cultural history. The purpose is for students to critically analyze their relationship to language as a cultural process implicated in relations of power. This assignment has the effect of defamiliarizing language and shifts student attention to language as a cultural formation in which they, too, play a role. Interpreting their findings invites them to become meaning-makers about their experience of language.

While students research and write their autoethnographies, we read two texts that highlight the significance of language to representation and interpretation, and the way that revision changes meaning. The first is a feature film from Burkina Faso, *Keita*,[15] in which a middle school student is caught between his initiation into a French education, and his initiation into the Mande people by a traditional griot. The second is Achebe's novel, *Things Fall Apart*,[16] which many students have read in high school, although primarily for its content, rather than its discursive aspects. Both texts represent contact zones and the negotiation of conflict—gendered, familial, intergenerational, national, and international—within asymmetrical power relations, and although *Things Fall Apart* is written in English, it is an English adapted to the purpose of representing Ibo society to multiple audiences. The devastating closing paragraph of the novel, in which Achebe represents a British colonial administrator's intention to summarize the life of the hero, Okonkwo, in a single paragraph of a book on the pacification of "African tribes," demonstrates the ways that rhetorical choices are implicated in power relations and the construction of knowledge and meaning. While the colonial administrator's writing can be seen as a revision of the novel Achebe has written, Achebe's novel can then also be read as a revision of colonial texts.

The theme of revision is also a factor in *Keita*. Mabo, the young student-hero, is a descendant of Sundiata, the founder of the Mali Empire in the early 1400's. His traditional initiation consists of his family's griot (traditional historian, genealogist, advisor; a walking library) coming to the city to tell him the epic of his ancestor. The film itself intercuts the contemporary situation with flashbacks that depict the episodes of the epic, as they are being narrated. As the film progresses, Mabo starts telling the story to his classmates. Each telling is a revision of the story, adapted to its context. Indeed, a full telling of the epic would take sixty hours, so the film itself represents the process of selection, and the ability to assess context and choose the most useful episode for different audiences. The central conflict in the film is between Mabo's French classroom education and his Mande initiation. This conflict is mirrored in the episodes of the epic chosen by the griot and by Mabo, and intensified between Mabo's parents, and the griot and the schoolteacher. Ways that such conflicts are negotiated are depicted in the incorporation of traditional Mande religion during the consolidation of Islam in the Sundiata epic, arguments between the contemporary players, and the eventual withdrawal of the griot from the field. However, Mabo has insisted that he wants both forms of initiation, and the ending of the film portrays his incorporation of the epic as an internally-persuasive discourse. Because the film's conclusion is open-ended, students are able to work through negotiations of the authoritative with the internally-persuasive, including those not represented in the film.

Thus, students participate in meaning-making in arguing for their interpretations of the text and the film in class discussions and in a short written response. The rhetorical considerations of these texts—language use, translation, selection, narration, audience, and revision—inform their ongoing autoethnography projects, which we discuss as a class throughout the writing process, including close reading and feedback in group peer-review conferences.

Working with African texts that foreground the tension between authoritative and internally-persuasive discourses foregrounds both the instability of language and the opportunity it offers for student agency. Writing an autoethnography, frankly terrifying to many students in its novelty, actually provides a relatively safe space for students to conduct that negotiation with their own acculturation processes. That is, if they can make the leap from their authoritative discourse of language as a natural and transparent event to language as a cultural and power-inflected process, the autoethnography provides an opportunity to make public their internally-persuasive discourses of their own language use. In the second section of the course, New World texts compel the more daunting and ethically-loaded task of writing about others.

To prepare for writing an ethnography, students read introductions to several ethnographies where the writers foreground the question of their relationship to the people they are researching. John Langston Gwaltney, in *Drylongso*, is both an insider and an outsider to the culture he writes about: urban working-class U.S. Black culture.[17] John Stewart, a Diasporic Trinidadian, introduces his ethnography of his home village, *Drinkers, Drummers, and Decent Folk*, by reviewing the history of anthropology.[18] He focuses on the audience for ethnographic research, the ways that anthropology has served the interests of domination, the crisis that the discipline has gone through, and the range of options in ethnographic research and writing that have subsequently emerged. His response to the subject-anthropologist-audience question is to publish everything: field notes, ethnographic reportage, and short stories based on his findings.

Thus, students enter the ethnography assignment, which requires them to describe and analyze a contact zone between two groups, aware of the changing authoritative discourses of a single discipline, anthropology. The ethnography assignment raises the stakes for their writing: they must confront the challenges of making meaning of what they are observing, contend with the possibility that those observed might make different meanings, question their own investment in their interpretation, and struggle with the necessary provisionality of their observations.

As students are conducting their research, we read two more texts as a class: Julie Dash's feature film *Daughters of the Dust*,[19] and Paule Marshall's novel *Praisesong for the Widow*.[20] Both texts examine the impact of the Black/White contact zone in the United States on Black communities. The film is set in 1903, and depicts a family reunion on the eve of the departure of half the family for the mainland to participate in the Great Migration. One of the central questions of the film is what, of the past, will the family carry into the future. Against the authoritative discourse of the mainland as progress and prosperity, different characters represent more marginalized perspectives: skepticism based on experience, love vs. material advancement, commitment to traditional religion, and commitment to the land. It is clear from the film that the characters who leave will have a dizzying array of new elements to choose among in creating a post-migration culture. The matriarch of the family, Nana Peazant, whose memories of enslavement are depicted, provides a model of re-negotiation for the family when she blesses them with a Bible bound with a sacred hand, or pouch filled with sacred objects. Most of the characters embrace her offering, but at least one character rejects it, and sees the migration as an opportunity to make a total break with the past. The film also depicts numerous cultural practices—grave-tending, martial arts, bottle trees, a letter under a glass of water under the bed—whose meanings are not self-evident. This becomes an important teaching tool as students are attempting to decipher the meanings of practices in the contact zone they are observing.

Praisesong for the Widow can be read as a narrative of the daughters of the post-Migration generation, and has an intertextual relationship with *Daughters of the Dust*, explicitly in the filmmaker's borrowing of a section of the novel's text for the film, and implicitly in the narrative of the protagonist, Avey Johnson. Avey is a retired upper middle-class African-American woman who, while taking a cruise through the Caribbean, abandons ship in Grenada. Her intention is to go straight home, back to the life that has become her authoritative discourse as the widow of a successful entrepreneur in White Plains, NY. But she becomes distracted by the emergence of long-suppressed internally-persuasive discourses from her childhood and young adulthood, triggered by the Grenadian landscape and sea. The rest of the novel reflects on the multiple informing discourses of her life, and the particular choice points where she, and particularly her husband Jerome, chose strategies that brought them material success while distancing them from belonging to, and participation in, Black community. The novel as a whole can be read as a rite of passage into elderhood and its responsibilities for Avey, and it closes with a ritual of reconciliation among the elders of Carriacou. Again, both works depict liminal areas, contact zones, and contention between forms of discourse, differently empowered. A thread that runs through all of the texts is the place of Africa in the historical imagination, the multiple forms of representing Africa, and the revision of African practices in the New World context. As the semester progresses, however, the texts become less explanatory and more ambiguous; students must work harder to elicit meanings and to write convincing interpretations. They must also begin to contend with alternative interpretations, and begin considering how to address them in their own work.

Students then enter the research process. The class proceeds along ever-expanding circles of inquiry, from the reliance on personal experience for evidence and analysis in the autoethnography to the increasing distance from direct experience in the ethnography and the culminating research paper. Students may choose to write about themes in African and African Diaspora culture, or about any subject analogous to our class material. Some students, who may have been persuaded of their agency in the autoethnography and ethnography assignments, are tempted to return to the familiar model of passive transmission of information when confronting work with secondary sources. The tension between authoritative and internally-persuasive discourses is highest in this assignment, and we use our readings to focus on how to create a productive relationship between student ideas and academic sources.

The texts that accompany the research project are *Drylongso*,[21] a feature film by Cauleen Smith, and *Freedom Dreams* by Robin D. G. Kelley.[22] *Drylongso*'s heroine, Pica, is a first-year student in a photography class at a fictional Oakland, California university. She is working class, and has taken on the task of documenting African-American men, in a project she calls "Evidence of Existence." Her negotiation of the authoritative discourses of her community, including suspicion of strangers taking one's picture, is to use a Polaroid, so there are no negatives. This brings her into conflict with her African American professor, who respects her ambitions, but wants her to work within the traditional confines of the assignment, a 35mm camera and a gallery space to display her work. Community violence interrupts her work: she befriends a woman who has been beaten by her boyfriend and who decides to dress as a man for protection, and Pica's artist-boyfriend is murdered by a serial killer who alternates between killing men and women. While Pica and her friend Toby occupy different class locations—Toby is middle-class—they share a strong sense of independence from their absentee mothers. The film deliberately challenges viewers by portraying stereotypical images of African-Americans and then subverting their meaning—three well-dressed young men standing by a Jeep appear first as drug dealers, but then turn out to be community protectors; Toby dresses like a gang member, but is really a middle-class young woman. Pica decides to exhibit her final project in the abandoned lot where her boyfriend was killed. She builds altars around the lot for the men—now dead, imprisoned, or otherwise missing—whose pictures she has taken, which remind viewers of some of the practices depicted in *Daughters of the Dust*.

Pica's professor and classmates come to the "opening" in the field, catered by her mother and friends for everyone in the community. Her professor acknowledges that she has shifted the authoritative discourse by her project, and that she has pushed him, when he thought he was pushing her. Pica's work is clearly no less rigorous or thoughtful for not employing a 35mm camera and a gallery; it meets and changes the authoritative discourse.

Robin Kelley's *Freedom Dreams* is a history of the place of imagination in Black movements for social change in the 20th century. Kelley argues that the imaginative has been the propulsive engine for social change in movements for Third World liberation, African American liberation, Black feminism, reparations, and the arts. His arguments are complex, and his evidence plentiful. Students who either disagree or agree with his claims analyze the text to identify his thesis and arguments, and to study the way he uses evidence to persuade the reader. In effect, we practice ways of reading Kelley's text as a model for reading the sources that students are using for their own research. Because much of the information in his text is new, students see him balancing conventional readings of events like the Civil Rights movement with the traditionally marginalized or ignored movements that he foregrounds. Thus his work demonstrates the kinds of negotiations they are conducting in their own research.

The purpose of reviewing how these African and African Diaspora texts can work in a university-level writing class is not to recommend them to all writing classes; rather, my intention is to broaden the discussion of the uses of such texts by adding to the current emphasis on their significance for students of African descent and as demonstrations of a specific culture's rhetoric. I argue that if writing is perceived as a process, and that process involves the negotiation of the usually highly-empowered known with the new, then such texts provide a rich range of demonstrations of the ways such negotiations can take place, beginning with the question of language, and building to engaged student dialogue with the body of authoritative texts to which their written work now becomes a contribution. The emphasis in these works on processes of change—for characters, cultures, languages, and meanings—invites students to become participants, or acknowledge their participation, in such processes in ways that they, too, become meaning-making contributors to the intellectual community, and sophisticated readers and writers, attentive to genre, discipline, expectations, and choices.

Similarly, as students enter the upper division Writing in the Disciplines classes, through their work with anthropology, Black Studies, and Cultural Studies in this version of the introductory class, they will have been exposed to the shifting dynamics of disciplinarity, and the kinds of political and cultural questions that are at stake in the rhetorical choices of, first, any discipline and, second, disciplinarity itself. A closing assignment I use now asks students to write about what has been left out of their research paper as a result of the research paper's disciplinary expectations of citation, logic, argument, and evidence. Students produce or find cartoons, photographs, poems, songs, stories and essays that represent that which was driven to the margins in their effort to fit the rhetorical context. This anti-disciplinary closing reminds them, and me, that important knowledge resides at the margins of authorized discourse, and our challenge as thinkers and writers is to be aware of the close relationship between discipline and displacement, and to continually challenge the gate-keeping functions of discourse.

Notes

1. Michael Omi and Howard Winant, *Racial Formations in the United States* (New York: Routledge, 1986), 57.

2. Audre Lorde, "Age, Race, Class, and Sex: Women Redefining Difference." *Sister Outsider* (Freedom, CA: The Crossing Press, 1984), 115.

3. W.E.B. DuBois, *The Souls of Black Folk* (Greenwich, CT: Fawcett, 1961 (1903)).

4. Mae G. Henderson, "'Where, By the Way, Is This Train Going?' A Case for Black (Cultural) Studies," *Callaloo* 19, no. 1 (1996): 60. See also Mario Azevedo, "African-American Studies and the State of the Art," in *Africana Studies: A Survey of Africa and the African Diaspora,* ed. Mario Azevedo (Durham, NC: Carolina Academic Press, 1993): 25-43; Manthia Diawara, "Black Studies, Cultural Studies: Performative Acts" in *What Is Cultural Studies? A Reader,* ed. John Storey. (London: Arnold, 1996), 300-6; Stuart Hall, "Cultural Studies and the Crisis of the Humanities," *October* 53 (1990): 11-90; Wahneema Lubiano, "Mapping the Interstices Between Afro-American Cultural Discourse and Cultural Studies: A Prolegomenon," *Callaloo* 19, no. 1 (1996): 68-77; Barbara Christian, "The Race for Theory," in *Hacienda Caras: Making Face, Making Soul: Creative and Critical Perspectives by Feminists of Color,* ed. Gloria Anzaldua (San Francisco: Aunt Lute Books, 1990): 335-45.

5. Manning Marable, "Living Black History: Black Intellectuals and the African-American Literary Tradition." April 2004, http://www.manningmarable.net/works/pdf/livingblackhistory.pdf (accessed November 20, 2006): 24.

6. Ella Shohat and Robert Stam, *Unthinking Eurocentrism: Multiculturalism and the Media,* (London and New York: Routledge, 1994), 241.

7. Victor Turner, *The Ritual Process: Structure and Anti-Structure* (Ithaca, NY: Cornell University Press, 1969), 94-5.

8. Mikhail Bakhtin. "Discourse in the Novel" in *The Dialogic Imagination: Four Essays by M.M. Bakhtin,* ed. Michael Holquist, trans. Caryl Emerson and Michael Holquist (Austin: University of Texas Press, 1981), 343.

9. Bakhtin, "Discourse," 346.

10. Bakhtin, "Discourse," 346.

11. For a critique of the uses of Pratt's concept of the contact zone, particularly in composition research, see R. Mark Hall and Mary Rosner, "Pratt and Pratfalls: Revisioning Contact Zones," in *Crossing Borderlands: Composition and Postcolonial Studies,* edited by Andrea A. Lunsford and Lahoucine Ouzgane (Pittsburgh: University of Pittsburgh Press, 2004), 95-109.

12. Mary Louise Pratt, "Arts of the Contact Zone" in *Ways of Reading,* 5th edition, ed. David Bartholomae and Anthony Petroksky (New York: Bedford/St. Martin's, 1999), 583.

13. Pratt, "Arts," 587.

14. Pratt, "Arts," 586.

15. *Keita,* dir. Dani Kouyate, California Newsreel, 1995.

16. Chinua Achebe, *Things Fall Apart* (London: Heineman, 1996 [1958]).

17. John Langston Gwaltney, *Drylongso* (NewYork: Vintage, 1981).

18. John Stewart, *Drinkers, Drummers and Decent Folk* (Albany: State University of New York Press, 1989).

19. *Daughters of the Dust,* dir. Julie Dash, prod. Julie Dash and Arthur Jafa. 1 hr. 53 mins., American Playhouse/Geechee Girls/WMG Film, 1991.

20. Paule Marshall, *Praisesong for the Widow* (New York: Plume, 1984).

21. *Drylongso*, dir. Cauleen Smith, prod. Cauleen Smith and Christine Gant. 1 hr. 26 mins., Nation Sack Filmworks Production, 1998.

22. Robin D.G. Kelley, *Freedom Dreams* (Boston: Beacon, 2002).

Chapter Eleven
Performing/Teaching/Writing:
Performance Studies in the
Critical Composition Classroom

Ryan Claycomb

The 2005 conference for the American Society of Theatre Research revolved around the theme of Writing and Performance, specifically:

> the dialectical frictions between writing and performance. Both terms have been pressed into an extraordinary array of meanings and uses—both in the dissemination of "textuality" as a metaphor for the operation of a wide range of signifying practices and in the migration of "performance" as a critical term throughout the humanities and social sciences.[1]

Yet, while many of the sessions and papers at the conference directly addressed the role of writing in creating, archiving, theorizing, teaching and understanding performance, little to no attention was expressly paid to the ways that performance and its discourses help us create, theorize, teach, or understand writing.

Existing inquiry into the relatively unmapped territory at the confluence of performance and composition is rare, but what exists is compelling. Of particular value is the recent contribution from investigators from the Stanford Study of Writing: Jenn Fishman, Andrea Lunsford, and two student writers. Their essay, "Performing Writing, Performing Literacy," lays out in persuasive ways how performance is already a significant system in developing student literacy, and the ways that it could be integrated more comprehensively into student writing and into our teaching of that writing. Essentially, the Stanford team proposes the same question that stimulated this project: "Can we expand our curricula and our pedagogies for performance in the writing classroom?" They conclude that "performance . . . stands to reinvigorate both teaching and learning in the writing classroom."[2] Further, they specifically identify affinities in performance with "the tradition of critical pedagogy established by Paolo Freire, Henry Giroux, and Peter McLaren."[3] I share this impulse to locate such affinities with a liberatory pedagogy, in that performance offers a site for literalizing Freire's emphasis on dialogue, acknowledging students' and teachers' bodies as constrained by specific social relations, and orienting learning toward action and socially resistant praxis. Indeed, when we integrate elements of embodied performance into a Freirian problem-posing framework—a pedagogy that the American academy in particular might otherwise conceive of in abstract terms—we take significant steps toward a praxis that moves beyond the classroom space and into the lived experience of students and teachers. This potentiality—to transform the classroom from a theatrical elsewhere of suspended disbelief into a performance lab for real social empowerment and resistance—drives this project.

In this essay, I would like to explore some of the avenues by which we might leverage the notion of performance for a critical writing pedagogy, both by raising questions to examine for others doing work on this confluence, and by suggesting a few approaches that may serve in practical ways in the writing-intensive classroom. While such approaches most directly engage those teaching writing courses, particularly early college composition, the questions, the potential answers, and their implications have ramifications for any number of others, including teachers of performance who bring writing into the classroom and Cultural Studies scholars themselves working against disciplinary structures, many of them embedded in academic writing. Indeed, composition is both uniquely amenable to a critical pedagogy, with its inherent interest in bringing students to voice and into personal agency, and at the same time remarkably subject to pressures from the academy at large to produce normative students whose value is measured in terms of marketable skills. In light of this, the exigence for a critical composition pedagogy is high and open to bold pedagogical interventions. Therefore, I imagine performance studies working with a critical writing pedagogy in three particular ways: as a lens to examine, assess and revitalize the complex performance dynamics of the writing-intensive classroom (the classroom as theater); as an empowering tool kit for students to reconfigure their own writing practice (the student writer as performance artist); and as a body of intellectual work that serves as subject matter for critical and anti-disciplinary inquiry through writing (performance as the course text).

However, performance is hardly a clearly defined concept and, in its various senses, presents a range of possibilities and quandaries for teachers of writing. In fact, a central tension within the field of performance studies is the notion of performance (particularly ritual performance) as consequential vs. the notion of performance (particularly theatrical performance) as hypothetical. This push and pull of the safe "as-if" space of the classroom against the meaningful yet risk-laden space of the classroom must condition any discussion about performances of writing for politically engaged learning. In what follows, I would like to argue that performance gives us a language of both theatricality and efficacy to pry open the writing classroom in multiple ways in service of a politicized, empowering, and potentially liberatory pedagogical stance. Therefore, we must actively imagine the classroom as a charged performance space, we must encourage our students to think about writing as performance in many ways, and we might (as I will sketch out in three assignments) use performance as a subject for teasing out these potentials.

I. The Classroom as Theater

The idea of the classroom as theater is hardly a new one, nor is it lost on me, as a middling former actor, the degree to which teaching is already like theatrical performance. But using the theatrical metaphor can help us explore the vectors of how power and knowledge flow through the writing classroom. Of course, certain obvious models for configuring the writing classroom are both limiting and retrograde: few in our profession would advocate the sage-on-the-stage model, with its authoritative teacherly performer holding forth to a passive student audience. Indeed, this model corresponds so closely to the banking model of education at the center of Freire's critique that it would seem to be antithetical to a critical pedagogy. Other, more complex models of how students often imagine the traditional classroom as theater may be no less stultifying, and perhaps more sinister. Disability and performance theorist Petra Kuppers raises the image of the medical teaching theater: a site for the surveillance, dissection and diagnosis of the aberrant and diseased body.[4] For some students, the writing classroom certainly seems like such a theater, though instead of watching from a distant gallery, students themselves are the medicalized subject. In such a model, the student offers a remarkably prone performance, one in which student agency has already been exercised and exhausted in the time leading up to the dissection. Drained of efficacy, the work is submitted to the antiseptic gaze of the teacher, who methodically surveys, dissects, and diagnoses the failures of writing in the student work.

Sadly, this is the notion of performance—as metric—that our students are most likely to bring to the writing classroom, and it is among the most deeply entrenched obstacles to a critical pedagogy in the university classroom. Ask most students what we mean when we discuss their performance in our classes, and they will generate some response that directly invokes grading. The system in which a writing product is assigned a grade that eventually solidifies into a mark on their permanent transcript at once reduces the act of writing to a quantity and drains the radical potential of that writing, even as it reifies the teacher as a power figure. In this model, performance becomes an extension of discipline and, as Jon McKenzie notes in *Perform or Else*, performance ultimately supersedes discipline as the prevailing matrix for social control in the twenty-first century.[5] McKenzie locates this shift from discipline to performance in (among other places) the drive for stock market performance in the 80s and 90s. This idea seems to underscore the degree to which the notion of grade performance is already oriented toward a market-driven understanding of higher education. Such an approach to education, then, only imagines the university as a labor source for a neo-liberal economy. By putting students in a position to perform in service of the demands of an increasingly corporatized higher educational system, this writing-as-quantity framework turns the act of writing into a marketable commodity rather than a tool for participating as an active citizen in a democracy, let alone activists in a global context.

Moreover, in many current writing systems, where writing pedagogy is being put in service of disciplinary training, the act of grading writing becomes a way to enforce disciplinary structures (in both the senses of academic disciplines and social discipline), which transforms the act of writing into a moment of confession (made all the more compulsory by curricular writing requirements). Writing for a grade admits the student into an academic subjectivity even as that student becomes subject to the power of the teacher as grader. One of the most inspiring feminist teachers of my education readily admitted that while she was deeply invested in a de-centered classroom, she feared that it masked the reality that she was the professor assigning the grade. The finality of her quantification of student performance thwarted many aspirations for a transformative classroom. Joe Parker, in this volume, considers the role of grading in a de-disciplinary pedagogy, and the challenges he raises there might usefully be echoed here: the difficulty in countermanding the foreclosures of student empowerment enforced by a systemic insistence upon performance as an objective and quantifiable metric of student value.

Indeed, the submission, review, and return of graded writing work are among the most powerful rituals of the daily life of higher education. In *Schooling as Ritual Performance*, Peter McLaren suggests ways that performance as ritual can be utilized to unpack the dynamics of the classroom. McLaren examines the classroom as a liminal space—one that sets the stage for rites of passage, of revitalization, of intensification, and importantly, of resistance—and follows both the structures of conformity and the anti-structures of *communitas* and resistance.[6] McLaren identifies these rituals as importantly symbolic and metaphorical, and yet simultaneously efficacious—having real, transformative consequences in the world beyond the classroom walls, beyond the boundaries of the rituals themselves.

We can easily imagine many of the ways that classroom performance and student writing are already ritualized. Many of those rituals reify existing power structures: the often subdued, reverent submission of work to the teacher's gaze is a moment of academic confession if ever there was one (*forgive me teacher, for I have sinned; I started this paper at midnight*). But McLaren is clear that reinforcing dominant power structures is not the only function of ritual in the classroom: "While classroom rituals embodied and transmitted ideological messages, they were recuperative to the extent that they additionally served as conduits of power and creativity (which had a revivifying influence on the students)."[7] Furthermore, he notes that "classroom rituals [are] neither enslaving nor liberating in their internal logic; while participation . . . altered the sensibilities of the participants (e.g. the way they coded reality), the creation of meaning was always subject to the ideological and material constraints surrounding the ritual."[8] Therefore, it is crucial, first of all, that we understand the rituals of the classroom, particularly those that shape student writing: comparing freewriting against quizzes as a daily warm-up, for example; or understanding the ways that various peer review and revision strategies, as repeated rituals, participate in structures of conformity or offer "conduits of power and creativity."

Importantly, McLaren notes that "A ritual has a distinct *form* in which its medium . . . is part of its message. The form gives the structure a subjunctive, or 'as if' quality."[9] The "as if" scenarios of writing, the imagined audiences who never read the work, the "practice scenarios" for such exercises often seem to undercut the sense that the writing classroom *matters*, an issue I take up more fully below. But perhaps what is most compelling about the ritualistic potential of schooling is that, contrary to many stereotypes of theatricality, the notion of ritual performance is imbued with a sense of efficacy, a sense that what happens matters to and transforms those who participate, even if their participation takes the "as if" form of mask (playing a role) or of self (with potential consequences to the self). Furthermore, as teachers in these spaces, we are both transformable participants and masked guides. Randi Kristensen, in this volume, suggests some of the ways that we might think about integrating the work of theorists of ritualistic performance into our pedagogy. Crucially, these performances are metaphorical and real, and the initiations into society that our students per-form—as passive subjects of state power, as public citizens in a democracy, as resistant activists—resonate well beyond the classroom.

Indeed, these rituals appear at the nexus of many complex systems of politi-cal economy and the multi-directional power flows of the university writing classroom: teachers wield power over students through grades, through credits, through cultural capital; students in turn hold power over teachers in the form of course evaluations, in their ability to lodge complaints and, less tangibly, in re-sponding to the work of the classroom; students hold power over one another by importing the socio-political contexts of the world beyond the classroom into that utopian space, so the political vectors of identity (class, race, gender, sexu-ality, and so forth) play out in the classroom. In the meantime, students and teachers alike are structured within an institutional framework that demands assessable and saleable performance, while larger state and national political and economic frameworks place discursive pressure on the classroom as a contested space, one designed to induct students into, alternately, national culture, democ-racy, and/or a capitalist marketplace. Indeed, we must constantly re-imagine (and ask our students to re-imagine) our authority as teachers as both negotiable and accessible, deploying multivalent approaches to assuming and abnegating authority, while at the same time acknowledging institutional limits on de-authorizing the teacher, from the persistence of grades, to control of rosters, to control of the syllabus. Certainly, it is true that most American students are far and away more privileged than those first students of Freire's liberatory peda-gogy. But it is no less true that these students are caught in a whirlwind of power and that few of them have any sense of how to operate effectively within it; the degree to which our students are bound up in the political economy of what McLaren calls a "predatory culture" makes engaging and empowering those students crucial, for their own well being and also, I would argue, for the transformation of the culture itself.

Of course, it is similarly true that as much as our students are on display in this classroom space, so are we as teachers. Our performances are similarly reviewed and scrutinized, by our students in evaluations, and by our departments through annual and tenure reviews (or for the huge number of adjunct and contract composition teachers, through course assignment and contract renewal). Regardless of teaching style, our bodies are spectacularized in the writing classroom, and we must at least acknowledge that the performances that take place there—and are under surveillance there—include our own. We therefore must be mindful of ourselves as actors on this stage even if we choose (with what control we have over the performance space) what model of theater we want to use.

That is, while the sage-on-the-stage and the medical theater models presuppose all sorts of hierarchical and passive learning scenarios, the most typical realist theater staging tactics offer us a metaphor for perhaps the most debilitating of all classroom dynamics: the suspension of disbelief. Indeed, the mimetic function of education, particularly writing education, has students imagining that what happens inside the classroom only *mimics* what will happen beyond those walls but has no direct bearing on "real life";[10] like the theater, the classroom is an "as if" scenario. This assumption can be useful to developing writers, but it also can drain the classroom, like the theater, of much of its transformative efficacy.[11] What is true for political theater is equally true of the critical classroom: the goal must be to create a sense of efficacy, one that has ripple effects beyond performance space and time. Avant-garde political performance of the last century offers many theatrical models of pedagogy that empower students to participate in the world beyond the theater. We can look to the epic theater tactics of Bertolt Brecht and Erwin Piscator, the environmental theater of Richard Schechner, the invisible theater of Augusto Boal, or the guerilla theater tactics of Teatro Campesino, each of which will inspire modes of analysis and teaching examples that I explore below.

II. Performing Writing

While it is important to locate theatrical dynamics of the classroom generally, we must also attend to the ways that an understanding of performance can and does inflect our understanding of writing and of the teaching of writing. A great number of important conversations have been happening in composition studies, many of them ongoing for years.

Audience

Of these conversations, work on audience is perhaps the most prominent. That is, though speech communication studies began to split off from English departments in the early twentieth century,[12] largely taking concern for *live* audiences out of the composition classroom with them, these discourses continue to inform one another. The ongoing presence of rhetoric studies in many writing curricula (re-invoking Aristotelian and Sophistic rhetoric) has already yielded a great deal of thought on how student writers and their teachers might attend to audience.[13] I would suggest that even greater attention could be paid to *what sorts of audiences* we and our students attend to. It is a simple exercise for students to address an audience of those familiar to them, even an audience that may care about the issues they write about. But such choices do not always accomplish much. We might think about making a shift: from asking students how to address a given audience to asking them how to choose an audience who must be addressed, or even more radically, asking them how to define, assemble and mobilize new audiences. Through revision guidance and reflective writing prompts, such a pedagogy must help students think more expansively about both embedding audience cues in their writing, and considering the context of the rhetorical situation and their potential control over that situation. Within a critical writing pedagogy, we must teach students to move beyond simply addressing audiences to strategically choosing audiences to engage and ultimately creating audiences for themselves.

In political performance, this shift has marked a move outward from theaters into street performance and other sorts of guerilla theater. Students may legitimately learn from these examples by being exposed to these sorts of audience interventions as subject matter and may duplicate these successes by considering which audiences outside the classroom, be they legislators or citizens on the streets, will most meaningfully effect change. Austrian playwright Peter Handke writes, for example, that:

> Committed theatre these days doesn't happen in theatres (those falsified domains of art where every word and movement is emptied of significance) but in lecture halls, for instance, when a professor's microphone is taken away, and professors blink through burst-open doors, when leaflets flutter down to the congregation from the galleries, and revolutionaries take their small children with them to the lectern. . . . In this way, theatre is becoming directly effective. There is now the Street Theatre, Lecture-hall Theatre, Church Theatre (more effective than 1,000 Masses), Department Store Theatre, etc.[14]

Importantly, Handke equates the most traditional forms of theater with the most traditional form of pedagogy—with his astonished, microphone-holding professor—and highlights ways that even such a classroom might be the place for student-generated theater to take place. But most crucial here is Handke's suggestion that the most successful political theater makes its audience where it finds it. Such theatrical work can also be found in the guerilla theater of El Teatro Campesino, a traveling Chicano troupe that grew out of the United Farm Workers' movement and the more general Chicano movement of the 60s and 70s. Their theater, a mix of powerful rhetoric and seemingly light entertainment, was more likely to play at picket lines, migrant camps, and union halls than in designated theater spaces.[15] Such efforts to invoke audiences where they are, in exigent spaces and times, can tell us and our students much about new ways to think through audiences, and we must learn (and teach) from radical theater about how such strategies might arise.

From a pedagogical vantage point, we might also think (as many of us already do) about how the positionalities of our students—as actors and audience members, writers and readers—might be best acknowledged, challenged, and mobilized for social action. This issue implicates not only individual classrooms but the institutions in which they are housed and the individual students who comprise the class. In virtually every writing classroom in a U.S. institution of higher education, students are often operating from positions of power relative to the majority of the global population. In some cases, the mere acknowledgement of this fact is enough to disrupt an easy entitlement to privilege. But at the most elite institutions, the necessity of challenging students' positionalities as deeply complicit with the operations of social dominance is as crucial for a liberatory curriculum as mobilizing those students for social justice. Bruce McConachie suggests using Augusto Boal's invisible theater, a foundational theatrical methodology for challenging economic, political, and symbolic tyranny, as a heuristic for engaging privileged students.[16] Specifically, Boal's invisible theater integrated staged theatrical improvisation into the fabric of everyday life: an actor playing a poor man goes to the supermarket and asks to pay in barter or in work, while other actors are placed strategically to draw other impromptu spectators into the action. Similarly, McConachie's pedagogy "stages" uncomfortable scenarios in the classroom in order to point out privilege, to get students to disengage the "as-if" impulses of the classroom and actually engage in the scenario being acted out, one that ideally has real consequences and not just hypothetical ones. Ultimately, then, whether we choose the theatrical tactics of El Teatro Campesino or Augusto Boal or we choose other less radical approaches, we must ourselves consider how we can leverage the attention to addressing, invoking, and creating audiences ourselves by learning from the efficacy-seeking tactics of political theater.

The Writing Body

Another vexing and recently very exciting conversation that incorporates the terms of both composition and performance presents the notion of performance as embodiment in the writing classroom. If we think of the classroom as a theatrical space, we must think of our students' bodies in those spaces; they are not disembodied minds telekinetically putting words onto a page. On this issue,

Fishman and Lunsford have already begun to theorize that "the embodied practices dropped out of composition's regular curriculum in the nineteenth century
[recitation, speechmaking, etc.] become significant tools for working powerful
classroom transformations."[17] They cite Della Pollock, whose writing pedagogy
"challenges students to incorporate time and space as well as the corporeal body
into the activity of writing," and Eve Kosofsky Sedgwick, who, in her course on
experimental critical writing, asks students to riff on the relationship between
physical voice and writing voice.[18] However, these examples come from graduate writing classes where students are exercising critical faculties that they are
already assumed to be using and, therefore, as the Stanford team suggests, we
still need to think about how to map these pedagogies of embodied performance
into early college writing classrooms. And while both of these examples invoke
what Elyse Lamm Pineau describes as "the performing body," we must also
consider what she calls "ideological bodies" in play, through the ways that students' corporeal identities come to bear.[19] This is merely one terminology that
we might use to call attention to the ideological body in the writing class. Many
others are certainly already in practice, each in a certain way engaging what Peter McLaren calls "enfleshment," the corporeal processes of repetition and ha-
bituation, where teachers and students physically internalize the dominant power
structures in the classroom, but which teachers and students may also use to
enact liberatory responses to those structures.[20] Such work, in both performance
studies and rhetoric and composition studies,[21] is already beginning to parse out
how students' bodies are in play not only in the classroom itself, but also outside
the classroom during the act of writing; here we find clues into ways that we
might begin to imagine an embodied liberatory pedagogy of writing.

Role Playing and Performative Writing

While we must consider both the audiences for, and bodies of, such performances of writing, it is crucial that we must also consider the nature of the
performance itself, of ritual, play, and masks. Of course, this raises a tension
discussed earlier: the pull of theatricality as an "as-if" proposition against the
efficacy of ritual performance. On the one hand, there can be specific uses of the
"as-if" scenario in the writing classroom; in fact, the notion of performance as
role-playing can be particularly freeing, particularly when the unpredictable
freedom of play is couched within rhetorical scenarios where the trickster has its
own rhetorical power.[22] That said, role-playing experiments with students hardly
prepare them for the academic writing they will confront in later courses, nor do
such exercises prepare them to powerfully enter the democracy that as young
adults they have legally already entered.[23] We can, therefore, usefully help students to imagine their own writing as a role-playing performance: one where
every piece of writing is already a pastiche of other writing, and where by playing a role, they can break out of the no-man's land of typical composition student anxieties.

Yet while an attention to writing as performance can play both sides of the tension between hypothetical play and efficacious action, we must work to push students toward the latter. In its simplest terms, performance is an action, a taking on of some act. This meaning invokes J. L. Austin's foundational grappling with the performative in *How to Do Things with Words*—the linguistic verb formation as an utterance that actually accomplishes what it metonymically represents (as in Whitman's "I celebrate myself, and sing myself"). Indeed, using Austin, we can easily imagine each piece of writing beginning with an implicit "I write," a silent invocation of the piece of writing as itself an *act* of writing. And if writing is always an action, it is also a performance. Performance theorist Richard Schechner glosses Derrida in this way, noting that "Because writing is always contested, a system of erasing as well as composing, meaning cannot 'be' once and for all. Meaning is always performed: always in rehearsal, its finality forever deferred, its actuality only provisional, played out in specific circumstances."[24] Similarly, Della Pollock argues, "At the brink of meaning, poised between abjection and regression, writing as *doing* displaces writing as meaning; writing becomes meaningful in the material dis/continuous act of writing."[25] Such performances are always bound up in power, and so to acknowledge writing as performance—as an act—is to acknowledge it as a political act, as one that engages, in complicated and shifting ways, the relationship of the individual to the discourses and structures of power, a fact we can and must leverage in the critical composition classroom. I suggested earlier that writing for a grade in a classroom setting admits students into a compromised academic subjectivity, but our place in that classroom must acknowledge the potential of student writing to exceed the reach of our classroom power as teachers, and to challenge the power of institutions that exercise it unethically.

While the "as if" of role-playing can be freeing for early college writers, the notion of efficacy can be empowering. This is particularly true if we are able to pry away quantitative notions of high and low performance that tend to bind students to a product-oriented notion of writing, one that tells them that their performance on a given piece of writing is finite and measurable. In a class in experimental critical writing, Eve Kosofsky Sedgwick asks students "whether it is really possible, even in theory, to divide utterances between the performative and the constative . . . calling attention to different senses in which all utterances *do* something *and* at the same time say something."[26] For students, this can and must underline the notion of writing as a process, that their writing becomes powerful in the act of doing, but also in the acts of re-iterating, of revising, of presenting, of re-thinking. If we initiate discussions of what writing can and does do as a constitutive act to both reify and challenge structures of power, our students are in better positions to both interrogate their own positions within the discourses of power and to work toward re-constituting them in ways that challenge the existing discourses. Working-class students may challenge corporate interests, or privileged students may work against the very forces which grant them privilege for a greater social good. Indeed, we might interrogate our own writing and teaching as constitutive acts that interpellate us into these same systems of power. We might just as easily use our positions of power to enable a liberatory learning experience as to reinforce dominant structures, or do one while paying lip-service to the other. By acknowledging the constitutive power of both writing and the teaching of writing as structures of and against power, we create spaces in which the structures of power might be reconfigured for more equitable ends. We must therefore encourage our students to think expansively about what their writing *does*, and in what ways their acts of writing might be at once more visible, meaningful, and powerful.

Reciprocally, we must strive to ask ourselves similar questions about our teaching: Inasmuch as we perform roles—and perform power—in the classroom and in our institution-sanctioned evaluations of student writing, what do our utterances in the classroom and in our written responses to student writing *do*, and how might an understanding of the performative value of our teaching processes change those processes? I recognize that these are questions already central to the discourse of critical pedagogy, but they bear repeating within this particular framework. Henry Giroux locates in both Cultural Studies and critical pedagogy an emphasis on "a performative pedagogy reflected in what social theorists such as Lawrence Grossberg call 'the act of doing,' the importance of understanding theory as the grounded basis for 'intervening into contexts and power . . . in order to enable people to act more strategically in ways that may change their context for the better.'"[27] Here, Giroux recognizes the pedagogical function of radical performance art alongside the performance functions of a radical pedagogy. He notes particularly that "The performative nature of the pedagogical recognizes the partial breakdown of, renegotiation, and repositioning of boundaries as fundamental to understanding how pluralization is linked to the shifting nature of knowledge, identities and the process of globalization."[28] He goes on to suggest that as teachers who perform a Cultural Studies or composition pedagogy, we must ourselves recognize the potential of performance to offer "new modes of symbolic and social practice . . . for expanding and deepening the processes of democratic education, social relations, and public life."[29]

The Theatrical and the Excessive

Giroux further acknowledges in the performative an element of the excessive. Several semesters ago, in a writing course entitled "The Rhetoric of Spectacle," I asked students to collectively work to define and debate the notion of spectacle, and one crucial element that we identified, beyond the visual and the performative, was this same notion of excess. Performance scholars from Erving Goffman to Judith Butler have usefully laid out ways that performance disappears seamlessly into everyday life. But while that very notion is already functioning in the traditional composition classroom, it might be useful to look to ways in which performance *does not* disappear—to ways that it makes a scene—to investigate how performance's theatricality might invigorate the writing classroom. I am not necessarily advocating the sort of tap-dancing teaching that, poorly used, turns into mere edutainment (although when skillfully used, such "tap-dancing" might be part of a useful set of pedagogical tactics).[30] That said, in the traditional higher education classroom, and the writing-intensive classroom in particular, we often pay close attention to written and verbal language while ignoring other expressive modes as keys to the kind of critical literacy we hope to prompt in the acts of writing we assign.

In their survey of the often ambiguous and contradictory concept of theatricality, Tracy Davis and Tom Postlewait define it as "characterized by histrionic actions, manners and devices, and hence a practice."[31] They locate in theatricality the concepts of excess and surplus, which are linked in conscious and unconscious ways to the kind of psychic excess that Judith Butler identifies as a particular key to dismantling and denaturalizing codes of normative behavior. And given that denaturalization and desocialization are keys to a critical pedagogy (particularly in the composition classrooms taught and described by Ira Shor in *Empowering Education*), we might look to ways in which the excessive, the spectacular, and the theatrical might help us invigorate our teaching. For example, educators such as McConachie and Jody Norton work from guerilla theater tactics toward a guerilla pedagogy. Norton specifically uses a co-teaching process where he and his co-teacher stage oppositional viewpoints in order to dislocate "the traditional univocal authority" of the professor, proposing the co-teachers as "provocateurs and interrogators—instigators, not didacts"[32] who, in staging dialogue, offer avenues for students to find ways to both disagree and to articulate their own positions.

The more difficult obstacle, one I ran up against frequently in the class on spectacle, was asking students themselves to engage in a rhetoric of excess, given the conventions of restraint that often govern students' sense of the traditional university writing classroom. The writing that happens in a performance-focused writing class need not be purely academic, purely expository. It can, and perhaps should, take on excessive forms. I often present my students with a quote from T.S. Eliot: "Only those who will risk going too far can possibly find out how far one can go."[33] Whatever we might call excellent writing (which is different from "good writing"), it often derives from risk, and risk and excess go hand in hand. Therefore, we must continue to ask ourselves: How can we suggest student excess through assignments, model theatricality in our classroom manner, or promote spectacle in ways that spill out beyond the boundaries of the curriculum?

Performance as Elusive

Throughout this piece, I have suggested that a performance-centered pedagogy is potent for empowering critical student writers because it offers both the freedom of the "as-if" circumstances of theatrical performance and the efficacy of ritual performance. This oscillation between play and power taps into precisely the possibility of performance in the critical composition classroom, a possibility that lies in the nature of performance as elusive, oppositional, and unusually amenable to an anti-disciplinary critique. Performance, with its ephemeral ability to disappear as it is happening and its essential difference from its own artifacts, is particularly resistant to discursive control. We cannot censor that which has already happened: what we discipline when we discipline performance is only ever a trace of that performance. Peggy Phelan argues that "the after-effect of [its] disappearance is the experience of subjectivity itself."[34] Under such a theoretical paradigm, we might suggest that we witness our students' entrance into subjectivity only after it has happened, in the performances of writing about which we can only guess at, armed only with traces of the performance. If we allow it to do so, this notion can radically decenter the power structure of the classroom, identifying students' writing performances—at the moment of doing—as under the control of the student and not the teacher. Indeed, many of us have experienced the difficulty of grading live performance, either non-traditional assignments or in-class presentations; while perhaps a mundane instance of performance's elusiveness, the difficulty nonetheless testifies to performative writing's greater radical potential.

We might, for example, suggest opportunities for performative writing, which Pollock describes as evocative, metonymic, subjective, nervous, citational, and consequential. "An itinerant in the land of good writing," she argues, "it travels side by side with normative performances of textuality, sometimes even passing for the same, but always drawing its energy from a critical difference, from the possibility that it may always be otherwise than what it seems."[35] Beyond the classroom, such performances and performative writings can empower our students to craft the sort of elusive radical interventions for which we ourselves often strive. They are powerful in their elusiveness, resistant, even challenging, to disciplinary conventions (which themselves govern texts far more rigorously than they can govern performances), different from normative writing while hiding the subversive potentiality of passing as "good writing." In teaching students through the vocabulary of performance, we can identify systems and codes that seek to wrest student performances into fixity and suggest ways of writing that might enable students to elude those institutional efforts. Similarly, our own pedagogies can perform against power in ways that are at once difficult, effective, and elusive. In what follows, I suggest several assignments that attempt to tap into precisely this potential of a critical, performance-aware composition curriculum.

III. Writing Performance—Three Assignments

I have suggested three primary avenues that we might use for performance studies as a way to think through the writing classroom: to examine and invigorate student writing as performance; to understand our own pedagogy as performative; and to a lesser degree, to explore performance as a subject matter for inquiry in the writing classroom. In the first two cases, anecdotal evidence abounds about assignments, exercises and lesson plans, both widespread and unique, that add performance aspects to the writing classroom. From my own pedagogy training at University of Maryland, I recall skits, oral presentations, and physical games all used and shared as ways to break the ice in the classroom. One assignment, introduced by instructor Scott Eklund and adapted from the work of George Chilcoat and Timothy Morrison, was a Living Newspaper assignment, drawing on the documentary theater work of the Federal Theater Project in the U.S. and, before that, of Brecht's contemporary Erwin Piscator in Germany.[36] Here students worked as a large group, chose a current issue, and divided into research roles and performance roles. The students then devised and performed scripts based on the debates they found in their issues. "Each script presented an issue," writes Eklund, "the stances taken on that issue (fictionalized and quoted, assigned to specific real participants); and [a] loudspeaker or one participant who could offer perspective and a resolution to the ongoing debate."[37]

Other anecdotes abound: Janine DeBaise, a writer in the academic blogosphere and composition instructor at SUNY-ESF, for example, describes how a short assignment designed to focus students on the thesis statement evolved from a metaphor about "the elevator pitch" that she had borrowed from another academic blogger.[38] DeBaise responded to student suggestions that the exercise actually be performed with the teacher on an elevator—situating the rhetorical situation in space and time, and highlighting the creation of audiences in unlikely spaces. These types of exercises, then, are more than mere gimmicks—they encourage students to think about the material contexts of rhetoric, of writing, and of the classroom in ways that can be leveraged by students and teachers alike to empower student writing beyond the classroom.

Other assignments, such as the three I will describe below, appear as more conventional writing assignments and involve less theatricalized live performance in the classroom, but they use the language (and sometimes the subject matter) of performance studies to introduce students to new ways of considering the material of the writing classroom, from writing their own identity, to imagining dialogue with research sources, to finding a public forum for analysis of public performances.

In my own teaching practice, using theatricality and spectacle as subject matter has been a uniquely denaturalizing case, often pointing out the exposed beams and trusses of ideology in a range of cultural productions students know all too well. In my course on the rhetoric of spectacle at George Washington University, I asked students over the course of several assignments and exercises to break down the degree to which shock-and-awe tactics (those in Iraq and those at home) contribute to the rhetorics we may already identify. In a semester with an inauguration, a Super Bowl, an Academy Awards, and a (muted) set of IMF protests, students had ample opportunities to pick apart the underlying ideologies of the spectacles in which they regularly participated as spectators. Because so many of the topics were immediate, contemporary, and local, I wanted students to take seriously their potential to begin to impact the discussion of these events, and used a course blog where students contributed the content. Students were required to post seven times over the course of the semester with entries on various spectacular events, and I worked to cultivate readers from beyond the classroom walls, inviting fellow faculty, their students, and readers of my own now-defunct blog to comment and interact with the students in this public space.

For the first assignment, in the early weeks of the course, I cancelled class (admittedly, a signal of the persistence of teacherly authority) so that students could attend some component of the presidential inauguration and then post an entry analyzing the spectacle they took part in and, finally, engage the analyses of other students in the comments sections of the posts. I and several outside readers commented as well. The activity was notable less for the quality of those individual posts than for the degree to which it incited dialogue and, in some cases, heated debate over the way that spectacle functioned in this event, from the rhetorical messages of power sent by the presidential motorcade (a post that went on to become a fascinating final paper studying motorcades and royal processions generally) to the "appropriateness" and effectiveness of protest strategies. Over the course of the semester, students contributed to the site over a wide range of topics, including television and film examples, the spectacles of airport security, celebratory fireworks, the purple finger of the Iraqi elections, and the Catholic Mass. While some posts were decidedly, even determinedly, credulous of the spectacles themselves, many students honed a vocabulary for critical thinking in a public forum that was attended by outside readers all semester long. Here, the study of theatricality and spectacle gave students a foothold to deploy this critical vocabulary that responded to many of the exercises of power—cultural and political alike—that they encountered over the space of a single semester.

In another case, while teaching a 2003 writing course on performing identity, I asked students to read Judith Butler's foundational essay on gender performance, "Performative Acts and Gender Constitution." We then discussed the idea of performativity and identity, the notion of fluid categories of identity, and the many categories of identity that involved performance, including not only race, class and sexuality but also other "roles" students believed they played in everyday life. We went on to read several other essays that attempted to lay out the shifting terms of various identity categories, each time asking how performance and performativity (a distinction that students were just beginning to grasp) constituted those identities. The writing assignment that followed was nothing radical on its surface: a traditional definition essay, as conventional as it gets. And yet, by injecting the notion of the performativity of identity into an otherwise standard essay prompt, students moved from sketching out an abstract and disengaged term to mapping the contested territories of their own existence: one student wrote meaningfully about being a scholarship and financial aid student on a campus populated largely by wealthy students, invoking the performativity of class, while another integrated discourses of race and class to define the term "boojie" (a colloquialization of bourgeois). In both cases, students grappled with

the material circumstances of their own lives, with the degree to which responding to those circumstances involved performances, and with the agency they had
in performing their way out of deterministic notions of identity. Other students
took similarly interesting routes: one young woman sought to reclaim the word
"slut" from the vicious double standard of gendered sexuality, and another made
interesting strides in defining the performative elements of being an adoptee.
While the assignment involved few non-traditional instances of performance in
the writing itself, the notion of identity performance at once empowered students' sense of themselves outside the classroom and set up avenues through
which they might more powerfully modulate their performances in the classroom as well.

Another writing assignment I use does not necessarily involve live performance either (though it certainly could) but does draw on a literalization of a
popular performance metaphor in composition studies: Kenneth Burke's famous
parlor metaphor. In *The Philosophy of Literary Form*, Burke writes:

> Imagine that you enter a parlor. You come late. When you arrive, others have
> long preceded you, and they are engaged in a heated discussion, too heated for
> them to pause and tell you exactly what it is about. In fact, the discussion had
> already begun long before any of them got there, so that no one present is quali-
> fied to retrace for you all the steps that had gone before. You listen for a while,
> until you decide that you have caught the tenor of the argument; then you put in
> your oar. Someone answers; you answer him; another comes to your defense;
> another aligns himself against you, to either the embarrassment or gratification
> of your opponent, depending on the quality of your ally's assistance. However,
> the discussion is interminable. The hour grows late, you must depart. And you
> do depart, with the discussion still vigorously in progress.[39]

Not only is this notion frequently used to introduce students to the idea of academic writing generally, it is often taught as a way of introducing students to the
research process. The writing assignment I do at this stage in the process leads
up to their longer research argument. The assignment brings a literal version of
Burke's metaphor to the performance dramaturgy of Anna Deavere Smith and
other oral history performers. In such oral history performance, the primary
means of "playwriting" is to collect interviews from sources involved in a community—often one that has recently weathered a polarizing event, such as the
Rodney King riots in Los Angeles, which Smith transformed into her most famous piece, *Twilight: Los Angeles, 1992.*

By this point in the semester, I have often taught Smith's work as a text for
rhetorical analysis, so students are familiar with her methodology. In other cases, I have shown a video of the performance as a way of introducing the idea of
multiple voices in a discourse. Either way, between Burke's parlor and Smith's
oral history performance, students bring to their research process an understanding of the idea of multiple voices in the conversation, and that the sources they
collect represent precisely these voices. They understand the importance of collecting many different sorts of sources, and the imperative to look deeper (as

Smith does) for the sorts of voices that are not typically found or are actively silenced in most dominant representations of public discourse. But these metaphors sometimes remain distressingly abstract for the students, so I have them use Smith's oral history format as a way of mapping out their own sense of the dialogue in the parlor. As I have written elsewhere, the oral history form represents a dialogue crafted out of sources composed as monologues; for many students, reading individual sources still feels decidedly monologic, and decidedly authoritative.[40] The assignment, then, asks students to survey their sources and excerpt twelve to fifteen of them for important passages that contribute to the dialogue on their subject. Their first task is to arrange the passages so the authors seem to be responding to one another and to the central concerns. I ask them to choose passages carefully to make sure that most of the major arguments are represented and that most of the parties with an investment in the issue are similarly given voice. Their next task is to write a two- or three-sentence introduction to each passage identifying who the speaker is, how the speaker is invested in the discussion and, if necessary, what context surrounds the words quoted. These tasks of choosing, arranging, and introducing are of course important in teaching simple skills in presenting evidence, but the tasks also suggest important ways that students' own understanding of the material can shape the debate and, by extension, how every representation of discourse is shaped.

The third task is a crucial one: in the final passage, the student joins the discussion. Just as the student has gotten a sense of the conversation in the parlor and developed an understanding of the shape of that conversation, she must write her own contribution. She must introduce herself, just as she has introduced the other speakers. In doing so, she invests herself with the authority to speak, to join in. Placing this passage in relation to others encourages the student to add something new to the discussion, to contribute to it in meaningful ways and in ways that tell the student implicitly that her voice is important and does contribute. The fourth task, finally, is to write a reflective memo that discusses the choices made: why specific passages were chosen; how those passages isolated and identified certain issues; how students struggled with representing many voices equitably; and finally, what space was left for the student's voice. While it is not practical for all students to perform the piece they craft, they still produce what ends up being a script for dialogue, one that includes the writer as an equal and engaged participant in the conversation.

Conclusion

Many of the elements and ideas of a performance-based writing pedagogy that I have briefly touched on here are already in play in writing classrooms around the country, both classrooms that are overtly striving to enact a liberatory critical pedagogy and those with no such aspirations. What I have sought to do here is to pull together and constellate some of those notions and practices. While this article is by no means an exhaustive consideration of the confluence of performing, teaching, and writing, this particular moment seems perched on the outset of a thoughtful, complicated, and thorough exploration of what we might find at this particular intersection. I hope therefore that future work at this intersection—by the work of the Stanford Study of Writing, by other scholars exploring this confluence, and by readers of this chapter—can take up these questions and individually and collectively fashion answers to them in our classrooms.

Admittedly, while I have argued for the potentials of a performance based critical writing pedagogy, the argument dances around the difficult issue of the teacher as classroom authority. This is an issue that applies to virtually any theory of critical teaching within traditional academic settings and, in many ways, this chapter cannot adequately grapple with the scope of those questions—how do we effectively de-center the classroom? How do we empower students without the viable possibility of completely de-authorizing the teacher? How can a teacher assess writing in ways that both meet basic institutional demands and affirm student empowerment? These remain crucial questions, and ones whose solutions are neither easily answered nor even particularly easily addressed by the potentials of a performance-based critical lens. All of that said, if we are to perform power in the classroom, we do well to acknowledge it as a performance and, at the same time, work to teach such performative tactics to our students, empowering them against discipline, against unethical exercises of power, and against injustice.

Notes

1. "2005 American Society for Theatre Research and the Theatre Library Association Annual Conference." *American Society for Theatre Research.* November 10, 2005. http://www.astr.org/conference2005/ASTRConference.html (accessed September 8, 2006).
2. Jenn Fishman, et al., "Performing Writing, Performing Literacy," *College Composition and Communication* 52, no. 7 (December 2005): 226-27.
3. Fishman, et al., "Performing Writing," 232.
4. Petra Kuppers, *Disability and Contemporary Performance: Bodies on Edge* (New York: Routledge, 2004), 39.
5. Jon McKenzie, *Perform or Else* (London: Routledge, 2001).
6. McLaren relies heavily on the work of anthropologist Victor Turner, who gives us the notion of *communitas*, as well as other performance theorists working in ritual studies, such as Richard Schechner. In the notion of *communitas*, Turner describes a notion of community that allows for the peaceful confrontation of individual identities and that incorporates them all into the potentially utopian space of the ritual. Turner defines it as "'a direct, immediate and total confrontation of human identities,' a deep rather than intense style of personal interaction. It has something 'magical' about it. Subjectively there is a feeling of endless power.'" See Victor Turner, *From Ritual to Theatre: The Human Seriousness of Play* (New York: PAJ Publications, 1982), 47-48.

7. Peter McLaren, *Schooling as Ritual Performance: Towards a Political Economy of Educational Symbols and Gestures* (London and New York: Routledge, 1986), 218.

8. McLaren, *Schooling*, 218.

9. McLaren, *Schooling*, 47.

10. Perhaps more accurately, students learn that the only trace of that performance that consistently survives beyond the classroom walls is the grade, which reifies the status of grades as the only performance that is "important."

11. Performance theorist Baz Kershaw defines efficacy as "the potential that theatre may have to make the immediate effects of performance influence, however minutely, the general historical evolution of wider political and social realities." See Baz Kershaw, *The Politics of Performance* (London: Routledge, 1992), 1. Similarly, Victor Turner makes the distinction between "liminoid" performance (such as traditional theater), in which the impact of the performance is cordoned off from the real world, and "liminal" performance (such as ritual) in which the results of the performance have a direct impact on the world beyond the performance boundaries (Turner, *From Ritual*, 33-35).

12. Stephen Mailloux, *Disciplinary Identities* (New York: Modern Language Association of America, 2006), 10-16.

13. Lisa Ede and Andrea Lunsford's article, "Audience Addressed/Audience Invoked," has been a touchstone for thinking about audience in composition, and their dual understanding of invoking and addressing the rhetorical audience is a powerful one for thinking through the invention of writing for transformative purposes; that is, their model takes into equal account how to craft writing to mobilize already existing audiences, as well as how writing always invokes its own audiences which may or may not correspond to those that exist outside the text. See Lisa Ede and Andrea Lunsford, "Audience Addressed/Audience Invoked: The Role of Audience in Composition Theory and Pedagogy," *College Composition and Communication* 35 (1984): 155-71.

14. Peter Handke, "Theatre in the Theatre and Theatre in the Streets," in *Radical Street Performance: An International Anthology*, ed. Jan Cohen-Cruz (New York: Routledge, 1998), 9.

15. Yolanda Broyles-Gonzáles, "From El Teatro Campesino and the Mexican Popular Performance Tradition," in *Radical Street Performance: An International Anthology*, ed. Jan Cohen-Cruz (New York: Routledge, 1998), 245.

16. Bruce McConachie, "Theatre of the Oppressed with Students of Privilege," in *Teaching Performance Studies*, eds. Nathan Stucky and Cynthia Wimmer (Carbondale, IL: Southern Illinois UP, 2002), 247-60.

17. Fishman, et al., "Performing Writing," 232-33.

18. Fishman, et al., "Performing Writing," 233.

19. Elyse Lamm Pineau, "Critical Performative Pedagogy," in *Teaching Performance Studies*, eds. Nathan Stucky and Cynthia Wimmer (Carbondale, Ill: Southern Illinois UP, 2002), 41-54.

20. McLaren, *Schooling as Ritual Performance*, 47.

21. Both Debra Hawhee and Kristie S. Fleckenstein import these discussions in different ways into their important work on embodied writing and literacy. Hawhee's work draws on the intertwined traditions of classical Greece to postulate "Three Rs" of sophistic pedagogy which "emphasized the materiality of learning, the corporeal acquisition of rhetorical movements through rhythm, repetition, and response [the three Rs]. This manner of learning-doing involves 'getting a feel for' the work" (Hawhee 160). Similarly, Fleckenstein's work incorporates writing with both bodies and images, which connect discourse and writing with lived, embodied experience. Jay Dolmage, in his review of these two texts, does note crucially the way these approaches privilege normative bodies,

and calls for further work in embodied writing that imagines a multi-abled rhetoric to account for different bodies in its pedagogy. See Debra Hawhee, *Bodily Arts: Rhetoric and Athletics in Ancient Greece* (Austin, TX: University of Texas Press, 2004); Kristie Fleckenstein, *Embodied Literacies: Imageword and a Poetics of Teaching*, (Carbondale, IL: Southern Illinois University Press, 2003); and Jay Dolmage, "The Teacher, The Body," *College Composition and Communication* 58, no. 2 (December 2006): 267-77.

22. We know all too well that students are frequently caught up between an anxiety that what they write is a reflection of some essential self, an anxiety that they must con-form to what the teacher wants—to "sound smart"—and the lessons (positive and nega-tive) that they have learned about writing. Students often feel so bound by these anxieties that they rarely feel that they have access to an authentic voice. Though the notion of a student's authentic voice has at different times garnered a good deal of attention in the study of writing pedagogy, a performance-oriented understanding of student writing sug-gests that an attention to, even fetishization of, an authentic voice is limiting, both stylis-tically and rhetorically.

23. Here, I integrate a performance pedagogy with more traditional rhetorical ap-proaches, particularly in the neo-Aristotelian appeals, and especially in the notion of ethos. While students typically have no trouble understanding what it means to build a strong logos, and can identify a pathetic appeal a mile away, the notion of crafting an ethos is often obscured by uncritical adolescent notions of writing as mere self-expression, coupled with a secondary school insistence on good writing as "objective" third-person prose. While some assignments might ask students to try on the voice of the "Other," an attention to crafting an ethos in a more traditional argument asks them to think about "another" voice for themselves, one that is tailored to the role they are assum-ing. That role may be citizen, constituent, insider in a specific community, or simply the role of an interested and informed researcher, as a student who must claim authority (and acknowledge a lack of authority) from the weeks of reading, researching and writing she has performed.

24. Richard Schechner, *Performance Studies: An Introduction* (New York: Rout-ledge, 2002), 127.

25. Della Pollock, "Performing Writing," in *The Ends of Performance* (New York: New York University Press, 1998), 75.

26. Eve Kosofsky Sedgwick, "Teaching 'Experimental Critical Writing,'" in *The Ends of Performance*, ed. Peggy Phelan and Jill Lane (New York: New York University Press, 1998), 106-7.

27. Henry Giroux, *Impure Acts: The Practical Politics of Cultural Studies* (New York: Routledge, 2000), 128.

28. Giroux, *Impure Acts*, 130.

29. Giroux, *Impure Acts*, 130-31.

30. In Jyl Felman's *Never a Dull Moment: Teaching and the Art of Performance* (New York: Routledge, 2001), the author explores and narrates the potentialities and (sometimes unintentional) pitfalls of this sort of pedagogy. Recognizing that such a peda-gogy is not universally applicable for all personalities, I would submit that theatricality can be useful in the classroom when handled judiciously and, importantly, with an eye toward disrupting its propensity to re-center the teacher.

31. Tracy Davis and Thomas Postlewait, eds. *Theatricality* (Cambridge University Press, 2003), 1.

32. Jody Norton, "Guerilla Pedagogy: Conflicting Authority and Interpretation in the Classroom," in *Beyond the Corporate University: Culture and Pedagogy in the New Mil-*

lennium, ed. Henry A. Giroux and Kostas Myrsiades (Lanham, MD: Rowman and Little-field, 2001), 292.

33. T. S. Eliot, "Preface," Harry Crosby, *Transit of Venus: Poems* (Paris: Black Sun Press, 1931), ix. This is the original appearance of the quotation, although it appears widely in collections and on websites listing inspirational quotes.

34. Peggy Phelan, *Unmarked: The Politics of Performance* (New York: Routledge, 1994), 148.

35. Pollock, "Performing Writing," 97.

36. Timothy G. Morrison and George W. Chilcoat, "The 'Living Newspaper Theatre' in the Language Arts Classroom," *Journal of Adolescent & Adult Literacy* 42, no. 2 (October 1998): 2-14.

37. Scott Eklund, letter to author, 19 June 2007.

38. Janine DeBaise writes her blog under a pseudonym, Jo(e), at *Writing as Jo(e)*. Her post can be found at http://writingasjoe.blogspot.com/2006/09/why-i-am-bringing-dramamine-to-class.html, which also links to Julie's post at *No Fancy Name*: http://nofancyname.blogspot.com/2006/08/modifying-guy-kawasakis-silicon-valley.html.

39. Kenneth Burke, *Philosophy of Literary Form* (Berkeley: University of California Press, 1973), 110-111.

40. Ryan Claycomb, "(Ch)oral History: Docudrama, the Communal Subject, and Progressive Form," *Journal of Dramatic Theory and Criticism* 17, no. 2 (Spring 2003): 95-121.

Appendix

Founders' Day

for Farmworkers

A reflection on Duke University's Heritage

October 3, 2002

Take a Look into the Lives of Farmworkers...

Organizations That Have Endorsed the Mt. Olive Pickle Boycott

- Student Action With Farmworkers
- United Students Against Sweatshops
- North Carolina Occupational Health and Safety Project
- Jobs With Justice
- Catholic Diocese of Raleigh
- Church Women United
- North Carolina AFL–CIO
- Triangle Friends
- Duke Students Against Sweatshops
- Duke's Sanford Deli
- Eno River Unitarian Universalist Fellowship
- All Souls Unitarian Universalist Church
- Durham Food Coop
- Durham Witness for Peace
- National Farm Worker Ministry
- National Interfaith Committee for Worker Justice
- Pesticide Action Network
- Rainbow–PUSH Coalition
- American Postal Workers Union
- Black Workers for Justice
- Campaign for Labor Rights
- Atlanta Labor Solidarity Network

and hundreds of others....

For more information visit:

www.floc.com
www.usasnet.org
www.duke.edu/web/uss

Figure 2.1: "Founders' Day for Farmworkers" Brochure (exterior).
Source: Pegeen Reichert Powell

Mt. Olive Corporation: The Facts

- Mt. Olive is the 4th largest pickle producer in the United States and the number one brand in the southeast.

- One half of the 10,000 immigrant farmworkers in North Carolina in the H2A guest workers program harvest cucumbers processed by Mt. Olive.

- Farmworkers picking for Mt. Olive in North Carolina make $1.80 per hundred pounds of cucumbers harvested, putting them well below the national hourly minimum wage.

- Farmworkers are exposed to dangerous pesticides in the fields and in 1998 there were only 7 pesticide field inspectors, requiring 43 years to inspect all farms in the state.

- Farmworkers are excluded from federal protections on their right to organize and collectively bargain as declared in the National Labor Relations Act.

- 44% of migrant camps tested in 1992 had contaminated water supplies and portable toilets and handwashing facilities were rare.

- Several thousand farmworkers have signed authorization cards for the Farm Labor Organizing Committee, but Mt. Olive refuses to recognize their union.

Why Duke Should Boycott Mt. Olive Pickles

- Supporting the worker-called boycott of Mt. Olive affirms the right of farmworkers to organize themselves and have a voice in the decisions that affect their lives.

- Over 300 organizations and dozens of retailers across the country have formally endorsed the boycott.

- Over 1200 Duke students, faculty, employers, and community members signed a petition in support of the Mt. Olive boycott within 48 hours.

- President Keohane's proposed solution of establishing a coalition of the university, Mt. Olive Company, and the state government to improve the conditions of farmworkers excludes the voices of workers and promotes paternalism instead of empowerment.

- Duke has set a precedent for supporting the struggles of workers through our code of conduct for apparel suppliers. We should continue to take a stand on this important issue.

Chronology of Duke's involvement with the Mt. Olive Pickle Boycott

1997– FLOC approaches Mt. Olive with a proposal to negotiate with their farmworkers. Mt. Olive refuses to recognize workers' union

March 1999– FLOC calls boycott on Mt. Olive Pickle Company

Fall 1999– Duke Students Against Sweatshops (SAS) pressures Duke to withdraw Mt. Olive from Dining Services

March 2002– Duke publicity and fully endorses the Mt. Olive boycott

June 2002– Duke administrators begin secret dialogue with Mt. Olive Company officials without consulting either students or workers

Aug 2002– President Keohane rescinds Duke's endorsement of the boycott and announces her ineffective 3-part solution

Aug 2002– Various members of student and community groups denounce President Keohane's decision

Figure 2.2: "Founders' Day for Farmworkers" Brochure (interior).
Source: Pegeen Reichert Powell

Gay Marriage: A Panel Discussion

Monday, April 19th, 2004

Schedule

7:30 pm:
Opening Remarks
Hali Cooperman-Dix

7:35 – 8:00 pm:
Panelist Presentations
(in alphabetical order)
Meg Bourdillon – Newman Catholic Student Center
John Korman – Duke Conservative Union
Ian Millhiser – Duke Law Democrats
Jessie Rosario and Micah Schnoor – AQUA Duke
Brian Schroeder and Mary Grant – Duke Undergrad ACLU

8:00 – 8:30 pm:
Open Mic Question and Answer

Hosted by:
Seeking Deliberation
Lindsay Bressler
Hali Cooperman-Dix
Marco Salmen
Mark Sembler
Jessica Stone
Emily Znamierowski

We ask you to please be respectful in all of your discourse (the evening and) to refrain from any violent or hate speech.

Staying Involved

Contact an Organization:

AQUA Duke:
Website – http://www.duke.edu/web/aquaduke/
Email - aquaduke-owner@duke.edu

Newman Catholic Student Center:
Website – http://www.duke.edu/web/catholic/
Phone - (919) 684-8959
Director – Fr. Joe Vetter – joev@duke.edu

Duke Undergraduate ACLU:
National Website – http://www.aclu.org
Duke Undergrad President – Brian Schroeder
bas18@duke.edu

Duke Law Democrats:
Website - www.law.duke.edu/student/acldem.htm
Co-chair – Artemis Malekpour –
artemis.malekpour@law.duke.edu

Duke Democrats:
Website – http://www.duke.edu/web/dukedems/
President – Jared Fish – jbf8@duke.edu

Duke Conservative Union:
Website – http://www.dukeconservativeunion.org/
President – Jeff Railcanu –
jsr9@DukeConservativeUnion.org

Upcoming Events:
- Presidential Election – November 2nd, 2004
Register to vote at http://www.election.com

Visit Website Debating Gay Marriage:
http://www.duke.edu/~kwc8/

Tell The Chronicle What You Think:
Email – letters@chronicle.duke.edu

Panelists

- **Meg Bourdillon – Newman Catholic Student Center**

Meg Bourdillon is from the Newman Catholic Student Center, which works "to provide a welcoming Catholic community on campus, to nurture faith and intellectual growth within the Catholic tradition, to foster full Christian participation and leadership in and beyond Duke and society, to inspire lives of service, stewardship and social justice, and to promote integration of spiritual and intellectual life at Duke."

- **John Korman – Duke Conservative Union**

John Korman is the current secretary of the DCU, a "student organization that strives to promote conservative and libertarian principles, policies and candidates at Duke University." Among other principles, the DCU believes in the quote from conservative philosopher Russell Kirk: "Recognition that change may not be arbitrary reform; hasty innovation may be a devouring conflagration, rather than a torch of progress."

- **Ian Millhiser – Duke Law Democrats**

Ian Millhiser is the incoming chairperson of the 2004-2005 Duke Law Democrats, an "organization of law students interested in democratic issues." They "promote progressive ideals by participating in the political process, exploring democratic issues in the legal profession, and providing a forum for political discussion."

- **Jessie Rosario and Micah Schnoor – AQUA Duke**

Jessie Rosario and Micah Schnoor are president and member, respectively, of the Alliance of Queer Undergraduates at Duke, a student organization that works "to create open and supportive social spaces for the Duke community in order to spread awareness of LGBTQ issues, provide support for LGBTQ members of our community, and deal with issues facing the LGBTQ community on and off the Duke University campus."

- **Brian Schroeder and Mary Grant – Duke Undergrad ACLU**

Brian Schroeder and Mary Grant are the president and vice-president, respectively, of the undergraduate chapter of the American Civil Liberties Union, which strives to "work daily in courts, legislatures and communities to defend and preserve the individual rights and liberties guaranteed to every person in this country by the Constitution and laws of the United States." The ACLU's mission includes preserving First Amendment rights, the right to equal protection under the law, the right to due process, and the right to privacy.

Characteristics of Deliberation

"A commitment to dialogue in the face of important differences and disagreements;

A willingness to negotiate over time, to accept ambiguity, and to acknowledge both partial agreements and incommensurable beliefs and positions;

A commitment to clarifying the underlying assumptions that shape judgments;

A willingness to explore the unanticipated consequences of both one's own positions and those of others;

An effort to offer mutually justifiable or recognizable reasons;

A commitment to reciprocity and an ethos of accountability;

A preference for participatory and inclusive approaches to political decision-making;

An ethic of civility in interpersonal interactions, even in the face of heated and passionate disagreement."[1]

From http://breeze.Ashoka.edu/Deliberation/whatis/why.htm

Important Questions Embedded In the Gay Marriage Debate

o Is marriage a fundamental right or a privilege?

o Is banning gay marriage an act of discrimination?

o Is endorsing gay marriage harmful to society?

o Does marriage have an explicit definition? If so, what is it?

o What is the purpose of marriage?

o Does same-sex parenting have harmful social and psychological effects on children?

o Is a constitutional amendment an appropriate method for resolving this issue?

o Is a civil union a viable alternative to gay marriage? What are other alternatives?

o Would legalizing gay marriage lead to the endorsing of incestuous and polygamous marriage?

Recent Developments

December 3rd, 1996 - Hawaii

Hawaii's Circuit Court lifts the ban on same-sex marriage in Hawaii, which legalizes the practice and forces the state to recognize same-sex couples who attain a marriage license. According to the Honolulu Star Bulletin, "The justices presumed that same-sex couples have a right to marry unless the state could offer a reason compelling enough to justify sex discrimination in the state law." The ruling is immediately appealed and later overturned.

January 16th, 1997 - DOMA

Under the Clinton administration, the Defense of Marriage Act (DOMA) is passed into law. The DOMA relieves states from being bound by the same-sex marriage laws of other states and also amends the U.S. Code to make explicit the definition of marriage as the legal union of a man and a woman.

November 18th, 2003 - Massachusetts

The Massachusetts Supreme Court rules that homosexuals have a constitutional right to marry based on the stability that loving relationships bring to society. Almost three months later the courts have an appeal, the Massachusetts Supreme Court states that there have no adequate reason presented to deny homosexual couples the right to marry. They give the Massachusetts state legislature six months to rewrite state marriage laws to include same-sex couples.

February 12th 2003 - San Francisco

The mayor of San Francisco defies state law and issues marriage licenses to same-sex couples, 118 on the first day alone. One month later the California Supreme Court rules that the city has to cease issuing the licenses. Between that time, 4,037 same-sex couples obtain marriage licenses in San Francisco.

February 24th, 2003 – President Bush

In a speech from the White House, President Bush calls for an amendment to the Constitution which would "protect the meaning of marriage from being changed forever." He cites the 1997 Defense of Marriage Act as having set a precedent which is being ignored by "activist judges and local officials" in Massachusetts, San Francisco, and New Mexico. He calls marriage the "union of a man and a woman," and says that America's "commitment to freedom does not require the redefinition of one of our most basic social functions."

March 22nd 2003 – Durham, NC

After being denied a marriage license in Durham, NC, a gay couple decides to file a lawsuit against the county. The couple argues that they have the right to a legally recognized commitment. In defense, the state argues that North Carolina law does not provide marriage licenses for same-sex couples. The issue is headed for the North Carolina Supreme Court.

Figure 1.2: "Gay Marriage: A Panel Discussion" brochure (interior).
Source: Pegeen Reichert Powell

Bibliography

"2005 American Society for Theatre Research and the Theatre Library Association Annual Conference." *American Society for Theatre Research.* 10 November 2005. http://www.astr.org/conference2005/ASTRConference.html (accessed September 8, 2006).

Achebe, Chinua. *Things Fall Apart.* London: Heineman, 1996 (1958).

Althusser, Louis. "Ideology and Ideological State Apparatuses: Notes Toward an Investigation." Pp. 127-86 in *Lenin and Philosophy.* London: Monthly Review Press, 1978.

Andersen, Jack. "Information Criticism: Where Is It?" *Progressive Librarian* 25 (Summer 2005): 12-22.

Ang, Ien. "Who Needs Cultural Research?" Pp. 477-83 in *Cultural Studies and Practical Politics: Theory, Coalition Building and Social Activism,* edited by Pepi Leystina. New York, Blackwell. 2005

Appadurai, Arjun. "Diversity and Disciplinarity as Cultural Artifacts." Pp. 23-36 in *Disciplinarity and Dissent in Cultural Studies,* edited by Cary Nelson and Dillip Prameshwar Gaonkar. New York: Routledge. 1996.

Archer, Wesley, and Milton Gray. "The Crepes of Wrath." In *The Simpsons*: Fox Network, 1990.

Aronson, Anne and Craig Hansen. "Writing Identity: The Independent Writing Department as a Disciplinary Center." Pp. 50-61 in *Field of Dreams: Independent Writing Programs and the Future of Composition Studies,* edited by Peggy O'Neill, Angela Crow, and Larry W. Burton. Logan, UT: Utah State University Press, 2002.

Association for College and Research Libraries, *Information Literacy Competency Standards for Higher Education,* American Library Association, http://www.ala.org/ala/acrl/acrlstandards/informationliteracycompetency.cfm (accessed July 2, 2008).

Azevedo, Mario, "African-American Studies and the State of the Art." Pp. 25-43 in *Africana Studies: A Survey of Africa and the African Diaspora,* edited by Mario Azevedo. Durham, NC: Carolina Academic Press, 1993.

Bakhtin, Mikhail. "Discourse in the Novel." Pp. 259-422 in *The Dialogic Imagination: Four Essays by M.M. Bakhtin,* edited by Michael Holquist. translated by Caryl Emerson and Michael Holquist. Austin: University of Texas Press, 1981.

Balestraci, Mary, et al. *Writing for Academic and Professional Situations: Exploring Experience Through Research.* Boston, MA: Pearson Custom Publishing, 2002. Reprint, 2003.

Barnard, Ian. "Anti-ethnography?" *Composition Studies* 34, no. 1 (Spring 2006): 95-107.
Barthes, Roland. *The Pleasure of the Text*, translated by Richard Miller. New York: Hill and Wang, 1992.
———. *Roland Barthes*, translated by Richard Howard. Berkeley: California, 1994.
Bartholomae, David. "Inventing the University." Pp. 134-65 in *When a Writer Can't Write: Studies in Writer's Block and Other Composing-Process Problems*, edited by Mike Rose. New York: Guilford, 1985.
Bartholomae, David. *Writing on the Margins: Essays on Composition and Teaching*. Boston: Bedford/St. Martin's, 2005.
Bernstein, Charles. "Charles Bernstein: Interview." *readme* no. 1 (1999), http://home.jps.net/~nada/issueone.htm, (accessed November 15, 2007).
Bérubé, Michael. *The Employment of English: Theory, Jobs, and the Future of Literary Studies*. New York and London: New York University Press, 1998.
———. "Why Inefficiency is Good for Universities," *The Chronicle of Higher Education* (March 27, 1998): B4-B5.
Bizzell, Patricia. *Academic Discourse and Critical Consciousness*. Pittsburgh: University of Pittsburgh Press, 1992.
Borges, Jorge Luis. *Ficciones*, translated by Anthony Kerrigan. New York: Grove, 1963.
Bousquet, Marc. *How the University Works*. New York: New York University Press, 2008.
Breton, André. *Manifestoes of Surrealism*, translated by Richard Seaver and Helen R. Lane. Ann Arbor: University of Michigan Press, 1969.
Brooker, Peter. "Why Brecht, Or, Is There English After Cultural Studies?" *Essays and Studies* 40 (1987): 20-31.
Brotchie, Alastair, ed. *Surrealist Games*. Boston: Shambhala, 1995.
Broyles-Gonzáles, Yolanda. "From El Teatro Campesino and the Mexican Popular Performance Tradition." Pp. 245-54 in *Radical Street Performance: An International Anthology*, edited by Jan Cohen-Cruz. New York: Routledge, 1998.
Burke, Edmund. *A Philosophical Enquiry into the Origins of Our Ideas of the Sublime and the Beautiful*, edited by Adam Phillips. Oxford: Oxford University Press, 1990.
Burke, Kenneth. *A Rhetoric of Motives*. New York: Prentice Hall, 1950.
———. *Philosophy of Literary Form*. Berkeley: University of California Press, 1973.
Burton, Robert. *The Anatomy of Melancholy*, edited by Holbrook Jackson. New York: New York Review of Books, 2001.
Canaan, Joyce E. "Examining the Examination: Tracing the Effects of Pedagogic Authority on Cultural Studies Lecturers and Students." Pp. 157-77 in *A Question of Discipline*, edited by Joyce E. Canaan and Debbie Epstein. Boulder, CO: Westview Press, 1997.
Canaan, Joyce E. and Debbie Epstein, "Questions of Discipline/Disciplining Cultural Studies." In *A Question of Discipline*, edited by Joyce E. Canaan and Debbie Epstein. Boulder, CO: Westview Press, 1997.
———. eds., *A Question of Discipline: Pedagogy, Power, and the Teaching of Cultural Studies*. Boulder, CO: Westview Press, 1997.
Carey-Webb, Allen. *Literature and Lives: A Response-Based Cultural Studies Approach to Teaching English*. Urbana: National Council of Teachers of English, 2001.
Carr, Jean Ferguson. "Rereading the Academy as Worldly Text." *College Composition and Communication* 45 (1994): 93-97.

Carter, Michael. "Ways of Knowing, Doing, and Writing in the Disciplines." *CCCC* 58, no. 3 (2007): 385-418.

Chow, Rey. "Introduction: Leading Questions," Pp. 1-26 in *Writing Diaspora: Tactics of Intervention in Contemporary Cultural Studies*. Bloomington: Indiana University Press, 1993.

———. "Theory, Area Studies, Cultural Studies: Issues of Pedagogy in Multiculturalism." Pp 11-16 in *A Question of Discipline*, edited by Joyce E. Canaan and Debbie Epstein. Boulder, CO: Westview Press, 1997.

———. "The Resistance of Theory; or, The Worth of Agony." Pp. 95-105 in *Just Being Difficult? Academic Writing in the Public Arena*, edited by Jonathan Culler and Kevin Lamb, Cultural Memory in the Present. Stanford: Stanford University Press, 2003.

Christian, Barbara. "The Race for Theory." Pp. 335-45 in *Hacienda Caras: Making Face, Making Soul: Creative and Critical Perspectives by Feminists of Color*, edited by Gloria Anzaldua. San Francisco: Aunt Lute Books, 1990.

Cintron, Ralph. *Angel's Town: Chero Ways, Gang Life and the Rhetorics of Everyday*. New York: Beacon Press, 1998.

Claycomb, Ryan. "(Ch)oral History: Docudrama, the Communal Subject, and Progressive Form," *Journal of Dramatic Theory and Criticism* 17, no. 2 (Spring 2003): 95-121.

Claycomb, Ryan and Rachel Riedner. "Cultural Studies, Rhetorical studies, and Composition: Towards an Anti-Disciplinary Nexus." *Enculturation* 5, no. 2 (2004), http://enculturation.gmu.edu/5_2/claycomb-riedner.html (accessed November 16, 2006).

Clayton, Jay. "Dickens and the Genealogy of Postmodernism." *Nineteenth-Century Literature* 46, no. 2 (1991): 181-95.

———.*Charles Dickens in Cyberspace: The Afterlife of the Nineteenth Century in Postmodern Culture*. Oxford: Oxford University Press, 2003.

Clifford, James. "Introduction: Partial Truths." Pp. 1-26 in *Writing Culture: The Poetics and Politics of Ethnography*. Eds. James Clifford and George E. Marcus. Berkeley, CA: University of California Press, 2000.

Cody, Dean E. "Critical Thoughts on Critical Thinking." *Journal of Academic Librarianship* 32, no. 4 (July 2006): 403-407.

Coleman, Lisa and Lorien Goodman. Introduction. "Rhetoric/Composition: Intersections/Impasses/Differends." *Enculturation* 5, no. 1 (Fall 2003): http://enculturation.gmu.edu/5_1/intro.html (accessed May 11, 2009).

Connors, Robert. "The New Abolitionism: Toward a Historical Background." Pp. 3-26 in *Reconceiving Writing, Rethinking Writing Instruction*, edited by Joseph Petraglia. Mahwah, NJ: Lawrence Erlbaum Associates, 1995.

Cooper, Kelly, and Annie Lipsitz. *knowing feminism? Hurricane Katrina "Refugees," Rigoberta Menchú, and Subcomandante Insurgente Marcos*. Typescript. Lanham, MD: Lexington Books, forthcoming.

Crowley, Sharon. "Composition Is Not Rhetoric." *Enculturation* 5, no.1 (Fall 2003): http://enculturation.gmu.edu/5_1/crowley.html (accessed September 5, 2008).

Cvetkovich, Ann. "Histories of Mass Culture: From Literary to Visual Culture." *Victorian Literature and Culture* 27, no. 2 (1999): 495-99.

Daniel, Sir John. "Lessons from the Open University: Low-Tech Learning Often Works Best," *The Chronicle of Higher Education*. September 2001: 24.

Darwin, Charles. *Origin of Species*. New York: Gramercy Books, 1995.

Daughters of the Dust, dir. Julie Dash, prod. Julie Dash and Arthur Jafa. 1 hr. 53 mins., American Playhouse/Geechee Girls/WMG Film, 1991.

Davis, Diane. Breaking Up [at] Totality: A Rhetoric of Laughter, Rhetorical Philosophy and Theory. Carbondale: Southern Illinois University Press, 2000.

Davis, Tracy, and Thomas Postlewait, eds. *Theatricality.* Cambridge: Cambridge University Press, 2003.

De Certeau, Michel. *The Practice of Everyday Life,* translated by Steven Rendall. Berkeley: University of California Press, 1988.

Deal, Terrence and Allan Kennedy. *Corporate Cultures.* New York: Addison Wesley, 2000 (1982).

———. *The New Corporate Cultures: Revitalizing the Workplace After Downsizing, Mergers, and Reengineering.* New York: Basic Books, 1999.

Derrida, Jacques. *Glas,* translated by James Leavey and Richard Rand. Lincoln: Nebraska, 1986.

Devi, Mahasweta, "'Draupadi' by Mahasweta Devi, Translated with a Foreword by Gayatri Chakravorti Spivak," *Critical Inquiry* 8, no. 2 (Winter 1981): 381-402.

Diawara, Manthia. "Black Studies, Cultural Studies: Performative Acts." Pp. 300-6 in *What Is Cultural Studies? A Reader,* edited by John Storey. London: Arnold, 1996.

Dolmage, Jay. "The Teacher, The Body." *College Composition and Communication* 58, no. 2 (December 2006): 267-277.

Downing, David B. "Beyond Disciplinary English: Integrating Reading and Writing by Reforming Academic Labor." Pp. 23-38 in *Beyond English Inc.: Curricular Reform in a Global Economy,* edited by David B. Downing, Claude Mark Hurlbert, and Paula Mathieu. Portsmouth, NH: Boynton/Cook, 2002.

Drylongso, dir. Cauleen Smith, prod. Cauleen Smith and Christine Gant. 1 hr. 26 mins., Nation Sack Filmworks Production, 1998.

DuBois, W.E.B. *The Souls of Black Folk.* Greenwich, CT: Fawcett, 1961 (1903).

During, Simon. "Introduction." Pp. 1-30 in *The Cultural Studies Reader,* edited by Simon During. New York: Routledge, 1993.

Durst, Russel K. "Can We be Critical of Critical Pedagogy?" *College Composition and Communication* 58, no. 1 (2006): 110-14.

———. *Collision Course: Conflict, Negotiation, and Learning in the Composition Classroom.* Urbana: National Council of Teachers of English, 1999.

Ede, Lisa and Andrea Lunsford. "Audience Addressed/Audience Invoked: The Role of Audience in Composition Theory and Pedagogy." *College Composition and Communication* 35 (1984): 155-71.

Elbow, Peter. "Being a Writer vs. Being an Academic: A Conflict in Goals." *College Composition and Communication* 46, no. 1 (1995): 72-83.

Eliot, T.S. Preface to Harry Crosby. *Transit of Venus: Poems.* Paris: Black Sun Press, 1931.

Ellsworth, Elizabeth. "Why Doesn't This Feel Empowering? Working Through the Repressive Mythos of Critical Pedagogy." Pp. 90-119 in *Feminisms and Critical Pedagogy,* edited by Carmen Luke and Jennifer Gore. New York: Routledge, 1992.

Emmons, Kimberly. "Rethinking Genres of Reflection: Student Portfolio Cover Letters and the Narrative of Progress." *Composition Studies* 31, no. 1 (2003): 43-62.

Evans, Mary. "A Good School Revisited." Pp. 173-84 in *Women's Lives into Print: The Theory, Practice and Writing of Feminist Auto/Biography,* edited by Pauline Polkey. New York: St. Martin's Press, 1999.

Fairclough, Norman. *Discourse and Social Change.* Cambridge, UK: Polity Press, 1992.
Felman, Jyl. *Never a Dull Moment: Teaching and the Art of Performance.* New York: Routledge, 2001.
Feyerabend, Paul. *Against Method.* London: New Left Books, 1978.
Fishman, Jenn, et al. "Performing Writing, Performing Literacy." *College Composition and Communication* 52, no. 7 (December 2005): 224-252.
Flecha, Ramón and Victòria dels Àngels Garcia. "Mirrors, Paintings, and Romances." Pp. 131-56 in *A Question of Discipline*, edited by Joyce E. Canaan and Debbie Epstein. Boulder, CO: Westview Press, 1997.
Fleckenstein, Kristie. *Embodied Literacies: Imageword and a Poetics of Teaching.* Carbondale, IL: Southern Illinois University Press, 2003.
Flint, Kate. "Counter-Historicism, Contact Zones, and Cultural History." *Victorian Literature and Culture* 27, no. 2 (1999): 507-511.
Forster, E. M. *Howards End.* New York: Signet Books, 1992.
Foucault, Michel. *The Archaeology of Knowledge*, translated by Alan Sheridan. New York: Pantheon, 1972.
———. "The Discourse on Language." translated by Alan Sheridan. *The Archaeology of Knowledge & the Discourse on Language.* New York: Pantheon, 1972: 215-38.
———. *Discipline and Punish: The Birth of the Prison*, translated by Alan Sheridan. New York: Vintage Books, 1995 (1975).
———. "La Poussière et le Nouage." In *L'Impossible Prison: Recherches sur le Système Pénitentiaire au XIXᵉ Siècle Réunies par Michelle Perrot*, edited by Michelle Perrot. Paris: Éditions du Seuil, 1980.
———. "Two Lectures." Pp. 78-108 in *Power/Knowledge: Selected Interviews and Other Writings, 1970-1977*, edited by Colin Gordon. New York: Pantheon, 1980.
———. "Of Other Spaces." translated by Jay Miskowiec. *Diacritics* 16, no. 1 (Spring 1986): 22-27.
———. "Questions of Method." Pp. 73-86 in *The Foucault Effect: Studies in Governmentality*, edited by Graham Burchell, Colin Gordon, and Peter Miller. Chicago: The University of Chicago Press, 1991.
Freire, Paulo. *Pedagogy of the Oppressed.* New York: Continuum International Publishing Group Inc., 2000.
———. *Teachers as Cultural Workers: Letters to Those Who Dare Teach.* Boulder, CO: Westview Press, 2005.
Freire, Paolo, and Donaldo Macedo. *Literacy: Reading the Word and the World.* London: Bergin & Garvey, 1987.
Frith, Simon. "Literary Studies as Cultural Studies—Whose Literature? Whose Culture?" *Critical Quarterly* 34, no. 2 (1992): 3-26.
Giroux, Henry A. "Disturbing the Peace: Writing in the Cultural Studies Classroom." *College Literature* 20, no. 2 (June 1993): 13-26.
———. "Reading Texts, Literacy, and Textual Authority." 63-74 in *Falling into Theory: Conflicting Views on Reading Literature*, edited by David H. Richter. Boston: Bedford Books, 1994.
———. "Doing Cultural Studies: Youth and the Challenge of Pedagogy," *Harvard Educational Review* 64, no. 3 (Fall 1994): 278-308.
———. "Who Writes in a Cultural Studies Class? or, Where is the Pedagogy?" Pp. 3-16 in *Left Margins: Cultural Studies and Composition Pedagogy*, edited by Karen Fitts and Alan W. France. Albany: State University of New York Press, 1995.

————. "Is There a Place for Cultural Studies in Colleges of Education?" Pp. 231-48 in *Education and Cultural Studies: Toward a Performative Practice*, edited by Henry A. Giroux and Patrick Shannon. Routledge: New York and London, 1997.

————. "Vocationalizing Higher Education: Schooling and the Politics of Corporate Culture." Pp. 29-44 in *Beyond the Corporate University: Culture and Pedagogy in the New Millennium*, edited by Henry Giroux and Kostas Myrsiades. Lanham: Rowman and Littlefield, 1999.

————. *Impure Acts: The Practical Politics of Cultural Studies*. New York: Routledge, 2000.

————. "The Corporate War Against Higher Education," *Workplace*. 5, no. 1 (October 2002). http://www.cust.educ.ubc.ca/workplace/issue5p1/5p1.html (accessed September 5, 2008).

————. *The Abandoned Generation: Democracy Beyond the Culture of Fear*. New York: Palgrave Macmillan, 2003.

————. "Academic Repression in the First Person: The Attack on Higher Education and the Necessity of Critical Pedagogy," *The Advocate* (February 2007) http://gcadvocate.org/index.php?action=view&id=124

Giroux , Henry A. and Susan Searls Giroux. *Take Back Higher Education: Race, Youth, and the Crisis of Democracy in the Post-Civil Rights Era*. New York: Palgrave Macmillan, 2004.

Giroux, Henry, David Shumway, Paul Smith, and James Sosnoski. "The Need for Cultural Studies: Resisting Intellectuals and Oppositional Public Spheres." *Dalhousie Review* 64, no. 2 (1986): 472-86.

Gleason, Barbara. "Self-Reflection as a Way of Knowing: Phenomenological Investigations in Composition." Pp. 60-71 in *Into the Field: Sites of Composition Studies*, edited by Anne Ruggles Gere. New York, NY: Modern Language Association of America, 1993.

Goleman, Judith. *Working Theory: Critical Composition Studies for Students and Teachers*. New York: Bergin & Garvey, 1995.

Gopen, George D. "Why So Many Bright Students and So Many Dull Papers?: Peer-Responded Journals as a Partial Solution to the Problem of the Fake Audience." *The WAC Journal* 16 (2005): 22-48.

Gore, Jennifer. *The Struggle for Pedagogies: Critical and Feminist Discourses as Regimes of Truth.* New York: Routledge, 1993.

————. "Disciplining Bodies: On the Continuity of Power Relations in Pedagogy." Pp. 231-51 in *Foucault's Challenge: Discourse, Knowledge and Power in Education*, edited by Thomas Popklewitz and Marie Brennan. New York: Teachers College, Columbia University, 1998.

Grossberg, Lawrence. *Bringing It All Back Home: Essays on Cultural Studies*. Durham & London: Duke University Press, 1997.

Gwaltney, John Langston. *Drylongso*. New York: Vintage, 1981.

Habermas, Jürgen. *The Structural Transformation of the Public Sphere: An Inquiry into a Category of Bourgeois Society.* translated by Thomas Burger (Cambridge: MIT University Press, 1989).

Hall, R. Mark and Mary Rosner, "Pratt and Pratfalls: Revisioning Contact Zones." Pp. 95-109 in *Crossing Borderlands: Composition and Postcolonial Studies*, edited by Andrea A. Lunsford and Lahoucine Ouzgane. Pittsburgh: University of Pittsburgh Press, 2004.

Hall, Stuart. "Cultural Studies and the Crisis of the Humanities." *October* 53 (1990): 11-90

Halloran, Michael S. "Rhetoric in the American College Curriculum." *Pre/Text* 3 (1982): 245-69.

Handke, Peter. "Theatre in the Theatre and Theatre in the Streets." Pp. 7-12 in *Radical Street Performance: An International Anthology,* edited by Jan Cohen-Cruz. New York: Routledge, 1998.

Harris, Joseph. "The Idea of Community in the Study of Writing." *College Composition and Communication* 40, no. 1 (1989): 11-22.

Harrison, Charles and Paul Wood, eds. *Art in Theory.* London: Blackwell, 2005.

Harvey, David. *Jutice, Nature & the Geography of Difference.* Cambridge: Blackwell, 1996.

Hawhee, Debra. *Bodily Arts: Rhetoric and Athletics in Ancient Greece.* Austin, TX: University of Texas Press, 2004.

Hayles, N. Katherine. "The Condition of Virtuality," Pp. 68-95 in *The Digital Dialectic: New Essays on New Media,* edited by Peter Lunenfeld. Cambridge: MIT Press, 2000.

Haynes, Cynthia. "Rhetoric/Slash/Composition." *Enculturation* 5, no. 1 (Fall 2003): http://enculturation.gmu.edu/5_1/haynes.html.

Henderson, Mae G. "'Where, By the Way, Is This Train Going?' A Case for Black (Cultural) Studies." *Callaloo* 19, no 1 (1996): 60-67.

Hesford, Wendy S. and Eileen E. Schell. "Introduction: Configurations of Transnationality: Locating Feminist Rhetorics." *College English* 7, no. 5 (May 2008): 461-70.

Hesse, Herman. *Steppenwolf,* translated by Basil Creighton. New York: Picador, 2002).

Highlander Research and Education Center "Grassroots Think Tank." http://www.highlandercenter.org/p-grassroots.asp (accessed September 10, 2007).

Hillard, Van. "Navigating the Social Turn: Information Literacy as Situated Literacy." In *Teaching Literary Research: Challenges in a Changing Environment,* edited by Steven Harris and Kathleen Johnson. Chicago: American Library Association, forthcoming.

hooks, bell. *Talking Back: Thinking Feminist, Thinking Black.* Boston: South End Press, 1989.

———. *Yearning: Race, Gender, and Cultural Politics.* Boston: South End Press, 1990.

Horner, Bruce. *Terms of Work for Composition: A Materialist Critique.* Albany: State University of New York Press, 2000.

Jameson, Frederic. *Marxism and Form: Twentieth-Century Dialectical Theories of Literature.* New ed. Princeton: Princeton University Press, 1974.

Joyce, Michael. *Of Two Minds: Hypertext Pedagogy and Poetics.* Ann Arbor: University of Michigan Press, 1995.

JSTOR, "The Archives," 2008. http://www.jstor.org/page/info/about/archives/ index.jsp. (accessed July 3, 2008).

Kaufer, David S., and Patricia L. Dunmire. "Integrating Cultural Reflection and Production in College Writing Curricula." Pp. 217-38 in *Reconceiving Writing, Rethinking Writing Instruction,* edited by Joseph Petraglia. Mahwah, NJ: Lawrence Erlbaum Associates, 1995.

Keep, William. "Rewriting Business as Usual." Pp. 9-17 in *Direct from the Disciplines: Writing Across the Curriculum,* edited by Mary T. Segall and Robert A. Smart. Portsmouth, NH: Boynton/Cook, 2005.

Keita. Dir. Dani Kouyate. California Newsreel, 1995.

Kelley, Robin D.G. *Freedom Dreams*. Boston: Beacon, 2002.

Kellogg, David, and Susan Soroka, eds. *The AWD Toolkit*. Second ed. Kendall/Hunt: Dubuque, IA, 2007.

Kershaw, Baz. *The Politics of Performance*. London: Routledge, 1992.

Krueger, Christine L. "Introduction." Pp. xi-xx in *Functions of Victorian Culture at the Present Time*, edited by Christine L. Krueger. Athens, OH: Ohio University Press, 2002.

Kucich, John. "Cultural Studies, Victorian Studies, and Graduate Education." *Victorian Literature and Culture* 27, no. 2 (1999): 477-80.

Kucich, John and Dianne F. Sadoff, eds. *Victorian Afterlife: Postmodern Culture Rewrites the Nineteenth Century*. Minneapolis: University of Minnesota Press, 2000.

Kuhn, Thomas. *The Structure of Scientific Revolutions*. Chicago: University of Chicago Press, 1970.

Kuppers, Petra. *Disability and Contemporary Performance: Bodies on Edge*. New York: Routledge, 2004.

Kurzman, Karen. "Reflection." *The English Journal* 87, no. 3 (1998): 28-29.

Langstraat, Lisa. "Gender Literacy in the Cultural Studies Composition Classroom: 'Fashioning' the 'Self' Through an Analysis of Popular Magazines." *Works and Days* 14 (1996): 169-76.

Lefebvre, Henri. *The Production of Space*. Translated by Donald Nicholson-Smith. Oxford: Basil Blackwell, 1991.

Leitch, Vincent. "Postmodern Interdisciplinarity." Pp. 165-71 in *Theory Matters*. New York: Routledge, 2003.

Lipsitz, George. "Class and Consciousness: Teaching about Social Class in Public Universities." Pp. 9-21 in *Class Issues: Pedagogy, Cultural Studies, and the Public Sphere*, edited by Amitava Kumar, New York and London: New York University Press, 1997.

Lorde, Audre. "Age, Race, Class, and Sex: Women Redefining Difference." Pp. 114-23 in *Sister Outsider*. Freedom, CA: The Crossing Press, 1984.

Lorentzen, Eric G. "Why the Novel (Still) Matters: Doing Student-Centered Cultural Studies in the Literature Classroom." *The Review of Education/Pedagogy/Cultural Studies* 26, no. 4 (October-December 2004): 289-311.

Lubiano, Wahneema. "Mapping the Interstices Between Afro-American Cultural Discourse and Cultural Studies: A Prolegomenon." *Callaloo* 19, no. 1 (1996): 68-77.

Luke, Carmen and Jennifer Gore, eds. *Feminisms and Critical Pedagogy*. New York: Routledge, 1992.

Lyotard, Jean-François. *The Postmodern Condition: A Report on Knowledge*, translated by Geoff Benington and Brian Massumi. Minneapolis, MN: University of Minnesota, 1999.

Mailloux, Stephen, *Disciplinary Identities*. New York: Modern Language Association of America, 2006.

Marable, Manning. "Living Black History: Black Intellectuals and the African-American Literary Tradition." April 2004. http://www.manningmarable.net/works/pdf/living blackhistory.pdf (accessed November 20, 2006).

Marcos, Subcomandante. "The Story of the Tiny Mouse and the Tiny Cat." Pp. 308-9 in *Our Word is Our Weapon: Selected Writings*, edited by Juana Ponce de Leon. New York: Seven Stories, 2001.

Marshall, Paule. *Praisesong for the Widow*. New York: Plume, 1984.

McComiskey, Bruce. *Teaching Composition as a Social Process.* Logan, UT: Utah State University Press, 2000.

McConachie, Bruce. "Theatre of the Oppressed with Students of Privilege." Pp. 247-60 in *Teaching Performance Studies,* edited by Nathan Stucky and Cynthia Wimmer. Carbondale, IL: Southern Illinois University Press, 2002.

McKenzie, Jon. *Perform or Else.* London: Routledge, 2001.

McLaren, Peter. *Schooling as Ritual Performance: Towards a Political Economy of Educational Symbols and Gestures.* London and New York: Routledge, 1986.

McRuer, Robert. "Composing Bodies; or, De-Composition: Queer Theory, Disability Studies, and Alternative Corporealities." *Journal of Advanced Composition* 24, no. 1 (2004): 47-78.

———. *Crip Theory: Cultural Signs of Queerness and Disability.* New York: New York University Press, 2006.

Menand, Louis. "The Marketplace of Ideas." *American Council of Learned Societies,* Occasional Paper No. 49. 2001. http://archives.acls.org/op/49_Marketplace_of_Ideas.htm (accessed July 22, 2008).

Messer-Davidow, Ellen, David R. Shumway, and David J. Sylvan, eds. *Knowledges: Historical and Critical Studies in Disciplinarity.* Charlottesville: University Press of Virginia, 1993.

———. *Disciplining Feminism: From Social Activism to Academic Discourse.* Durham: Duke University Press, 2002.

Monroe, Jonathan. *Writing and Revising the Disciplines,* Ithaca, NY: Cornell University Press, 2002.

Morrison, Timothy G. and George W. Chilcoat. "The 'Living Newspaper Theatre' in the Language Arts Classroom." *Journal of Adolescent & Adult Literacy* 42, no. 2 (October 1998): 2-14.

Murphy, Peter F. "Cultural Studies as Praxis: A Working Paper." *College Literature* 19, no. 2 (1992): 31-43.

National Commission on Writing. "Writing: A Ticket to Work . . . or a Ticket Out: A Survey of Business Leaders." College Board, 2004.

Nelson, Cary and Dilip Parameshwar Gaonkar. "Cultural Studies and the Politics of Disciplinarity." Pp. 1-19 in *Disciplinarity and Dissent in Cultural Studies,* edited by Cary Nelson and Dilip Parameshwar Gaonkar. New York: Routledge, 1996.

Nelson, Cary and Stephen Watt. *Academic Keywords: A Devil's Dictionary for Higher Education.* Routledge, 1999.

Noble, David. "The Future of the Digital Diploma Mill," *Academe* 87:5 (September-October 2001): 29.

Norton, Jody. "Guerilla Pedagogy: Conflicting Authority and Interpretation in the Classroom." Pp. 287-307 in *Beyond the Corporate University: Culture and Pedagogy in the New Millennium,* edited by Henry A. Giroux and Kostas Myrsiades. Lanham, MD: Rowman and Littlefield, 2001.

O'Neill, Peggy, and Angela Crow, "Introduction: Cautionary Tales about Change." Pp. 1-48 in *Field of Dreams: Independent Writing Programs and the Future of Composition Studies,* edited by Peggy O'Neill, Angela Crow, and Larry W. Burton. Logan, Utah: Utah State University Press, 2002.

Omi, Michael and Howard Winant. *Racial Formations in the United States.* New York: Routledge, 1986.

Orner, Mimi. "Interrupting the Calls for Student Voice in 'Liberatory' Education: A Feminist Poststructuralist Perspective." Pp. 74-89 in *Feminisms and Critical Pedagogy*, edited by Carmen Luke and Jennifer Gore. New York: Routledge, 1992.

"Overview of the Changes." Texas Tech TOPIC webpage: http://ttopic.english.ttu.edu/manual/manualread.esp. Accessed on June 7, 2006.

Parker, Joe and Ranu Samantrai. "Interdisciplinarity and Social Justice: An Introduction." In *Interdisciplinarity and Social Justice: Revisioning Academic Accountability*, edited by Ranu Samantrai, Joe Parker, and Mary Romero. Albany: State University of New York Press, forthcoming.

Pennell, Michael. "'If Knowledge is Power, You're About to Become Very Powerful': Literacy and Labor Market Intermediaries in Postindustrial America." *College Composition and Communication* 58, no. 3 (2007): 345-84.

Perlstein, R. "'Funny Doctor, I don't *feel* antidisciplined': Cultural Studies as Disciplinary Habitus (or, Reading *Cultural Studies*)." *parallax: a journal of metadiscursive theory and cultural practices* 1 (1995): 131-41.

Phelan, Peggy. *Unmarked: The Politics of Performance*. New York: Routledge, 1994.

Pineau, Elyse Lamm. "Critical Performative Pedagogy." Pp. 41-54 in *Teaching Performance Studies*, edited by Nathan Stucky and Cynthia Wimmer. Carbondale, IL: Southern Illinois University Press, 2002.

Pollock, Della. "Performing Writing." Pp. 73-103 in *The Ends of Performance*, edited by Peggy Phelan and Jill Lane. New York: New York University Press, 1998.

Poovey, Mary. "Cultural Criticism: Past and Present." Pp. 3-15 in *Understanding Others: Cultural and Cross-Cultural Studies and the Teaching of Literature*, edited by Joseph Trimmer and Tilly Warnock. Urbana: National Council of Teachers of English, 1992.

Pratt, Mary Louise. "Arts of the Contact Zone." Pp. 582-95 in *Ways of Reading*, 5th edition, edited by David Bartholomae and Anthony Petroksky. New York: Bedford/St. Martin's, 1999.

Prior, Paul A. *Writing/Disciplinarity: A Sociohistorical Account of Literate Activity in the Academy*. Mahwah, NJ: Erlbaum, 1998.

Qualley, Donna. *Turns of Thought: Teaching Composition as Reflexive Inquiry*. Hanover, NH: Boynton/Cook, 1997.

Ratcliffe, Krista. "The Current State of Composition Scholar/Teachers: Is Rhetoric Gone or Just Hiding Out?" *Enculturation* 5, no. 1 (Fall 2003): http://enculturation.gmu.edu/5_1/ratcliffe.html

Ray, Robert. *How A Film Theory Got Lost and Other Mysteries in Cultural Studies*. Bloomington: Indiana, 2001.

Riedner, Rachel and Kevin Mahoney. *Democracies to Come*. Lanham, MD: Lexington Books, 2008.

Rizzolatti, Giacomo, Leonardo Fogassi, and Vittorio Gallese. "Mirrors in the Mind." *Scientific American* (November 2006): 54-61.

Rohrs, Kelly. "Mt. Olive Boycott Ends after 5 Years." *The Chronicle Online*. 2004. http://www.dukechronicle.com/media/storage/paper884/news/2004/09/16/News/Mt.Olive.Boycott.Ends.After.5.Years-1471088.shtml?norewrite200605091308 (accessed December 14, 2006).

Russell, David R. *Writing in the Academic Disciplines, 1870-1990: A Curricular History*. Carbondale and Edwardsville, IL: Southern Illinois University Press, 1991.

Ryan, Rory. "The Social Life of Literature: Cultural Studies, Cultural Ethnography and the Future of Literary Studies." *Journal of Literary Studies* 12, nos. 1-2 (1996): 1-39.

Sadker, David. "Foreword," Pp. xix-xxxix in *Women in Literature: Reading Through the Lens of Gender*, edited by Jerilyn Fisher and Ellen S. Silber. Westport, CT: Greenwood Press, 2003.

Santayana, George. *Skepticism and Animal Faith*. New York: Dover, 1955.

Sassen, Saskia. *A Sociology of Globalization*. New York: W.W. Norton, 2007.

Schechner, Richard. *Performance Studies: An Introduction*. New York: Routledge, 2002.

Scholes, Robert, Nancy R. Comley and Gregory L. Ulmer, eds. *Text Book*. New York: St. Martin's, 1995.

Sedgwick, Eve Kosofsky. "Teaching 'Experimental Critical Writing'." Pp. 104-15 in *The Ends of Performance*, edited by Peggy Phelan and Jill Lane. New York: New York University Press, 1998.

Shohat, Ella, and Stam, Robert. *Unthinking Eurocentrism: Multiculturalism and the Media*. London and New York: Routledge, 1994.

Shor, Ira. *Empowering Education: Critical Teaching for Social Change*. Chicago: University of Chicago Press, 1992.

Sloan Consortium. *Growing by Degrees: Online Education in the United States, 2005*.

Soja, Edward. *Postmodern Geographies: The Reassertion of Space in Critical Social Theory*. New York: Verso, 1989.

Spivak, Gayatri Chakravorty. "The Politics of Translation." Pp. 179-200 in *Outside in the Teaching Machine*. New York: Routledge, 1973.

Spivak, Gayatri Chakravorty, "Can the Subaltern Speak?" Pp. 271-317 in *Marxism and the Interpretation of Culture*, edited by Cary Nelson and Larry Grossberg. Urbana: University of Illinois Press, 1988.

———. "More on Power/Knowledge." Pp. 25-52 in *Outside in the Teaching Machine*. New York: Routledge, 1993.

———. "Scattered Speculations on the Question of Culture Studies." Pp. 255-84 in *Outside in the Teaching Machine*. New York: Routledge, 1993.

———. "Explanation and Culture: Marginalia." Pp. 29-51 in *The Spivak Reader*, edited by Donna Landry and Gerald MacLean. New York: Routledge, 1996.

———. "Subaltern Studies: Deconstructing Historiography." Pp. 203-36 in *The Spivak Reader*, edited by Donna Landry and Gerald Maclean. New York: Routledge, 1996.

———. "Thinking Cultural Questions in 'Pure' Literary Terms." Pp. 333-57 in *Without Guarantees: In Honour of Stuart Hall*, edited by Paul Gilroy, Lawrence Grossberg, and Angela McRobbie. London: Verso Press, 2000.

———. "Thinking Academic Freedom in Gendered Post-Coloniality." Pp. 453-59 in *The Anthropology of Politics: A Reader in Ethnography,Theory, and Critique*, edited by Joan Vincent. Maiden, MA: Blackwell, 2002.

———. "Righting Wrongs." Pp. 168-227 in *Human Rights, Human Wrongs: The Oxford Amnesty Lectures 2001*, edited by Nicholas Owen. New York: Oxford University Press, 2003.

———. *Death of a Discipline*, The Wellek Library Lectures in Critical Theory. New York: Columbia University Press, 2003.

———. http://www.arts.cornell.edu/sochum/sct/html/courses.html#spivak (accessed January 20, 2007).

Stabile, Carol. "Pedagogues, Pedagogy, and Political Struggle." in *Class Issues: Pedagogy, Cultural Studies, and the Public Sphere*, edited by Amitava Kumar, 208-20. New York and London: New York University Press, 1997.

Steig, Michael. "*David Copperfield* and Shared Reader Response." Pp. 140-8 in *Approaches to Teaching Dickens' David Copperfield*, edited by Richard J. Dunn. New York: The Modern Language Association of America, 1984.

Steinberg, Deborah Lynn. "All Roads Lead to . . . Problems with Discipline." Pp. 192-204 in *A Question of Discipline*, edited by Joyce E. Canaan and Debbie Epstein. Boulder, CO: Westview Press, 1997.

Stewart, John. *Drinkers, Drummers and Decent Folk.* Albany: State University of New York Press, 1989.

Strickland, Ronald. "Pedagogy and Public Accountability." Pp. 163-78 in *Class Issues: Pedagogy, Cultural Studies, and the Public Sphere*. Edited by Amitava Kumar. New York and London: New York University Press, 1997.

Sullivan, Nikki. *An Introduction to Queer Theory.* New York: New York University Press, 2003.

Swales, John M. *Genre Analysis: English in Academic and Research Settings.* Cambridge, UK: Cambridge University Press, 1990.

Taylor, Marvin. "'I'll be your mirror, reflect what you are': Postmodern Documentation and the Downtown New York Scene from 1975 to the Present." *RBM* 3, no. 1 (2002): 32-51.

Thaiss, Chris, and Terry Myers Zawacki. *Engaged Writers and Dynamic Disciplines: Research on the Academic Writing Life.* Portsmouth, NH: Boynton/Cook, 2006.

Thelin, William H. "Understanding Problems in Critical Classrooms." *College Composition and Communication* 57, no. 1 (2005): 114-41.

———. "William H. Thelin's Response to Russel Durst." *College Composition and Communication* 58, no. 1 (2006): 114-118.

Trimbur, John. "Composition and the Circulation of Writing." *College Composition and Communication* 52 (2000): 188-219.

———. "Delivering the Message: Typography and the Materiality of Writing." Pp. 188-202 in *Rhetoric and Composition as Intellectual Work*, edited by Gary A. Olson. Carbondale: Southern Illinois University Press, 2002.

Turner, Victor. *The Ritual Process: Structure and Anti-Structure.* Ithaca, NY: Cornell University Press, 1969.

———. *From Ritual to Theatre: The Human Seriousness of Play.* New York: PAJ Publications, 1982.

"UCF Distributed Learning: Scope and Policies" http://online.ucf.edu/cdl/dlp_plain.htm. (accessed June 1, 2006).

Ulmer, Gregory. *Applied Grammatology.* Baltimore: Johns Hopkins University Press, 1985.

———. *Teletheory.* New York: Routledge, 1989.

Weisser, Christian R. *Moving Beyond Academic Discourse: Composition Studies and the Public Sphere.* Carbondale: Southern Illinois University Press, 2002.

Welch, Nancy. "Living Room: Teaching Public Writing in a Post-Publicity Era." *College Composition and Communication* 56 (2005): 470-92.

Wells, Susan. "Rogue Cops and Health Care: What Do We Want from Public Writing?" *College Composition and Communication* 47 (1996): 325-41.

White, Edward M. "The Scoring of Writing Portfolios: Phase 2." *College Composition and Communication* 56, no. 4 (2005): 581-600.

Willard-Traub, Margaret K. "Reflection in Academe: Scholarly Writing and the Shifting Subject." *College English* 68, no. 4 (2006): 422-32.

Williams, Carolyn. "Introduction: Victorian Studies and Cultural Studies." *Victorian Literature and Culture* 27, no. 2 (1999): 355-63.

Williams, Raymond. *Marxism and Literature*. New York: Oxford University Press, 1977.

Yancey, Kathleen Blake. "Making Learning Visible: What You Can't See Can Change Response." Pp. 69-71 in *The WAC Casebook: Scenes for Faculty Reflection and Program Development*, edited by Chris M. Anson. New York: Oxford University Press, 2002.

Young, Jeffrey. "'Hybrid' Teaching Seeks to End the Divide between Traditional and Online Instruction: By blending approaches, colleges hope to save money and meet students' needs." *The Chronicle of Higher Education*. Information Technology. March 22, 2002.

Index

academic freedom, 148–50
academy, critique of, Foucault on, 35–37
Achebe, Chinua, 175
ACRL Information Literacy Competency Standards, 131–32, 140
action, writing and, 26, 28
activism:
    distance learning and, 121;
    public writing and, 57–72
administration, and anti-disciplinary pedagogy, 29–30
African and Diaspora literature, 171–81
agency, Goleman on, 92–93
alternative literacies, 153
Althusser, Louis, 93–95, 158
Analogy Cards game, 79, 81–82
Andersen, Jack, 134
Ang, Ien, 22–24, 27
anti-disciplinary pedagogy, 21–33, 75–89;
    definition of, 5-6;
    distance learning and, 122;
    literature and, 147–69;
    omissions and, 179–80;
    practices in, 30–31;
    public writing and, 63–64;
    recommendations for, 29;
    writing and, 1–18
antonomasia, 82
Appadurai, Arjun, 19
Armstrong, Nancy, 158

Aronson, Anne, 10
assessment. *See* grading
assimilation, naming and, 47
audience:
    performance and, 189–90;
    public writing and, 57–72;
    reflective writing and, 103–4
Austin, J. L., 192
authoritative discourse, Bakhtin on, 174
autoethnography, 175
Azevedo, Mario, 173

Bakhtin, Mikhail, 93, 174
banking model of education, 151, 185
Barthes, Roland, 141
Bartholomae, David, 95, 111, 136
Bernstein, Charles, 133
Bérubé, Michael, 152–53
Birmingham school, 22, 53, 173
Bizzell, Pat, 95, 107n22
Black Studies, and Cultural Studies, 50, 171–81
Bleak House (Dickens), 158–60
Boal, Augusto, 190
body:
    performance and, 190–91;
    power and, 36
border writing, 7
Borges, Jorge Luis, 135
Bousquet, Marc, 8–9
Brady, Laura, 119
Brecht, Bertolt, 86, 196

225

Contributors

Ryan Claycomb is an Assistant Professor of English at West Virginia University, where he teaches courses in drama, performance, contemporary literature, and composition. In addition to writing on performance studies in the composition classroom, he also works on gender studies, narrative theory, and modern drama. His work has appeared in *Enculturation, Modern Drama, JNT: Journal of Narrative Theory*, and *Journal of Dramatic Theory and Criticism*, as well as other journals and collections.

Alan Ramón Clinton received his Ph.D. in English at the University of Florida in 2002. He has taught interdisciplinary writing courses at Georgia Institute of Technology, Northeastern University, and University of Miami. He is the author of *Mechanical Occult: Automatism, Modernism, and the Specter of Politics* (Peter Lang: 2004).

Cathy Eisenhower is an Instruction and Collection Development Librarian at Gelman Library, George Washington University. For several years she has collaborated closely with faculty in the University Writing Program at GW to integrate research instruction into the writing classroom. She also has two collections of poetry: *clearing without reversal* (Edge Books: 2008) and *would with and* (Roof Books: 2009).

Catherine Gouge is an Assistant Professor of English at West Virginia University. She has designed courses for, taught in, and coordinated an online Professional Writing and Editing undergraduate program since 2001. Dr. Gouge's research interests include online pedagogy, program administration, disciplinarity, and technology and Cultural Studies. She has published articles about web-based writing and editing course design, program administration, and the cultural influences of new technologies. Her future projects will consider web-based writing program administrative structures and assessment approaches.

David Kellogg is Assistant Professor of English and Director of Advanced Writing in the Disciplines at Northeastern University. He has published articles and reviews in various journals including *CCC: College Composition and Communication* and *Pedagogy*. His essay "Toward a Post-Academic Science Policy: Scientific Communication and the Collapse of the Mertonian Norms," published in *The International Journal of Communications Law and Policy*, won the 2007 NCTE award for best article on philosophy or theory of technical or scientific communication.

Randi Gray Kristensen is Assistant Professor of University Writing at the George Washington University. Her publications include creative non-fiction in *Under Her Skin: How Girls Experience Race in America*, fiction in *Electric Grace: Still More Fiction by Washington Area Women*, and poetry in *Creation Fire: Caribbean Women Poets*. She also publishes book reviews and articles on African and African diaspora literature, and is currently writing a novel on female sex tourism in Jamaica.

Eric G. Lorentzen is Assistant Professor of English at the University of Mary Washington in Fredericksburg, Virginia, where he teaches a wide variety of courses including nineteenth-century British literature and culture, cultural studies, narrative theory and the novel genre, critical pedagogy, and the multinational short story. His research interests include the rise of mass literacy and dangerous modes of education in the nineteenth-century British novel, the exigency and efficacy of employing a Cultural Studies methodology in the university literature classroom, and critical and inter-disciplinary pedagogy. His publications have appeared in such journals as *Dickens Studies Annual, The Review of Education, Pedagogy and Cultural Studies, Victorian Newsletter*, and *The Virginia Woolf Miscellany*.

Joe Parker is Associate Professor of East Asian Thought at Pitzer College and Adjunct Professor at Claremont Graduate University. He teaches International and Intercultural Studies, Gender and Feminist Studies, Media Studies, and Asian Studies. He has published articles in Asian Studies journals and in edited volumes, including *Japanese Women Writers: A Bio-Critical Source Book and Theorizing Scriptures: New Critical Orientations to a Cultural Phenomenon*. He is the co-editor for a forthcoming collection from State University of New York Press, *Interdisciplinarity and Social Justice: Revisioning Academic Accountability*.

Pegeen Reichert Powell received her Ph.D. in English from Miami University (Oxford, OH), and is currently a faculty member in the English department at Columbia College Chicago. Her research includes work on pedagogy, basic writing, critical discourse analysis, and feminist mothering studies. She has published articles in *CCC: College Composition and Communication* and *JAC: Journal of Advanced Composition*, as well as chapters in edited collections. In addition to her recent work on the relationship between writing instruction and retention in higher education, she is co-editing, with Jocelyn Fenton Stitt, a collection titled *Mothers Who Deliver: Feminist Interventions in Interpersonal and Public Discourse* (under contract with SUNY Press).

Rachel Riedner is Assistant Professor of University Writing at the George Washington University. Her research interests include transnational feminisms, cultural studies, and feminist rhetorics. She has recently published articles about affect and pedagogy, and her co-authored book, *Democracies to Come: Rhetorical Action, Neoliberalism, and Communities of Resistance*, was published by Lexington in 2008. Her next project is on transnational feminist pedagogy.

Dolsy Smith is a Librarian at the George Washington University, where he works closely with faculty and students in the university's first-year writing program, incorporating research practice into the writing classroom. Prior to becoming a librarian, he received an MFA in poetry from Washington University in St. Louis, where he also taught creative and expository writing.

Breinigsville, PA USA
12 March 2010
234108BV00002B/23/P